BEHAVIOR SCIENCE OUTLINES

VOLUME I

OUTLINE OF CULTURAL MATERIALS

4th REVISED EDITION

FIFTH PRINTING WITH MODIFICATIONS

GEORGE P. MURDOCK

CLELLAN S. FORD

ALFRED E. HUDSON

RAYMOND KENNEDY

LEO W. SIMMONS

JOHN W. M. WHITING

D1697452

PUBLISHED BY

HUMAN RELATIONS AREA FILES, INC.

755 PROSPECT STREET

NEW HAVEN

4th REVISED EDITION
FIFTH PRINTING WITH MODIFICATIONS, 1971

ISBN 0-87536-652-X

LIBRARY OF CONGRESS CATALOG CARD NUMBER: 61-11509

© COPYRIGHT 1961
HUMAN RELATIONS AREA FILES, INC.
NEW HAVEN, CONNECTICUT

TABLE OF CONTENTS

PREFACE

000 MATERIAL NOT CATEGORIZED

10 ORIENTATION
    101 Identification
    102 Maps
    103 Place Names
    104 Glossary
    105 Cultural Summary

11 BIBLIOGRAPHY
    111 Sources Processed
    112 Sources Consulted
    113 Additional References
    114 Comments
    115 Informants
    116 Texts
    117 Field Data

12 METHODOLOGY
    121 Theoretical Orientation
    122 Practical Preparations
    123 Observational Role
    124 Interviewing
    125 Tests and Schedules
    126 Recording and Collecting
    127 Historical Research
    128 Organization and Analysis

13 GEOGRAPHY
    131 Location
    132 Climate
    133 Topography and Geology
    134 Soil
    135 Mineral Resources
    136 Fauna
    137 Flora

14 HUMAN BIOLOGY
    141 Anthropometry
    142 Descriptive Somatology
    143 Genetics
    144 Racial Affinities
    145 Ontogenetic Data
    146 Nutrition
    147 Physiological Data

15 BEHAVIOR PROCESSES AND PERSONALITY
    151 Sensation and Perception
    152 Drives and Emotions
    153 Modification of Behavior
    154 Adjustment Processes
    155 Personality Development
    156 Social Personality
    157 Personality Traits
    158 Personality Disorders
    159 Life History Materials

16 DEMOGRAPHY
    161 Population
    162 Composition of Population
    163 Birth Statistics
    164 Morbidity
    165 Mortality
    166 Internal Migration
    167 Immigration and Emigration
    168 Population Policy

17 HISTORY AND CULTURE CHANGE
    171 Distributional Evidence
    172 Archeology
    173 Traditional History
    174 Historical Reconstruction
    175 Recorded History
    176 Innovation
    177 Acculturation and Culture Contact
    178 Socio-Cultural Trends

18 TOTAL CULTURE
    181 Ethos
    182 Function
    183 Norms
    184 Cultural Participation
    185 Cultural Goals
    186 Ethnocentrism

19 LANGUAGE
    191 Speech
    192 Vocabulary
    193 Grammar
    194 Phonology
    195 Stylistics
    196 Semantics
    197 Linguistic Identification
    198 Special Languages

20 COMMUNICATION
   201 Gestures and Signs
   202 Transmission of Messages
   203 Dissemination of News and Information
   204 Press
   205 Postal System
   206 Telephone and Telegraph
   207 Radio and Television
   208 Public Opinion

21 RECORDS
   211 Mnemonic Devices
   212 Writing
   213 Printing
   214 Publishing
   215 Photography
   216 Sound Records
   217 Archives
   218 Writing and Printing Supplies

22 FOOD QUEST
   221 Annual Cycle
   222 Collecting
   223 Fowling
   224 Hunting and Trapping
   225 Marine Hunting
   226 Fishing
   227 Fishing Gear
   228 Marine Industries

23 ANIMAL HUSBANDRY
   231 Domesticated Animals
   232 Applied Animal Science
   233 Pastoral Activities
   234 Dairying
   235 Poultry Raising
   236 Wool Production
   237 Animal By-products

24 AGRICULTURE
   241 Tillage
   242 Agricultural Science
   243 Cereal Agriculture
   244 Vegetable Production
   245 Arboriculture
   246 Forage Crops
   247 Floriculture
   248 Textile Agriculture
   249 Special Crops

25 FOOD PROCESSING
   251 Preservation and Storage of Food
   252 Food Preparation
   253 Meat Packing Industry
   254 Refrigeration Industry
   255 Canning Industry
   256 Cereal Industry
   257 Confectionery Industries
   258 Miscellaneous Food Processing
       and Packing Industries

26 FOOD CONSUMPTION
   261 Gratification and Control of Hunger
   262 Diet
   263 Condiments
   264 Eating
   265 Food Service Industries
   266 Cannibalism

27 DRINK, DRUGS, AND INDULGENCE
   271 Water and Thirst
   272 Nonalcoholic Beverages
   273 Alcoholic Beverages
   274 Beverage Industries
   275 Drinking Establishments
   276 Narcotics and Stimulants
   277 Tobacco Industry
   278 Pharmaceuticals

28 LEATHER, TEXTILES, AND FABRICS
   281 Work in Skins
   282 Leather Industry
   283 Cordage
   284 Knots and Lashings
   285 Mats and Basketry
   286 Woven Fabrics
   287 Nonwoven Fabrics
   288 Textile Industries
   289 Paper Industry

29 CLOTHING
   291 Normal Garb
   292 Special Garments
   293 Paraphernalia
   294 Clothing Manufacture
   295 Special Clothing Industries
   296 Garment Care

30 ADORNMENT
   301 Ornament
   302 Toilet
   303 Manufacture of Toilet Accessories
   304 Mutilation
   305 Beauty Specialists
   306 Jewelry Manufacture

31 EXPLOITATIVE ACTIVITIES
   311 Land Use
   312 Water Supply

313 Lumbering
314 Forest Products
315 Oil and Gas Wells
316 Mining and Quarrying
317 Special Deposits

32 PROCESSING OF BASIC MATERIALS
   321 Work in Bone, Horn, and Shell
   322 Woodworking
   323 Ceramic Industries
   324 Stone Industry
   325 Metallurgy
   326 Smiths and Their Crafts
   327 Iron and Steel Industry
   328 Nonferrous Metal Industries

33 BUILDING AND CONSTRUCTION
   331 Construction
   332 Earth Moving
   333 Masonry
   334 Structural Steel Work
   335 Carpentry
   336 Plumbing
   337 Electrical Installation
   338 Miscellaneous Building Trades
   339 Building Supplies Industries

34 STRUCTURES
   341 Architecture
   342 Dwellings
   343 Outbuildings
   344 Public Structures
   345 Recreational Structures
   346 Religious and Educational Structures
   347 Business Structures
   348 Industrial Structures
   349 Miscellaneous Structures

35 EQUIPMENT AND MAINTENANCE OF BUILDINGS
   351 Grounds
   352 Furniture
   353 Interior Decoration and Arrangement
   354 Heating and Lighting Equipment
   355 Miscellaneous Building Equipment
   356 Housekeeping
   357 Domestic Service
   358 Maintenance of Nondomestic Buildings

36 SETTLEMENTS
   361 Settlement Patterns
   362 Housing
   363 Streets and Traffic
   364 Sanitary Facilities
   365 Public Utilities

366 Commercial Facilities
367 Parks
368 Miscellaneous Urban Facilities
369 Urban and Rural Life

37 ENERGY AND POWER
   371 Power Development
   372 Fire
   373 Light
   374 Heat
   375 Thermal Power
   376 Water Power
   377 Electric Power
   378 Atomic Energy
   379 Miscellaneous Power Production

38 CHEMICAL INDUSTRIES
   381 Chemical Engineering
   382 Petroleum and Coal Products Industries
   383 Rubber Industry
   384 Synthetics Industry
   385 Industrial Chemicals
   386 Paint and Dye Manufacture
   387 Fertilizer Industry
   388 Soap and Allied Products
   389 Manufacture of Explosives

39 CAPITAL GOODS INDUSTRIES
   391 Hardware Manufacture
   392 Machine Industries
   393 Electrical Supplies Industry
   394 Manufacture of Heating and
       Lighting Appliances
   395 Manufacture of Optical and
       Photographic Equipment
   396 Shipbuilding
   397 Railway Equipment Industry
   398 Manufacture of Vehicles
   399 Aircraft Industry

40 MACHINES
   401 Mechanics
   402 Industrial Machinery
   403 Electrical Machines and Appliances
   404 Household Machines and Appliances
   405 Weighing, Measuring, and
       Recording Machines
   406 Weight-moving Machinery
   407 Agricultural Machinery

41 TOOLS AND APPLIANCES
   411 Weapons
   412 General Tools
   413 Special Tools

414 Miscellaneous Hardware
415 Utensils
416 Appliances
417 Apparatus

42 PROPERTY
421 Property System
422 Property in Movables
423 Real Property
424 Incorporeal Property
425 Acquisition and Relinquishment of Property
426 Borrowing and Lending
427 Renting and Leasing
428 Inheritance
429 Administration

43 EXCHANGE
431 Gift Giving
432 Buying and Selling
433 Production and Supply
434 Income and Demand
435 Price and Value
436 Medium of Exchange
437 Exchange Transactions
438 Domestic Trade
439 Foreign Trade

44 MARKETING
441 Mercantile Business
442 Wholesale Marketing
443 Retail Marketing
444 Retail Businesses
445 Service Industries
446 Sales Promotion
447 Advertising

45 FINANCE
451 Accounting
452 Credit
453 Banking
454 Saving and Investment
455 Speculation
456 Insurance
457 Foreign Exchange
458 Business Cycles

46 LABOR
461 Labor and Leisure
462 Division of Labor by Sex
463 Occupational Specialization
464 Labor Supply and Employment
465 Wages and Salaries
466 Labor Relations

467 Labor Organization
468 Collective Bargaining

47 BUSINESS AND INDUSTRIAL ORGANIZATION
471 Ownership and Control of Capital
472 Individual Enterprise
473 Corporate Organization
474 Cooperative Organization
475 State Enterprise
476 Mutual Aid
477 Competition

48 TRAVEL AND TRANSPORTATION
481 Locomotion
482 Burden Carrying
483 Weight Moving
484 Travel
485 Travel Services
486 Regulation of Travel
487 Routes
488 Warehousing
489 Transportation

49 LAND TRANSPORT
491 Highways
492 Animal Transport
493 Vehicles
494 Highway Transport
495 Auxiliary Highway Services
496 Railways
497 Rail Transport
498 Terminal Facilities
499 Highway and Railway Construction

50 WATER AND AIR TRANSPORT
501 Boats
502 Navigation
503 Waterways Improvements
504 Port Facilities
505 Water Transport
506 Aircraft
507 Aviation
508 Airport Facilities
509 Air Transport

51 LIVING STANDARDS AND ROUTINES
511 Standard of Living
512 Daily Routine
513 Sleeping
514 Elimination
515 Personal Hygiene
516 Postures
517 Leisure Time Activities

52 RECREATION
    521 Conversation
    522 Humor
    523 Hobbies
    524 Games
    525 Gambling
    526 Athletic Sports
    527 Rest Days and Holidays
    528 Vacations
    529 Recreational Facilities

53 FINE ARTS
    531 Decorative Art
    532 Representative Art
    533 Music
    534 Musical Instruments
    535 Dancing
    536 Drama
    537 Oratory
    538 Literature
    539 Literary Texts

54 ENTERTAINMENT
    541 Spectacles
    542 Commercialized Sports
    543 Exhibitions
    544 Public Lectures
    545 Musical and Theatrical Productions
    546 Motion Picture Industry
    547 Night Clubs and Cabarets
    548 Organized Vice
    549 Art and Recreational Supplies Industries

55 INDIVIDUATION AND MOBILITY
    551 Personal Names
    552 Names of Animals and Things
    553 Naming
    554 Status, Role, and Prestige
    555 Talent Mobility
    556 Accumulation of Wealth
    557 Manipulative Mobility
    558 Downward Mobility

56 SOCIAL STRATIFICATION
    561 Age Stratification
    562 Sex Status
    563 Ethnic Stratification
    564 Castes
    565 Classes
    566 Serfdom and Peonage
    567 Slavery

57 INTERPERSONAL RELATIONS
    571 Social Relationships and Groups
    572 Friendships

    573 Cliques
    574 Visiting and Hospitality
    575 Sodalities
    576 Etiquette
    577 Ethics
    578 Ingroup Antagonisms
    579 Brawls, Riots and Banditry

58 MARRIAGE
    581 Basis of Marriage
    582 Regulation of Marriage
    583 Mode of Marriage
    584 Arranging a Marriage
    585 Nuptials
    586 Termination of Marriage
    587 Secondary Marriages
    588 Irregular Unions
    589 Celibacy

59 FAMILY
    591 Residence
    592 Household
    593 Family Relationships
    594 Nuclear Family
    595 Polygamy
    596 Extended Families
    597 Adoption

60 KINSHIP
    601 Kinship Terminology
    602 Kin Relationships
    603 Grandparents and Grandchildren
    604 Avuncular and Nepotic Relatives
    605 Cousins
    606 Parents-in-Law and Children-in-Law
    607 Siblings-in-Law
    608 Artificial Kin Relationships
    609 Behavior toward Nonrelatives

61 KIN GROUPS
    611 Rule of Descent
    612 Kindreds and Ramages
    613 Lineages
    614 Sibs
    615 Phratries
    616 Moieties
    617 Bilinear Kin Groups
    618 Clans
    619 Tribe and Nation

62 COMMUNITY
    621 Community Structure
    622 Headmen
    623 Councils
    624 Local Officials

625 Police
626 Social Control
627 Informal Ingroup Justice
628 Inter-community Relations

63 TERRITORIAL ORGANIZATION
631 Territorial Hierarchy
632 Towns
633 Cities
634 Districts
635 Provinces
636 Dependencies

64 STATE
641 Citizenship
642 Constitution
643 Chief Executive
644 Executive Household
645 Cabinet
646 Parliament
647 Administrative Agencies
648 International Relations

65 GOVERNMENT ACTIVITIES
651 Taxation and Public Income
652 Public Finance
653 Public Works
654 Research and Development
655 Government Enterprises
656 Government Regulation
657 Public Welfare
658 Public Education
659 Miscellaneous Government Activities

66 POLITICAL BEHAVIOR
661 Exploitation
662 Political Intrigue
663 Public Service
664 Pressure Politics
665 Political Parties
666 Elections
667 Political Machines
668 Political Movements
669 Revolution

67 LAW
671 Legal Norms
672 Liability
673 Wrongs
674 Crime
675 Contracts
676 Agency

68 OFFENSES AND SANCTIONS
681 Sanctions

682 Offenses against Life
683 Offenses against the Person
684 Sex and Marital Offenses
685 Property Offenses
686 Nonfulfillment of Obligations
687 Offenses against the State
688 Religious Offenses
689 Social Offenses

69 JUSTICE
691 Litigation
692 Judicial Authority
693 Legal and Judicial Personnel
694 Initiation of Judicial Proceedings
695 Trial Procedure
696 Execution of Justice
697 Prisons and Jails
698 Special Courts

70 ARMED FORCES
701 Military Organization
702 Recruitment and Training
703 Discipline and Morale
704 Ground Combat Forces
705 Supply and Commissariat
706 Navy
707 Air Forces
708 Auxiliary Corps

71 MILITARY TECHNOLOGY
711 Military Engineering
712 Military Installations
713 Ordnance
714 Uniform and Accouterment
715 Military Vehicles
716 Naval Vessels
717 Military Aircraft
718 Special Military Equipment
719 Munitions Industries

72 WAR
721 Instigation of War
722 Wartime Adjustments
723 Strategy
724 Logistics
725 Tactics
726 Warfare
727 Aftermath of Combat
728 Peacemaking
729 War Veterans

73 SOCIAL PROBLEMS
731 Disasters
732 Defectives
733 Alcoholism and Drug Addiction

734 Invalidism
735 Poverty
736 Dependency
737 Old Age Dependency
738 Delinquency

74 HEALTH AND WELFARE
741 Philanthropic Foundations
742 Medical Research
743 Hospitals and Clinics
744 Public Health and Sanitation
745 Social Insurance
746 Public Assistance
747 Private Welfare Agencies
748 Social Work

75 SICKNESS
751 Preventive Medicine
752 Bodily Injuries
753 Theory of Disease
754 Sorcery
755 Magical and Mental Therapy
756 Psychotherapists
757 Medical Therapy
758 Medical Care
759 Medical Personnel

76 DEATH
761 Life and Death
762 Suicide
763 Dying
764 Funeral
765 Mourning
766 Deviant Mortuary Practices
767 Mortuary Specialists
768 Social Readjustments to Death
769 Cult of the Dead

77 RELIGIOUS BELIEFS
771 General Character of Religion
772 Cosmology
773 Mythology
774 Animism
775 Eschatology
776 Spirits and Gods
777 Luck and Chance
778 Sacred Objects and Places
779 Theological Systems

78 RELIGIOUS PRACTICES
781 Religious Experience
782 Propitiation
783 Purification and Expiation

784 Avoidance and Taboo
785 Asceticism
786 Orgies
787 Revelation and Divination
788 Ritual
789 Magic

79 ECCLESIASTICAL ORGANIZATION
791 Magicians and Diviners
792 Holy Men
793 Priesthood
794 Congregations
795 Sects
796 Organized Ceremonial
797 Missions
798 Religious Intolerance

80 NUMBERS AND MEASURES
801 Numerology
802 Numeration
803 Mathematics
804 Weights and Measures
805 Ordering of Time

81 EXACT KNOWLEDGE
811 Logic
812 Philosophy
813 Scientific Method
814 Humanistic Studies
815 Pure Science
816 Applied Science

82 IDEAS ABOUT NATURE AND MAN
821 Ethnometeorology
822 Ethnophysics
823 Ethnogeography
824 Ethnobotany
825 Ethnozoology
826 Ethnoanatomy
827 Ethnophysiology
828 Ethnopsychology
829 Ethnosociology

83 SEX
831 Sexuality
832 Sexual Stimulation
833 Sexual Intercourse
834 General Sex Restrictions
835 Kinship Regulation of Sex
836 Premarital Sex Relations
837 Extramarital Sex Relations
838 Homosexuality
839 Miscellaneous Sex Behavior

84 REPRODUCTION
    841 Menstruation
    842 Conception
    843 Pregnancy
    844 Childbirth
    845 Difficult and Unusual Births
    846 Postnatal Care
    847 Abortion and Infanticide
    848 Illegitimacy

85 INFANCY AND CHILDHOOD
    851 Social Placement
    852 Ceremonial During Infancy
        and Childhood
    853 Infant Feeding
    854 Infant Care
    855 Child Care
    856 Development and Maturation
    857 Childhood Activities
    858 Status of Children

86 SOCIALIZATION
    861 Techniques of Inculcation
    862 Weaning and Food Training
    863 Cleanliness Training
    864 Sex Training

    865 Aggression Training
    866 Independence Training
    867 Transmission of Cultural Norms
    868 Transmission of Skills
    869 Transmission of Beliefs

87 EDUCATION
    871 Educational System
    872 Elementary Education
    873 Liberal Arts Education
    874 Vocational Education
    875 Teachers
    876 Educational Theory and Methods

88 ADOLESCENCE, ADULTHOOD, AND OLD AGE
    881 Puberty and Initiation
    882 Status of Adolescents
    883 Adolescent Activities
    884 Majority
    885 Adulthood
    886 Senescence
    887 Activities of the Aged
    888 Status and Treatment of the Aged

INDEX

PREFACE

First Edition

The first draft of the present <u>Outline</u> was prepared in 1937 through the cooperative effort of its authors. Copies were sent out for criticism to leading specialists in many fields, and nearly one hundred responded with helpful suggestions. In the meantime, each of the authors submitted the proposed classification to a practical test by attempting to organize the materials in a standard ethnography in accordance with it. On the basis of the defects revealed in these tests, and of the suggestions received, the preliminary draft was substantially modified, and was subsequently published in a first edition in 1938.

To the following, whose suggestions proved particularly influential in the preparation of the first edition, the authors acknowledge a special indebtedness: Roland H. Bainton, Raymond V. Bowers, Peter H. Buck, Edwin G. Burrows, John M. Cooper, Arthur L. Corbin, John Dollard, Leonard W. Doob, Fred Eggan, Fred R. Fairchild, Ellsworth Huntington, Eugen Kahn, Albert G. Keller, Clyde Kluckhohn, William Ewart Lawrence, Neal E. Miller, Maurice Parmelee, Wilson D. Wallis, and Benjamin L. Whorf.

A Spanish translation of the first edition, by Rádames A. Altieri, entitled "Guía para la investigación etnológica," was published in Tucuman, Argentina in 1939 as part of Volume I of the <u>Notas del Instituto de Antropología</u> of the Universidad Nacional de Tucumán.

Second Edition

Three years of use by the staff of the Cross-Cultural Survey (see below), during which time the materials on some ninety societies were processed and classified, revealed certain gaps and other deficiencies in the <u>Outline</u>. These were corrected in a second edition, first issued in a private printing for office use in 1942 and reprinted in 1945 as Volume II of the <u>Yale Anthropological Studies</u>.

Third Edition

During World War II the <u>Outline</u> was extensively used on government projects. Experience in classifying information on complex modern societies, notably the Latin American republics and the Japanese Empire, revealed the desirability of splitting certain categories, e.g., those on technology and government, into smaller and more manageable units. The opportunity to do this appeared with the establishment in 1949 of the Human Relations Area Files (see below). Since this necessitated reproducing all the existing Files for distribution to other institutions, it seemed a particularly opportune time to modify the Outline on the basis of the experience accumulated over twelve years. The third edition was the result. It differed from previous editions in a considerable increase in the number of sections and categories and in the elimination of subcategories.

For invaluable suggestions which were incorporated in the third revision the authors are indebted to Selden D. Bacon, Irvin L. Child, Yehudi A. Cohen, Leonard Doob, Cora Du Bois, John Gillin, Ward H. Goodenough, A. Irving Hallowell, Clyde Kluckhohn, Martin Knowlton, Floyd Lounsbury, Stephen W. Reed, John M. Roberts, Betty Clark Rosenthal, John Sirjamaki, Katherine Spencer, and Joseph E. Weckler. Thanks are also due to the many others who have assisted in one way or another in the development of the Outline and its use, in particular to Wendell C. Bennett, Allan R. Holmberg, Alfred Métraux, Alois M. Nagler, Willard Z. Park, and Benjamin Paul.

Since the authors of the first edition had become widely scattered, the primary responsibility for the third revision was assumed by George P. Murdock and Clellan S. Ford, who received substantial assistance from John W.M. Whiting.

Fourth Edition

The fourth edition of the Outline in 1961 and the present second printing with modifications incorporates changes suggested by various staff members of HRAF during the period from 1950 to 1965. These changes are relatively minor. In twelve cases category titles have been altered. In every case the original first word of the original title has been retained. Category 147 (Physiological Data), which was added to the Outline in the form of an insert after the original edition was printed, has now been incorporated. The most extensive change has been the addition of numerous cross-references and an expanded index. The format has been changed slightly to emphasize the importance of the two-digit categories, and to make cross-references easier to use. Minor changes in wording have been made in the category descriptions in many cases. The intent has been to clarify and make explicit rather than to modify. The third edition is not rendered obsolete by the present edition.

HRAF staff members participating in the revision under the general supervision of Frank M. LeBar included George R. Bedell, John Beierle, Robert Lee, and Timothy J. O'Leary, as well as M. L. Bartlett, who earlier made many valuable suggestions. Frank W. Moore directed the preparation of final drafts of changes, all of which were reviewed and approved by George P. Murdock and Clellan S. Ford.

The Outline was originally developed as a tool for the Cross-Cultural Survey, an organization established in 1937 by the Institute of Human Relations at Yale University as part of its program of interdisciplinary research in the social sciences. Under the direction of George P. Murdock, and after 1945 of Clellan S. Ford, this organization engaged in assembling and classifying the basic information on a sample of the peoples of the earth. Its ultimate objective was to organize in readily accessible form the available data on a statistically representative sample of all known cultures -- primitive, historical, and contemporary -- for the purpose of testing cross-cultural generalizations, revealing deficiencies in the descriptive literature, and directing corrective field work.

By 1943 the Survey had excerpted from the literature, translated into English where necessary, classified according to the system in the Outline and systematically filed some 500,000 slips with full or substantial information on nearly 150 cultures. Although most of these represented primitive peoples in all parts of the world, a number of Files had been assembled on more complex civilizations, including a few modern communities and such historical societies as the Imperial Romans and the Elizabethan English.

This body of materials was sufficient for preliminary comparative studies, and a number were undertaken by members of the research staff of the Institute of Human Relations. Among those published to date are the following:

Ford, C.S. "A Comparative Study of Human Reproduction." Yale University Publications in Anthropology, XXXII, 1-111. 1945.

Horton, D. "The Functions of Alcohol in Primitive Societies: A Cross-Cultural Study." Quarterly Journal of Studies on Alcohol, IV, 199-320. 1943.

Murdock, G.P. Social Structure. New York: Macmillan, 1949.

In addition, the Survey attracted an increasing number of scholars in various fields to New Haven to utilize its resources in their own research.

After the entry of the United States into World War II the Cross-Cultural Survey concentrated its efforts largely on areas of probable combat operations, especially in the Pacific. With its budget from the Institute of Human Relations expanded by a grant from the Carnegie Corporation, it assembled considerable information which proved useful to national war agencies. In addition, from materials in its Files it published a series of seven Strategic Bulletins of Oceania on such subjects as meteorology, food and water supply, and the distribution of diseases. These were widely distributed by the Ethnogeographic Board of the Smithsonian Institution.

Strategic Index of the Americas

The increasing use of the Files by government agencies, who frequently sent representatives to New Haven for specific information on particular areas and topics, brought the Survey to the attention of the Coordinator of Inter-American Affairs. This agency entered into a contract with Yale University by which was established, on July 1, 1942, the Strategic Index of Latin America, subsequently renamed the Strategic Index of the Americas. A competent staff was assembled, and the cultures and subcultures of Latin America were classified into approximately one hundred regional units. Using this classification and the Outline of Cultural Materials, the Strategic Index processed, before it was discontinued on September 30, 1943, an estimated third of the major sources on the geography and civilization of modern Latin America. In all, 488 sources totaling 22,663 pages were completely processed and 249 additional sources were translated or compiled in manuscript form but remained unprocessed at the conclusion of the project. Besides excerpting text material, the Index reproduced for the Files all relevant maps, charts, and photographs. It also issued fifteen factual and informative bulletins, including bibliographies, glossaries, and special reports on such subjects as geology, useful flora, food, health, and settlements.

Navy Project

The usefulness of the material in the Cross-Cultural Survey Files on the then Japanese-held islands of the Pacific led the United States Navy Department, in 1943, to contract with Yale University for the continuation of the work on an expanded scale. In addition, three members of the staff received commissions and were assigned the task of organizing the information in the Files, largely from Japanese and other foreign-language sources, in the form of practical handbooks for military government officers. Between August 1943 and November 1944 nine of these Military Government Handbooks were published, covering the Marshall, Caroline, Marianas, Izu, Bonin, Kurile, and Ryukyu Islands. Since the war these handbooks have been declassified and made available for distribution to civilian scholars by the Chief of Naval Operations, Office for Island Governments, Navy Department, Washington, D.C.

Nebraska Project

During 1946 and 1947 the University of Nebraska, in cooperation with the Institute of Human Relations at Yale, conducted a special project for assembling information on the Plains Indians. Using the Outline of Cultural Materials, this project, under the direction of Dr. John M. Roberts, produced complete Files on ten Plains tribes, of which copies are available at both institutions.

Human Relations Area Files

Despite its wide utility, the Cross-Cultural Survey possessed the serious disadvantage that the only complete File was located in one place, which was remote from many institutions of learning. During 1948 and 1949 the Social Science

Research Council, in collaboration with the Carnegie Corporation, undertook to explore the possibilities of duplicating the Files for wider distribution and of continuing the work on a broader basis. Following a careful assessment of the Survey by Dr. Brewster Smith of the Harvard Department of Social Relations, and a demonstration of interest from a number of institutions, an inter-university organization called HRAF (Human Relations Area Files, Inc.) was established and began operations on October 1, 1949. Controlled by an Executive Board representing the participating institutions, HRAF was established for the purpose of producing cross-cultural Files for its members through a grant from the Carnegie Corporation and processing and distributing additional materials through contributions from its participants and foundations. Member institutions at the end of 1960 were:

University of Chicago
University of Colorado
Cornell University
Ecole Pratique des Hautes
    Etudes, Paris
Harvard University
University of Hawaii
University of Illinois
Indiana University
State University of Iowa
Kyoto University
University of Michigan

State University of New York
    at Buffalo
University of North Carolina
University of Oklahoma
University of Pennsylvania
University of Pittsburgh
Princeton University
Smithsonian Institution
University of Southern California
Southern Illinois University
University of Utah
University of Washington

Yale University

Microfilm Edition

The need for a wider distribution of the Area Files than is possible with the twenty-three regular members, led to the production beginning in 1958 of a microfilm version utilizing unitized microfilm. About 100,000 File pages are filmed each year and distributed to participating institutions in the United States and foreign countries. A brochure, Microfiles, which gives full information on this program, is available on request from the Human Relations Area Files.

Physical Aspects of the Files

The HRAF Files of each participating institution are housed in filing cabinets with drawers accommodating slips of the dimensions of five by eight inches. There is a separate File for each distinctive culture or subculture and likewise for each major historical period in the case of societies with historical records extending over periods of substantial cultural change. Within each File the slips are arranged topically according to the categories of this Outline. Thus all the information on the land use practices of the early Aztecs, from all the sources processed, is to be found in a single block, between tabbed separator cards, under Category 311 of the NU7 Aztec File for this particular historical period.

Within such a block of notes the individual slips are arranged in a definite order, namely, 1) by bibliography number and 2) by page number. The bibliography number is the distinctive number assigned to each source processed for the particular File. Within a category, therefore, there will first appear in page order all slips from Source No. 1, followed by those from Source No. 2 in similar order, etc. Each slip carries its bibliography and page numbers.

Full bibliographical references to all sources processed for the particular File are given on separate slips under Category 111, where they are arranged in order of their bibliography numbers. Along with the reference, each bibliography slip includes a brief critique of the source and an analysis of its contents. It also carries a code number from the Outline of World Cultures, which relates the source to 1) a continent or other major geographical division, 2) a culture area or regional subdivision, and 3) a particular culture or subculture. Copies of all bibliographical references are also kept, in alphabetical order of authors, in a master bibliographical File of all sources processed by HRAF.

For each File, one copy of every slip is placed in Category 116 (Texts). This brings together a complete copy, in page order, of each source. By referring to Category 116, users of the Files can establish the complete original context for any statement.

Processing Procedure

The cultures to be processed and the order in which they are to be undertaken are determined by the HRAF staff in consultation with the Executive Board and in accordance with a world sample list drawn up by G. P. Murdock, J. W. M. Whiting, and other cross-cultural specialists. Once a culture has been selected, intensive bibliographical research is initiated to locate and evaluate as many sources as possible, published or in manuscript. The sources are then processed until a point has been reached where the law of diminishing returns makes it advisable to turn to the next culture rather than accumulate additional materials of lesser value.

If a source selected for processing is written in a foreign language, the next step is to prepare a complete and accurate translation. In addition to the translation, which is typed on Multigraph masters for reproduction as File slips, a complete copy of the original foreign text is also filed in Category 116 (Texts) for reference.

Sources selected for processing are photographed page for page onto Multigraph masters, which are then assigned to the researchers for annotation of the content of the source according to the numbered categories of this Outline. These research-analysts enter category numbers on the margins of the masters, first in nonreproducing pencil and later, after checking by another analyst, with a special pen which enables the numbers to be reproduced during the printing process along with the textual material. Annotation is done sentence by sentence, though most category numbers apply to at least a paragraph. Single-sentence references are indicated by category numbers enclosed by brackets. Most paragraphs contain information on more than one subject. Thus a statement to the effect that coiled baskets are made only by old women would be annotated with the numbers 285 and

887 to indicate that copies should be made for both Category 285 (Mats and Basketry) and Category 887 (Activities of the Aged), besides the usual copy for Category 116 (Texts).

It should be emphasized that sources are usually completely annotated, so that the Files contain, not abstracts, but the entire content of each source processed. Occasionally some sections are not processed, but in such case this fact is indicated on the bibliographic (111) slip and the general content of the omitted section is given. In a large collection of folktales, for example, it might seem sufficient to process only a few examples of each type of tale and to indicate for the specialist the location of unprocessed tales. A user of the Files may rest assured that a source contains nothing on a topic of interest to him if he finds no references to omitted materials under the pertinent categories and no indication on the bibliographic slip that the source has been only partially processed.

In the fourth step the Multigraph masters are run through Multigraph printing machines to produce as many copies as are needed for the Files of all HRAF members.

The facsimile File slip reproduced here illustrates the various features of the system. The heading, which is identical for all slips of any single source, gives first the assigned bibliographic number and last name of the author. The number has no significance except as identification. The source number prevents confusion between works by the same author and aids the researcher in locating the correct Category 116 or 111 entries.

The second feature of the heading is the evaluation in which a letter and a number (see below) are given to indicate to the researcher the author's background or field of specialization and the classification of the work as primary data, secondary data, etc.

A   Archeologist, Antiquarian
B   Folklorist
C   Technical Personnel (engineers, agricultural experts, Point Four advisors, etc.)
D   Physician, Physical Anthropologist
E   Ethnologist, Social Anthropologist (Formerly used also for Sociologist, see Z)
F   Foreign Resident
G   Government Official (administrator, soldier, foreign diplomat)
H   Historian
I   Indigene
J   Journalist
K   Geographer
L   Linguist
M   Missionary, Clergyman

N   Natural or Physical Scientist
O   Lawyer, Judicial Personnel
P   Psychologist
Q   Humanist (philosopher, critic, editor, writer, etc.)
R   Artisan (artist, musician, architect, dancer)
S   Social Scientist (other than those designated)
T   Traveler (tourist, explorer)
U   Unknown
V   Political Scientist, Propagandist
W   Organizational Documents and Reports (constitutions, law codes, government or UN reports and documents, censuses)
X   Economist, Businessman
Y   Educator (teacher, school administrator)
Z   Sociologist

SOURCE NUMBER   EVALUATION   AREA FILE CODE
        AUTHOR   FIELD DATE   PUBLICATION DATE

CATEGORY NUMBERS

Sex Status..........
Family Relationships...

Sex Status...........

Sex Status............
Funeral..............
Mourning............

(Punch indicates
this page to be
filed in category
764)

5: Malinowski E-5 (1914-1920) 1929 OLG Trobriands OL6

THE STATUS OF WOMAN

562 the main strands in the social fabric. But in their personal
593 relations the strictest taboo divides brother from sister—
and prevents any sort of intimacy between them.[1]

562 As woman is debarred from the exercise of power, land
ownership, and many other public privileges, it follows
that she has no place at tribal gatherings and no voice
in such public deliberations as are held in connection with
gardening, fishing, hunting, oversea expeditions, war, ceremonial trade, festivities and dances.

2

MORTUARY RITES AND FESTIVITIES

562 On the other hand, there are certain ceremonial and
• 764 festive activities in connection with which women have
765 a great deal both to say and to do. The most important
of these in solemnity and sanctity, as well as the most
imposing in display and extent, are the mortuary ceremonies. In the tending of the corpse, the parade of grief,
the burial with its manifold rites and long series of ceremonial food distributions: in all these activities, which
begin immediately after the death of any important tribes-
man and continue at intervals for months or even years
afterwards, women play a large part and have their own
definite duties to fulfil. Certain women, standing in a
special relationship to the deceased, have to hold the corpse
on their knees, and fondle it; and while the corpse is
tended in the hut, another category of female relatives
performs a remarkable rite of mourning outside: a number

[1] Cf. ch. xiii, sec. 6, and ch. xiv.

36

(File slip reduced 1/4)

1 Poor
2 Fair
3 Good, useful sources but not uniformly excellent
4 Excellent secondary data (e.g., compilations and/or interpretations of
   original data and primary documents)
5 Excellent primary data (e.g., traveler's accounts, ethnological studies,
   etc., as well as primary documents such as legal codes, legal documents, autobiographies etc.)

Thus in the facsimile slip "E" indicates the author was a trained ethnologist; "5" indicates his work is based on original field work. A fuller treatment of an author's qualifications can be found on the bibliographic (111) slip.

Following the evaluation is a date or dates enclosed in brackets. These dates indicate the period during which the field work was done. If no field work was done, or if the dates cannot be established, the entry (no date) appears.

After the field date, a date without brackets shows the time of publication.

The final portion of the heading is the Area File Code. The numbers and letters appearing before and after the name of the society refer to the Outline of World Cultures code symbols. The Outline of World Cultures systematically presents a separate code for the world's societies, areas, and historic periods. Details of this arrangement are explained in the preface to the Outline of World Cultures, or OWC (Human Relations Area Files, 1958).

In the example given, the symbols OL6 in front of the tribal name Trobriands indicate the text or Category 116 will be found in the Trobriands File. The post-posited numbers indicate the specific category slips will also be found in the Trobriands File. If this particular page of this source generally dealing with the Trobriands had contained information on the Louisades the heading would have been as follows:

> 5: Malinowski   E-5   (1914-1920) 1929   OL6 Trobriands
>   Louisades OL5

The "OL6 Trobriands" indicates that the entire page order copy of the text (Category 116) is to be found in the Trobriands File and the "Louisades OL5" indicates the location of specific category slips. In many cases, materials on two or more societies may appear on the same page. In such case the heading would be as follows:

> 5: Malinowski   E-5   (1914-1920) 1929   OL6 Trobriands OL6
>   D'Entrecasteaux OL4
>   Louisades OL5

The 116 or text would still be found only in the Trobriands File, but copies of the specific category slips would be found in all three Files. The initials "T," "D," or "L" would appear above the appropriate category numbers to indicate which material pertained to which File.

Further details on the heading system and other aspects of use of the Files can be found in Guide to the Use of the Files.

Plan of the Outline

The Outline has been devised with two primary purposes in mind: first, to assist the staff in annotating and classifying cultural materials from all societies and, second, to aid researchers in locating readily in the Files the material pertinent to their interests. These objectives have necessitated a single standard system of organization into which all cultural and background material can be fitted for any society from the simplest to the most complex. It is fully realized that cultures differ enormously, not only in the elements which they do or do not contain, but also in the configurations into which their elements are organized. However, the adoption of a distinctive system of classification for each culture, adapted to its particular content and institutions, would require a user of the Files to master the unique organization of each culture before he could locate any item of specific information about it. The authors have therefore been driven perforce to an elaboration of what Wissler called "the universal culture pattern." In consequence, the reader must expect to find classified under the same heading such superficially divergent phenomena as the Indian medicine man and the modern psychoanalyst under Category 756 (Psychotherapists), and the primitive quarrying of flint and the contemporary activities of the Anaconda Copper Company under Category 316 (Mining and Quarrying). Similarly, there can be no special category like "Christianity," pertaining to only a limited number of cultures, but only general categories like 779 (Theological Systems).

The system of classification adopted for the present edition of the Outline divides all cultural and background information into 79 major divisions or two-digit categories, numbered from 10 through 88, and into 631 minor divisions or three-digit categories, numbered by adding digits from 1 to 9 to the numbers of the sections under which they fall. These headings provide an appropriate place for every item of information encountered in the cultures processed by HRAF. Materials not readily classifiable under any existing three-digit category are filed under the appropriate two-digit category. Materials of a summary nature touching briefly on several specific three-digit categories will generally be classified under the major two-digit category.

Following the number and title of each category in the Outline is a brief descriptive statement indicating the range of information to be filed or sought under that particular heading. It is impossible, of course, to do more than suggest the immense variety of possible specific content. Beneath the statement there normally appears a list of cross-references to other categories under which related material is filed. These cross-references are presented in tabular form in numerical order.

Being designed for universal application, the categories are naturally not mutually exclusive for every individual culture. Some overlap is inevitable. For this reason closely related categories are normally grouped in the same section and, wherever possible, adjacent to one another. In the case of material which overlaps two or more categories, a decision is made as to which is the most appropriate and the material is classified there. Separate copies of a slip are not ordinarily made for two categories that are cross-referenced to each other or located in the same section unless a clear-cut distinction between categories of the same major division can be made.

The authors have frequently been asked to elucidate the theoretical principles underlying the system of classification. They admit only that they have attempted to group inherently related categories in the same section and that they have arranged the sections in an order that is not wholly without logic. Beyond this, however, they insist that the classification is wholly pragmatic. As a matter of fact, in earlier editions they attempted in several instances to institute classificatory innovations that seemed sounder on theoretical grounds than categories in general use. In practically every such case, however, they were compelled to abandon the innovation because the attempt to press the data into a new mold invariably necessitated splitting up passages in the sources and distributing the parts so widely that the context for each individual item evaporated. Through trial and error, therefore, the categories have come to represent a sort of common denominator of the ways in which anthropologists, geographers, sociologists, historians, and nonprofessional recorders of cultural data habitually organize their materials.

Types of Categories

Perhaps the chief theoretical assumption affecting the organization of the Outline is the recognition that any element of culture may have as many as seven major facets, any one of which can be taken as the primary basis of classification. Each of the seven is extensively used in the descriptive literature, and all seven have been employed in defining at least some of the categories in the Outline.

Every element of culture involves, in the first place, a patterned activity, i.e., a customary norm of motor, verbal, or implicit (covert or ideational) behavior. The nature of such an activity is the primary basis of classification for such categories as 484 (Travel), 521 (Conversation), and 674 (Crime).

Secondly, an activity is normally considered appropriate only under certain circumstances, e.g., of time or place. Categories like 527 (Rest Days and Holidays), 731 (Disasters), and 841 (Menstruation) embrace varied activities linked by their occurrence under similar circumstances.

In the third place, customary activities are frequently associated with a particular subject, i.e., a culturally defined class of persons, the occupants of a particular status, or the members of a specified social group. Categories like 462 (Division of Labor by Sex), 614 (Sibs), and 793 (Priesthood) depend more upon who performs an activity than upon what activity is performed or the circumstances of its performance.

Fourthly, an activity is commonly directed toward some object, which may be an inanimate thing, an animal, or a person. Such categories as 235 (Poultry Raising), 252 (Food Preparation), 602 (Kin Relationships), and 855 (Child Care) are oriented primarily around the objects of activities.

In the fifth place, many activities are accomplished by the use of some means external to both the subject and the object, e.g., an artifact or a human assistant. Categories like 206 (Telephone and Telegraph) and 411 (Weapons) are defined basically by means of the first type; those like 476 (Mutual Aid) and 676 (Agency) by means of the second type.

Sixthly, activities are normally performed with a purpose or goal in mind. It is the purpose, rather than any other criterion, that determines whether a particular item shall be assigned to such a category as 211 (Mnemonic Devices), 754 (Sorcery), or 861 (Techniques of Inculcation).

Finally, an activity commonly has some concrete result, affecting either the subject, the object, or both. The result often corresponds closely to the purpose, especially in technological activities. The two, however, may bear no relationship to each other. In the case of sorcery, for example, the purpose is to injure the object, but the usual result probably is merely to gratify or allay the aggressive impulses in the subject. Categories like 396 (Shipbuilding) and 681 (Sanctions) are defined primarily in terms of the results of activities.

To give full and separate expression to each of the above seven principles, though theoretically possible, would produce an intolerably cumbersome system of classification, and would seriously fragment the descriptive materials. The authors have consequently chosen in most instances to follow the sources, in which common-sense categories predominate. These reflect now one principle of classification, now another, oftentimes two or more in combination. When alternative principles are in widespread use these are recognized, even though they sometimes lead to assigning similar data to different categories. The same process of fashioning an iron blade, for example, might be filed under either 325 (Metallurgy), 326 (Smiths and their Crafts), or 391 (Hardware Manufacture), depending upon whether the particular source treated it from the point of view of the object (iron), the subject (smith), or the result (tool).

Some authors organize their data into broader or more abstract categories than do others. The Outline adopts a number of these, e.g., 181 (Ethos), 463 (Occupational Specialization), 511 (Standard of Living). It should be emphasized, however, that broad categories of this type will normally include only data thus organized in the sources, and that much pertinent information on such topics will be found only under the more specific categories employed in other sources.

To avoid overloading certain categories with masses of descriptive detail about the artifacts employed as means in the particular cultural activity, or produced as results thereof, it has seemed advisable to reserve a number of categories specifically for such descriptive data. The most important of these are found in Sections 29 (Clothing), 34 (Structures), 40 (Machines), 41 (Tools and Appliances), and 71 (Military Technology).

Some categories, e.g., those of Sections 77 (Religious Beliefs) and 82 (Ideas about Nature and Man), are reserved primarily for symbolic or ideational behavior. A number are concerned almost exclusively with organized social relationships and groups, e.g., those in Sections 47 (Business and Industrial Organization), 61 (Kin Groups), 64 (State), 70 (Armed Forces), and 79 (Ecclesiastical Organization).

A major distinction should be noted between those categories -- the great majority -- which describe the behavior, culture, or social structure of a people as it appears equally to the native and the outside observer, and other categories which present interpretations or conclusions involving a level of scientific knowledge and abstraction possible only in a highly trained observer. The latter type includes most of the categories in Sections 13 through 19 and such others as

435 (Price and Value), 511 (Standard of Living), 781 (Religious Experience), and 811 (Logic).

Use of the Outline in Field Research

Though not designed as a field manual, the Outline has been found a useful aid in the field. It calls attention to a very wide range of cultural, social, and background phenomena, some portions of which are all too often omitted in descriptive accounts. Moreover, its descriptive sections can suggest leads for inquiry that might otherwise be overlooked. Finally, it provides a useful system for the classification of field notes, bringing together data gathered at different times from different informants that would be widely scattered in a notebook, and thus drawing attention to inconsistencies and problems that demand clarification on the spot. Field workers should be warned, however, that no culture will fit precisely into the framework of the Outline, and should be prepared to modify the system of classification freely in adjustment to exigencies in the local situation. And under no circumstances should they organize the published report of their findings in slavish accordance with the sections and categories of the Outline.

In instances where field work is undertaken in societies for which HRAF has processed the earlier sources, a careful preliminary study of the material in the File should pay rich dividends. It will save the researcher from duplicating the sound work of his predecessors and reveal gaps which need to be filled. Above all, perhaps, it will call attention to inconsistencies which should be reconciled and to important problems which demand a solution.

Use of the Files for Scientific Research

Any problem in the human sciences requiring analysis of the literature on a number of different societies can usually be studied with the use of the Files in an inconsiderable fraction of the time needed to accomplish the same work through the ordinary techniques of library research. Even if its solution requires other methods, a brief pilot study in the Files will often indicate whether or not the project as conceived is feasible, or the hypothesis as formulated is likely to be validated. The suggestions below are designed to expedite the efficient use of the Files for scientific research.

The ready location of the data needed will be a primary requirement of all research. For this purpose the Outline provides two aids: a table of contents and an extensive index. Referred by these aids to particular categories, the researcher should carefully scrutinize the introductory statements at the head of each relevant section. These describe the content of the section and sometimes provide important definitions. The statements in the specific categories should also be closely examined to ascertain whether they are designed to include the kind of data sought, and note should be taken of other cross-referenced categories under which relevant material may be filed. Armed with a list of presumably pertinent categories, the researcher should then go to the Files and inspect the slips themselves. In addition to the cross-referenced categories, he should examine the slips in categories adjacent to the obviously pertinent ones. In this way he should be able to ascertain in a few minutes whether a particular File contains any information relevant to his subject, and if it does, to secure the packet of slips which he needs.

Scientists with a strong theoretical interest, but who are inexperienced in the use of the Files, are likely to be attracted first to the more generalized and theoretically oriented categories. They should recognize the fact, noted above, that it is precisely these categories that are least likely to contain all the relevant material. Careful analysis of what they seek, however, should readily lead them to the more concrete categories that contain the rest of the data. A researcher interested in standards and levels of living, for example, should not confine himself to Category 511 (Standard of Living) but should also turn to the categories on the specific components of such standards and levels, e.g., 262 (Diet), 291 (Normal Garb), 342 (Dwellings), 517 (Leisure Time Activities), 556 (Accumulation of Wealth), and 735 (Poverty).

Specialists in other human sciences who lack a grounding in anthropology or the theory of culture will frequently encounter difficulty in translating their hypotheses into cultural terms so they can be tested against the material in the Files. A psychologist investigating some aspect of the problem of aggression, for example, would be led by the index to only one category, 865 (Aggression Training), though he would doubtless turn of his own accord to Section 15 (Behavior Processes and Personality) and to Category 828 (Ethnopsychology). He might not be aware, however, that substantial material on his subject could be found under such categories as 186 (Ethnocentrism), 266 (Cannibalism), 477 (Competition), 522 (Humor), 526 (Athletic Sports), 578 (Ingroup Antagonisms), 586 (Termination of Marriage), 626 (Social Control), 628 (Informal Intergroup Justice), 668 (Political Movements), 683 (Offenses against the Person), 691 (Litigation), 721 (Instigation of War), 754 (Sorcery), and 798 (Religious Persecution). Such specialists would do well to discuss with an anthropologist or sociologist in their own institution how to translate their problem into cultural terms, or to communicate directly with a representative of HRAF.

The Files are intended as an aid to research in the human sciences, not as a substitute for other types of research. It is fully realized that they are likely to prove more useful in some fields than in others. Their utility will be least in the social sciences that are primarily concerned with behavior in a single society or in a small group of related societies, as is commonly the case in history, economics, political science, and applied sociology. These disciplines normally require specific data of a type not universally available and in quantities beyond the resources of HRAF to accumulate. Their practitioners will find the Files of substantial value only in special instances, particularly where comparative data are needed.

On the other hand, it must be emphatically denied that the Files are exclusively, or even predominantly, designed for the use of anthropologists. From the very outset the Cross-Cultural Survey was intended to serve all the sciences that are concerned with human behavior in broad perspective, i.e., with establishing valid principles not limited in time or space, and HRAF has committed itself to the same policy. The Executive Board of the latter organization, as a matter of fact, has officially decided to develop the Files so that they will serve alike all the universal, as opposed to the culture-bound, human disciplines, and it has defined the universal sciences as including sociology, cultural anthropology, psychology, human biology, and geography. The interests of these five disciplines, as reflected through the official representatives of the participating institutions, will determine the kinds of materials to be processed for the Files.

000 MATERIAL NOT CATEGORIZED

000 MATERIAL NOT CATEGORIZED--materials not pertinent to any specific category (e.g., personal reminiscences, conjectures, generalized predictions, etc.). Such materials will be found only in category 116 (Texts).

---

10 ORIENTATION

10 ORIENTATION--information especially likely to be needed by users of a file as a frame of reference for understanding the materials classified elsewhere; organization of the file, special coding decisions, and evaluation of the file.

101 IDENTIFICATION--name of the society or cultural group; alternative names bestowed by selves and others; meanings of names; location of group with reference to comparable and larger groups; names given by selves to other groups; affiliation with a culture area or subarea; period as of which the culture is described, and its relationship to other time periods; local and temporal subdivisions employed in the classification of data; specification of date and locale of field study; etc. See also:

Territorial organization	63	Intracultural differences	184
Location	131	Linguistic relationships	197
Cultural distributions	171	Ethnic stratification	563

102 MAPS--reproductions of all maps. Specific maps will also be found under the appropriate descriptive category. See also:

Descriptive geographical data	13	Route maps and charts	487
Settlement patterns	.361		

103 PLACE NAMES--lists of the names of settlements and geographical features; etymologies of place names; historical and cultural connotations; etc. See also:

Settlements	36	Territorial divisions	631
Personal names	551		

104 GLOSSARY--definitions of native terms frequently used in the sources; orthographies and transliteration systems. See also:

Word lists and vocabulary	192

105 CULTURAL SUMMARY--synopsis of the whole culture (as a background for specific information); references to summaries in other works. See also:

Cultural history   17   Ethos   181

---

11 BIBLIOGRAPHY

11 BIBLIOGRAPHY--sources of information on the particular society during the time period specified in the Outline of World Cultures, and data relevant to their evaluation.

111 SOURCES PROCESSED--complete bibliographical references to all sources actually processed, with a brief critique of each. Sources are numbered, and arranged numerically.

112 SOURCES CONSULTED--full bibliographical references to sources consulted but not processed. Sources are arranged by alphabetical order of authors' surnames.

113 ADDITIONAL REFERENCES--bibliographical lists; annotated bibliographies; works referred to in processed sources; etc.

114 COMMENTS--reviews; critiques of earlier sources; information about authors and their backgrounds; general statements on field experience; etc. See also:

Methodology   12   Date and locale of field study   101

115 INFORMANTS--identification and characterization of persons serving as sources of information. See also:

Use of informants and interpreters in field   Life histories   159
   research   124

116 TEXTS--a full set of pages from each processed source, arranged in page order, as a means of establishing the context for any particular slip. Sets are arranged in the numerical order of the sources. See also:

Literary texts   539

117 FIELD DATA--journals and diaries kept in the field; unorganized field notes; etc. This category is primarily designed for materials not adapted to distribution among other categories.

---

12 METHODOLOGY--descriptions and discussions of methods employed by the observers of the particular society. Generalized statements dealing with several of the specific subjects covered below.

121 THEORETICAL ORIENTATION--research aims and objectives (e.g., complete ethnographic description, study of a particular institution or culture complex, testing of a theoretical hypothesis); general theoretical approach (e.g., historical, functional, psychological); formulation of research program; reasons for choice of particular field site; etc. See also:
General information about the author 114

122 PRACTICAL PREPARATIONS--source of financial support; selection and assembly of equipment; arranging problems of transportation and bureaucratic red tape; familiarization with previous descriptive literature; learning language, etc.

123 OBSERVATIONAL ROLE--techniques for establishing rapport; assumption or ascription of a status in the community; methods of altering the observer's status; adoption of the technique of participant observation; degree of participation in community life actually achieved; effect of the observer's presence on the life of the community; limitations imposed by sex of observer; etc.

124 INTERVIEWING--methods of selecting informants or subjects (e.g., sampling); use and selection of interpreters; methods of checking and rewarding informants and interpreters; group interviewing; methods of interviewing (e.g., question and answer, nondirective, use of topical outlines); special techniques (e.g., life history, genealogical, event centered); use of documents prepared by informants; etc. See also:
Informants 115

125 TESTS AND SCHEDULES--description of tests used (e.g., intelligence, projective); schedules and questionnaires employed (e.g., preparation, pretesting); administration of tests, schedules, and questionnaires; sampling techniques; methods of scoring; use of control groups; special experiments; census-taking by author; etc. See also:
Results of tests of sensation and perception . . 151   Results of personality tests 157, 159
Results of aptitude and intelligence tests. . . 153

126 RECORDING AND COLLECTING--methods of note taking (e.g., verbatim, post-interview summaries); taking of native texts; use of diaries and journals; utilization of sound and photographic equipment; preparation of sketches, charts, and maps; collection of field specimens.

127 HISTORICAL RESEARCH--extent to which original field research was supplemented or replaced by the use of records; types of records utilized (e.g., archeological remains, unpublished documents, museum collections, census data, literary sources, earlier published materials); techniques of analysis and criticism applied in assessing source materials; etc. See also:

History   17

128 ORGANIZATION AND ANALYSIS--methods of processing raw data (e.g., analysis, classification, quantification); special techniques of analysis (e.g., sociometric); preparation of tables and graphs; methods of determining consistency, reliability, and validity of results (e.g., statistical, use of ratings and scales); organization of materials for presentation in published form; etc. See also:

Orthographies and transliteration systems . . .   104

---

13 GEOGRAPHY

13 GEOGRAPHY--general statements covering several aspects of geographical description and analysis. For conceptions of natural phenomena see 82.

131 LOCATION--latitude and longitude; position in relation to land and sea (e.g., insular, coastal, interior); area of territory occupied; accessibility by land and sea routes; boundaries; etc. See also:

Territorial organization.   63   Maps   102
Location of group in relation to others . . .   101

132 CLIMATE--type of climate; seasons (e.g., number, dates, character); temperature (e.g., annual mean, extreme range, diurnal and seasonal variations); precipitation (e.g., mean annual rainfall, seasonal distribution, snowfall); humidity; frosts; winds (e.g., prevailing winds, cyclonic storms); etc. See also:

Heat   374   Reaction to typhoons and tornadoes.   731
Meteorological research and weather stations .   654   Ethnometeorology   821

133 TOPOGRAPHY AND GEOLOGY--altitude above sea level; relief (e.g., hills, mountains, plateaus, passes); bodies of water (e.g., lakes, rivers, arms of the sea, swamps); subsurface water; character of seacoast and adjacent marine floor; tides and currents; floods; areas of volcanic and seismic activity; etc. See also:

Land and water transport . . . .   49, 50   Seismic and volcanic disasters   731
Water supply   312   Ethnogeography   823
Routes   487

134 SOIL--physical and chemical characteristics of the soil; erosion; soil types and soil fertility; area susceptible of cultivation (e.g., by local methods, by modern scientific methods); etc. See also:

Soil science. 242   Land use 311

135 MINERAL RESOURCES--availability or significant lack of mineral deposits (e.g., metals, stone, coal, petroleum, clay, salt); quantity, quality, and distribution of minerals; etc. See also:

Exploitation of mineral resources 31   Metallurgy 325
Salt manufacture 258   Petroleum and coal products industries . . 382

136 FAUNA--principal native species, especially mammals, reptiles, birds, fish and shellfish, insects, and disease-bearing micro-organisms; historical changes (e.g., introduced species); etc. See also:

Hunting, fowling, and fishing 22   Ethnozoology. 825
Animal husbandry 23

137 FLORA--general type of flora (e.g., jungle, equatorial forest, tropical scrub, savanna, desert, steppe, prairie, deciduous forest, coniferous forest, tundra); types of wood; important species of land and marine flora; historical changes (e.g., introduced species); etc. See also:

Cultivated plants 24   Ethnobotany 824
Collecting 222

---

14 HUMAN BIOLOGY

14 HUMAN BIOLOGY--general statements dealing with several types of scientific biological data about the members of the society. For beliefs about the human organism see 82.

141 ANTHROPOMETRY--mean, range, and sex distribution of physical measurements (e.g., stature, weight, span, length of limbs); indices (e.g., cephalic, nasal); etc. See also:

Postures 516   Conception of ideal bodily proportions . . . 826

142 DESCRIPTIVE SOMATOLOGY--color of skin, hair, and eyes; form, length, and distribution of hair; musculature; secondary sexual characteristics; somatotype data; etc.

143 GENETICS--blood groupings; incidence of sex-linked characteristics (e.g., color blindness, hemophilia); other data of specific genetic significance (e.g., unusual response potentialities or limitations); etc. See also:

Notions about heredity 827

144 RACIAL AFFINITIES--indicated affiliation with established races and sub-races; supporting evidence; extent of race mixture; etc. See also:

Distribution of ethnic groups 162   Ideas about race 829
Ethnic stratification and status of racial
   hybrids 563

145 ONTOGENETIC DATA--evidence as to physical growth and mental development during infancy and childhood; eruption of teeth; age at puberty for each sex; age at menopause and onset of senile impotence; characteristics of menstruation and menopause; physical senescence; etc. See also:

Adolescence, adulthood, and old age. . . . 88   Development and maturation during
                                    infancy and childhood 856

146 NUTRITION--evidences of malnutrition and dietary deficiencies; adequacy of the diet of subgroups and of the population as a whole; chemical analyses of native foods; etc. See also:

Morbidity 164   Research in nutrition. 742
Customary diets 262   Infant feeding 853

147 PHYSIOLOGICAL DATA--evidence bearing upon physiological systems and their functions (e.g., cardio-vascular, respiratory, gastro-intestinal, genito-urinary, nervous, endocrine); metabolism; salt and water balance; indications of physiological stamina (e.g., strength and endurance); characteristic body odor; etc. See also:

Sexual behavior 83   Incidence of disease. 164
Occurrence of genetic traits. 143   Physical deformities. 732
Sensation and perception 151   Native ideas about physiology. 827
Drives and emotions 152

---

15 BEHAVIOR PROCESSES AND PERSONALITY

15 BEHAVIOR PROCESSES AND PERSONALITY--general statements dealing with several distinct types of mechanisms and manifestations of individual behavior and personality as these appear to the observer and the scientist. For their interpretation by members of the society see 828; for data on the socialization process see 86; for education see 87.

151 SENSATION AND PERCEPTION--acuity of vision, hearing, taste, smell, and touch (e.g., uncontrolled observations, reports of tests); evidence on sensory discrimination and perception (e.g., form configurations, color perception, optical illusions, tone discrimination); data on the cultural patterning of perception; etc. See also:

Food preferences	262	Rhythm in dancing	535
Use of perfumes	302	Defectives	732
Notions about heat and cold perception	374	Ideas about form, color, and sound	822
Optical instruments	416	Standards of sensory pleasantness and	
Appreciation of form and perspective in art	532	unpleasantness	828
Musical appreciation	533		

152 DRIVES AND EMOTIONS--evidence bearing upon the nature and intensity of basic impulses or drives (e.g., hunger, thirst, need for oxygen, sex, urination, defecation, pain, heat and cold discomfort, fatigue); information pertaining to the incidence and quality of derived drives and emotions (e.g., aggression, anger, hate, jealousy, fear, anxiety, depression, grief, disgust, homesickness, love, sympathy, elation, excitement, mirth, curiosity, greed, ambition, vanity, inferiority); expression and control of emotions (e.g., stoicism); etc. See also:

Thirst and narcotic cravings	27	Patterned expressions of emotions	201
Ornament and mutilation	30	Hunger	261
Sleep and elimination	51	Labor and leisure	461
Recreation	52	Leisure time activities	517
Legal offenses	68	Ingroup antagonisms	578
Socialization of impulses	86	Motives for waging war	721
Recurrent personality traits	157	Emotional reactions in religion	781
Profanity	195	Sexuality	831

153 MODIFICATION OF BEHAVIOR--specific evidence concerning the mechanisms of conditioning and habit formation (e.g., conditioned and unconditioned stimuli, configurations, response hierarchy, random behavior, positive and negative reinforcement, generalization, discrimination, anticipation); data on types of problem solution (e.g., trial and error, insight or intelligence, imitation); evidence as to special mechanisms in verbal or symbolic learning; results of aptitude and intelligence tests; data bearing upon conscious mental processes (e.g., memory, judgment, reasoning, conation, reactions in emergencie); etc. See also:

Culture change	17	Ethnopsychology	828
Attitudes	208	Techniques of inculcation	861
Logic	811	Educational methods	876

154 ADJUSTMENT PROCESSES--evidence bearing upon the incidence, nature, and cultural patterning of unconscious mental processes (e.g., free association, dreaming, fantasy, visions, inspiration, intuition); modes of resolving situations involving conflict, frustration, and anxiety; observations and inferences concerning adjustment mechanisms (e.g., repression, regression, displacement, projection, introjection, identification); etc. See also:

Ingroup antagonisms	578	Dream interpretation and vision quest	787
Sorcery	754	Rationalization	811

155 PERSONALITY DEVELOPMENT--evidences and inferences concerning the influence of constitutional factors, of physiological strains, and of social

pressures and physical environment on the development of personality; psychological and psychoanalytic interpretations of personality formation under particular sociocultural conditions; evidence as to levels of personality development (e.g., anal, oral); etc. See also:

Sex	83	Social control	626
Infancy and childhood	85	Legal sanctions	681
Socialization	86	Adolescent problems	883
Family relationships	593		

156 SOCIAL PERSONALITY--conception of the self in relation to others; enhancement and defense of the self; social participation and isolation; individual roles in relation to culturally defined statuses; interpretations of personality as reflecting social norms; conformity; etc. See also:

Social status and mobility	55	Kinship statuses	602
Social stratification	56	Social control	626
Occupational specialization	463	Cultural definition of the self	828
Social relationships and groups	571		

157 PERSONALITY TRAITS--occurrence of idiosyncratic habits (e.g., biting of lips or nails, twiddling of thumbs, wringing of hands); prevalence of cooperativeness and competitiveness; incidence and distribution of recurrent personality traits (e.g., leadership, submissiveness, aggressiveness); incidence and distribution of recognized types of personality (e.g., introvert, extrovert, obsessional, manic, paranoid, hypochondriac); generalized results of personality tests; indications of cultural selectivity with reference to personality traits and types; evidence bearing upon the existence of a modal or basic personality; etc. See also:

Mutual aid and competition	47	Humor	522
Social mobility	55	Statuses adapted to particular	
Derived drives and emotions	152	personality types	554
National character and ethos	181	Social interaction rates	571
Patterned expressions of emotion	201	Types of religious experience	781
Attitudes	208	Ethnopsychology	828
Postures	516		

158 PERSONALITY DISORDERS--incidence and distribution of hypertension and of symptoms of neurotic or functional disorders (e.g., hysteria, hypochondria, compulsive behavior, generalized anxiety), of motor disturbances (e.g., tics, stammering), of dissociative behavior (e.g., amnesia, somnambulism), of hallucinations and delusions, of manias (e.g., kleptomania, pyromania), of sadistic and masochistic behavior, of addiction (e.g., to drugs or alcohol), and of severe psychic disturbances (e.g., phobias, manic-depressive psychoses, involutional melancholia, schizophrenia); psychiatric interpretations of mental disorders; etc. See also:

Sexual perversions	83	Alcoholism and drug addiction	733
Socialization	86	Insane asylums	734
Incidence of organic diseases	164	Psychotherapy	755
Conception of conscience	577	Care of the insane	758
Crimes, torts, and sins	673	Suicide	762
Delinquency	674, 738	Ideas about abnormal mental states	828
Feeblemindedness	732	Adolescent problems	883

159 LIFE HISTORY MATERIALS--observations and interpretations of individual behavior, character, and personality; clinical analyses; case records; biographical materials; collections and interpretations of individual dreams; results of tests designed to measure acquired behavior or personality (e.g., tests of motor or verbal skills, projective tests); etc. Generalizations or conclusions relating to groups or classes of individuals will be filed elsewhere under appropriate headings. For specific professional or occupational biographies, see also under appropriate headings. See also:

Offenses and sanctions	68	Description of tests and schedules	125
Sex	83	Avenues of individual achievement	554
Socialization	86	Dependency	736
Data on informants	115	Types of religious experience	781
Unclassified field data	117	Interpretations of dreams	787

16 DEMOGRAPHY

16 DEMOGRAPHY--general statements covering several distinct types of information on population, including vital statistics.

161 POPULATION--enumerations and estimates (with dates); density (e.g., arithmetical, for arable land); population trends; etc. See also:

Population policy	168	Census taking	659

162 COMPOSITION OF POPULATION--distribution of population by age, sex, locality, marital status, mode of life (e.g., rural and urban, nomadic and sedentary), and by social groupings (e.g., occupation, religion, class, ethnic group); size of families; etc. See also:

Defectives and dependents	73	Ethnic stratification	563
Literacy	212	Age at marriage	582
Location and distribution of settlements	361	Incidence of plural marriages	595
Urban and rural differentiation	369	Statistics on crime	674
Occupational specialization	463	Educational statistics	871

163 BIRTH STATISTICS--birth rates; distribution of births (e.g., by season, locality, race, sex, occupation); incidence of stillbirths and multiple births; age of parents at birth of first child; spacing of children; number of children

per completed family; etc. See also:

Childbirth . . . . 844 Incidence of illegitimacy 848

164 MORBIDITY--incidence, nature, and distribution of various diseases and accidents (e.g., by location, season, sex, age, occupation); occurrence of epidemics; evidence of immunity or susceptibility to disease; dental ailments; etc. See also:

Morbidity as a social problem 73   Malnutrition and dietary deficiencies . . . 146
Theory and treatment of disease 75   Incidence of neuroses and psychoses 158
Care of infants and children 85   Public health 744

165 MORTALITY--death rates (crude and corrected); infant and maternal mortality; distribution of deaths (e.g., by cause, season, age, occupation, locality); life expectancy; authentic cases of extreme longevity; prevalent causes of death (e.g., illness, accident, old age); etc. See also:

Homicide 682   Suicide 762
Mortality in warfare 727   Infanticide and abortion 847

166 INTERNAL MIGRATION--shifting of residence between communities and districts within the society; organized resettlement; trends toward redistribution of the population; etc. See also

Seasonal migrations 221   Travel 484
Degree of permanence or impermanence   Rule of residence in marriage 591
   of settlements 361

167 IMMIGRATION AND EMIGRATION--extent and sources of immigration; extent and destination of emigration; reasons of migration; trends; restrictive regulation; colonization; etc. See also:

Prehistoric migrations 174   Colonial dependencies 636
Travel 484   Naturalization 641
Ethnic stratification 563   Transplantation of conquered populations . . . 728
Slave trade 567

168 POPULATION POLICY--theories and attitudes relating to the control of population; measures designed to stimulate or limit population growth; concepts of optimum population; etc. See also:

Specific data on cannibalism 266   Sterilization of defectives 732
Castration 304   Care of the sick and injured 734, 758
Land utilization 311   Human sacrifice 782
Living standards 511   Birth control 842
Marriage regulation 582   Abortion and infanticide 847
Celibacy 589   Child care 855
Capital punishment 681   Treatment of the aged 888

---

17 HISTORY AND CULTURE CHANGE--general statements dealing with several specific types of information on history and culture change. Since separate files will be prepared on each major historical period for societies with an appreciable known time depth, the categories below are designed to include only (a) information bearing upon the society's prehistory and (b) historical data for the specific time period which do not readily fall into particular categories elsewhere in the Outline.

171 DISTRIBUTIONAL EVIDENCE--occurrence of similar culture traits in other societies; inferences from trait distributions; etc. See also:

Distribution of biological traits   14   Linguistic relationships   197
Affiliation with particular culture areas
or subareas   101

172 ARCHEOLOGY--prehistoric culture sequences and chronology (e.g., as determined by geological and paleontological evidence, stratigraphy, typology, tree-ring dating); archeological supplementation of the historical record; evidence from epigraphy; historical inferences from archeological data; description of archeological sites or artifacts; etc. See also:

Archeology as a discipline.   814

173 TRADITIONAL HISTORY--oral historical traditions and evidence as to their reliability; dynastic lists and genealogies; historical inferences from myth and tradition; etc. See also:

Traditions of kin groups   61   Mythology.   773
Myth texts.   539   Historians and genealogists.   814
Kinship genealogies.   601

174 HISTORICAL RECONSTRUCTION--inferences as to origins, migrations, contacts, prehistory and culture history from various types of evidence (e.g., anthropometry and language); etc. See also:

Historical research   814

175 RECORDED HISTORY--written sources (e.g., chronicles, reports of travelers, official records and documents) and their evaluation; evidence and inferences about prehistoric events from such sources; summaries of historical development within the periods distinguished under 101; specific historical information pertinent to an understanding of culture change; etc. See also:

Records.   21   Historiography   814
Literary texts   539

176 INNOVATION--analyses or general summaries of discoveries and inventions originating within the cultural group; factors involved (e.g., accident, genius, cultural base); number, range, and frequency of innovations, inventors and innovators; etc. For specific inventions see the appropriate

descriptive category. See also:
Patents and copyrights 424

177 ACCULTURATION AND CULTURE CONTACT--number, character, and intensity of contacts with alien cultures; factors affecting cultural receptivity; instances of cultural borrowing; adaptive modification of introduced elements; agencies and agents of culture change; etc. See also:
Immigration 167   Colonial administration 636
Loan words 192   Foreign relations 648
Foreign trade 439   Missions 797
Ethnic stratification 563

178 SOCIOCULTURAL TRENDS--changes in fundamental underlying conditions; linear trends (e.g., cultural drift); cyclical trends (e.g., fashions and vogues); dynamic processes (e.g., integration, selective elimination, cultural evolution); evidence of cultural lag; evidence of cultural continuity or stability; etc. See also:
Demographic trends 161   Trends in urban development 369
Linguistic drift 197   Political movements 668
Clothing fashions 291

---

18 TOTAL CULTURE

18 TOTAL CULTURE--summary statements on the total culture as interpreted or described by an author. The categories below are intended to include descriptive and interpretive materials which pertain to the entire culture or which override a number of more specific categories. Consequently much of the material pertinent to the individual topics below will be found only under other headings.

181 ETHOS--general orientation of the culture; predominating interests, values, themes, and motivations; characterizations of the total culture (e.g., as "conservative," "competitive," "militaristic," "spirit-ridden," "Apollonian," "folk," "urban"); allegations and inferences as to national character; etc. See also:
Cooperation and competition 47   General character of religion 771
Prevalent personality types 157   Social philosophy 829
Ethics 577

182 FUNCTION--internal cultural consistency or its lack; allegations of integration or disintegration; adjustments of parts of the culture to one another; relation of cultural forms to biological and social needs and to physical environment; etc. See also:
Integrative process in culture change 178   Functional integration of kinship systems . . . 601

183 NORMS--native and scientific definitions of custom (e.g., as ideal patterns, as ranges of variation within limits, as statistical inductions from observed behavior); positive and negative norms (e.g., folkways, taboos); verbalized and covert norms; investment of norms with affect and symbolic value (e.g., mores, idealization); discrepancies between ideals and behavior; configurations of norms (e.g., culture complexes, institutions); etc. See also:

Attitudes	208	Taboos	784
Ethical ideals	577	Transmission of social norms	867
Legal norms	671		

184 CULTURAL PARTICIPATION--prevalence of "specialties" and "alternatives"; degree of proliferation of subcultures, intra-cultural differences, and special statuses; extent to which the entire culture is socially shared; etc. See also:

Social stratification	56	Occupational specialization	463
Individual roles within statuses	156	Differences in standard of living	511
Dialectic differentiation	197	Ascribed and achievable statuses	554
Urban and rural differences	369	Ethnic stratification	563
Regional specialization in production	438		

185 CULTURAL GOALS--social foresight; concept of progress; reform movements and utopian goals; prevention of waste; social planning; conservation policies; etc. See also:

Organization of production and distribution	47	Land reform	423
Individual achievement	55	Economic planning and development	433
Specific government projects	65	Saving and investment	454
Population policy	168	Political doctrines, policies, and programs	668
Dynamics of culture change	178	Social insurance	745
City planning	361	Social philosophy	829

186 ETHNOCENTRISM--exaltation of the ingroup (e.g., consciousness of kind, local pride, patriotism, class consciousness, old school tie); unfavorable judgments of other groups (e.g., race prejudice, religious intolerance, national antipathies); overt manifestations (e.g., snobbishness, discrimination, ethical dualism, nationalism); symbolic representation (e.g., flags, anthems, emblems, national heroes); channeling of hostilities (e.g., sports rivalry, ethnic scapegoats); etc. See also:

Sports and games	52	Citizenship	641
Prejudice and discrimination toward ethnic and other stratified groups	56	International relations	648
		Political parties	665
Ingroup antagonisms	578	Nationalistic and nativistic movements	668
Behavior toward nonrelatives, strangers, and aliens	609	Military morale	703
		Religious persecution	798
Moiety rivalries	616	Ideas about race	829
Development of nationalism	619		

19 LANGUAGE--general statements dealing with several aspects of language. The categories below are devoted to the use and scientific analysis of language. Terminology pertinent to special aspects of culture will commonly be found only under appropriate topical headings elsewhere. For examples of native text see 539.

191 SPEECH--notions about language; standards of correctness; individual speech idiosyncrasies; ideas about speech defects (e.g., stuttering); speech aids (e.g., megaphone); bilingualism; etc. See also:

Telephony.	206	Oratory	537
Radio	207	Vituperation	578
Writing	212	Deafmutism	732
Sound recording	216	Cursing	789
Conversation	521	Acquisition of speech	868
Vocal music.	533		

192 VOCABULARY--paucity or richness of vocabulary; range of vocabulary in ordinary use; receptivity to loan words; elaboration of vocabulary in particular directions; special vocabularies (e.g., sacred words, slang, legal language, technical words, occupational jargon); words and phrases with strong emotional connotations; etc. See also:

Place names	103	Kinship terms	601
Glossaries of native words frequently used in descriptive accounts	104	Numerals	802
		Native terms for plants and animals	824, 825
Personal names	551		

193 GRAMMAR--lexical elements (e.g., roots, stems, bases); composition (e.g., compounding, polysynthesis); morphology (e.g., prefixing, suffixing, infixing, ablaut, reduplication, extrusion); covert structure; word categories (e.g., gender, "parts of speech"); modulus categories (e.g., number, tense, comparison, voice, aspect, mode, case); predication; syntax (e.g., intra- and intersentential linkage); end and initial sentence marking; minimal and abbreviated sentences; etc. See also:

Linguistic studies 814

194 PHONOLOGY--phonetic range; list of phonemes; significant length, stress, pitch, and tone; positional variants; phonologic processes (e.g., contraction, fusion, ellipsis); etc. See also:

Transliteration systems and orthography. . . . 104

195 STYLISTICS--differentiation in styles (e.g., conversational, narrative, rhetorical); stylistic modifications in phonology, grammar, and vocabulary; styles typed according to sex, age, status, and social context; euphemisms and metaphorical usages; profanity; etc. See also:

Poetic, oratorical, dramatic, and song styles .	53	Word taboos	784
Social stratification	56	Curses and incantations	789
Etiquette.	576	Obscenity	831

196 SEMANTICS--general problems of meaning and linguistic symbolism; semantics of morphological and lexical elements; affectual connotation (e.g., tone of voice, rapidity of delivery); multiple contextual definitions of words and phrases; semantic drift; etc.

197 LINGUISTIC IDENTIFICATION--dominant language or languages; affiliation with other languages; position within a linguistic stock or family; dialectic differentiation; processes of linguistic change (e.g., drift); etc. See also:
Racial affiliations	144	Cultural affiliations	171

198 SPECIAL LANGUAGES--marginal languages (e.g., pidgin, trade languages); languages confined to a particular sex, occupation, social class, or ethnic group; special adaptations of speech (e.g., yodeling, whistling, ventriloquism); etc. See also:
Sign languages	201	Writing	212
Drum languages	202		

---

20 COMMUNICATION

20 COMMUNICATION--general statements dealing with several aspects of communication over space. For communication over time, by means of records, see 21.

201 GESTURES AND SIGNS--patterned expressions of emotion (e.g., affection, aggression, derision, fear, disgust); gestures of affirmation and negation; indications of size and shape; directive signs (e.g., beckoning, warning); sign languages and their use (e.g., by the deaf, in intertribal communication); etc. See also:
Recreation gestures	52	Greetings and obeisances	576
Gestures in dancing, drama, and oratory . . .	53	Numerical signs.	802
Nervous gestures	157	Ideas about facial reactions	827
Postures	516	Suggestive gestures	832
Humor	522		

202 TRANSMISSION OF MESSAGES--signaling devices (e.g., fire, smoke, blinker, semaphore); signal codes (e.g., drum language, flag codes, Morse code); cryptography; use of carrier birds and animals; messengers and courier systems; etc. See also:
Oral communication	191	Railway signaling systems	496
Travel	484	Embassies.	648
Post and relay stations	495	Scouts in warfare	726

203 DISSEMINATION OF NEWS AND INFORMATION--informal verbal transmission (e.g., rumor, grapevine); criers and heralds; bulletins and newsletters; etc. See also:

Advertising. 447   Conversation 521

204 PRESS--newspapers and magazines; gathering of news and information (e.g., reporters, press releases, news services); content (e.g., news, stories, features); publication and distribution; ownership, organization, and personnel; financial support (e.g., subscriptions, advertising, subsidies); regulation; etc. See also:

Printing 213   Typesetting and printing machinery. . . . 402
Publishing 214   Advertising 447
Printing supplies 218   Literature 538

205 POSTAL SYSTEM--mail services (e.g., collection, delivery); transportation of mail (e.g., by pony express, rail, air); special equipment; parcel post; postal organization and personnel; finance (e.g., postal rates, subsidies); etc. See also:

Express and freight transportation. . . . 48, 49, 50   Postal savings 454
Postoffice buildings   344   Government enterprises 655

206 TELEPHONE AND TELEGRAPH--technology; use of equipment; facilities and services; organization and personnel; public and private systems; finance (e.g., rates, subsidies); regulation; etc. See also:

Telegraphic codes 202   Description of equipment 403
Municipal telephone and telegraph systems . 365   Military signal corps 708
Manufacture of equipment 393   Military communications equipment 718

207 RADIO AND TELEVISION--radio, television, radar, sonar, etc.; technology; use of equipment; facilities and services; organization and specialized personnel; programs and their preparation; audience; finance (e.g., advertising, subsidies); regulation; etc. See also:

Electric power. 377   Advertising 447
Manufacture of radio and television equip-   Use of radio and radar in aviation 507
    ment. 393   Military radio and radar equipment 718
Description of equipment 403

208 PUBLIC OPINION--attitudes; importance accorded them; modes of expression; measurements (e.g., informal means, public opinion polls and surveys); molding of public opinion (e.g., publicity, propaganda); influence of various media; specialized personnel; etc. This category is designed primarily to cover the expression and molding of public opinions and attitudes; in nearly all instances information on specific attitudes will be classified elsewhere under the relevant subject categories. See also:

Political behavior 66   Motion pictures. 546
Education 87   Social control 626
Sociocultural trends 178   Psychological warfare 723
Advertising 447

21 RECORDS--general statements dealing with several aspects of communication over time, by means of more or less permanent records. For communication over space see 20.

211 MNEMONIC DEVICES--aids to memory; elaborated devices (e.g., wampum, quipu); uses; interpretation; commemorative monuments (e.g., statues); etc. See also:

Memorial structures 349   Tallies 802
Property marks 422

212 WRITING--picture writing (e.g., type, technique, use); written symbols (e.g., ideograms, phonograms); systematization (e.g., syllabary, alphabet); reading and spelling; incidence of literacy; writing materials (e.g., parchment, paper, ink); instruments (e.g., pen, brush); methods (e.g., shorthand, chirography); products (e.g., inscriptions, diaries, letters, manuscripts); clerical specialists (e.g., scribes, stenographers); etc. See also:

Communication 20   Representative art 532
Draftsmanship 341   Forms of literature 538
Description of typewriters 405   Signs for numerals 802
Description of writing instruments 413

213 PRINTING--methods (e.g., block printing, movable type, linotype, photographic reproduction); materials (e.g., paper, ink); typography; binding; products (e.g., sheet music, maps, pamphlets); specialists; etc. See also:

Newspapers and magazines 204   Description of printing and binding machinery. 402
Manufacture of printing and binding machinery. 392   Route maps and charts. 487

214 PUBLISHING--organized production and distribution of records; products (e.g., books, sheet music, phonograph records); personnel and organization; selection of material to be published; business arrangements with authors; (e.g., advances, royalties); sales promotion; finance (e.g., profits, subsidies); etc. See also:

Music, art, and literature. 53   Book dealers 549
Newspaper and magazine publishing 204   Humanistic studies 814
Copyrights 424

215 PHOTOGRAPHY--techniques of photographic reproduction; equipment used; products and their uses; specialists; business elaboration of photographic services; etc. See also:

News photographers. 204   Photography as a hobby 523
Manufacture of photographic supplies 395   Motion pictures 546
Description of photographic apparatus 416

216 SOUND RECORDS--techniques of sound recording; appliances used (e.g., phonographs, wire recorders); uses; products; specialists; etc. See also:

Radio 207   Music 533
Appliance manufacture 393   Sound records in motion pictures 546
Description of appliances 405

217 ARCHIVES--repositories of records (e.g., libraries, art galleries, museums); state archives (e.g., court records, administrative records); making collections; accessions; filing and indexing; curatorial activities; services (e.g., exhibits, loans); organization and specialized personnel; sources of support (e.g., public, private); etc. See also:

Library and museum buildings 346   Collecting hobbies 523
Land records 423   Exhibitions 543
Financial records 451   Archivists 814

218 WRITING AND PRINTING SUPPLIES--miscellaneous materials and supplies for offices, libraries, and museums; description and manufacture of expendable supplies not elsewhere classified (e.g., stationery, index cards); etc. See also:

Special tools and apparatus. 41   Printing machinery. 402
Paper manufacture 289

---

22 FOOD QUEST

22 FOOD QUEST--general statements dealing with several aspects of food gathering. For food production through animal husbandry and agriculture see 23 and 24. For the relative importance of various productive activities see 433.

221 ANNUAL CYCLE--seasonal distribution and succession of food-getting and other economic activities; seasonal migrations in the gathering or production of food (e.g., transhumance, nomadism). See also:

Migrations. . . . . 166, 167   Annual ceremonial calendar 796
Economic productivity. 433   Calendar 805

222 COLLECTING--edible materials gathered (e.g., roots, fruits, seeds, seaweed, insects, honey, sap, syrup, eggs); techniques and artifacts employed; economic importance of collecting; organization of activities; division of products; associated beliefs and practices; etc. See also:

Natural resources in fauna and flora. 13   Collection of marine fauna. 226
Collection of nonedible raw materials and salt . 31   Diet 262

223 FOWLING--birds sought; methods and techniques (e.g., nets, snares, birdlime, decoys); special elaborations (e.g., falconry); organization of labor and division of catch; associated beliefs and practices; regulation (e.g., game laws); etc. See also:

Native fauna 136   Weapons 411

224 HUNTING AND TRAPPING--animals sought; hunting methods and techniques (e.g., stalking, collective drive); description and use of traps and snares; use of domestic animals (e.g., dogs, ferrets); special elaborations (e.g., trapping for the fur trade); hunting trips; economic importance of hunting; organization of labor and division of catch; associated beliefs and practices; hunting for sport; regulation (e.g., game laws, open seasons); etc. See also:

Native fauna. 136   Transportation of animal carcasses 483

Weapons 411

225 MARINE HUNTING--animals sought (e.g., whale, alligator, seal, dugong, turtle); methods and techniques employed; special elaborations (e.g., whaling and sealing); organization of labor and division of catch; associated beliefs and practices; regulation; etc. See also:

Weapons 411

226 FISHING--species sought (e.g., fish, shellfish); gathering of marine fauna; fishing methods and techniques (e.g., hook and line, nets, poison); description and use of traps and weirs; special elaborations (e.g., fishing for sport); economic importance of fishing; organization of labor and division of catch; associated beliefs and practices; fishing for sport; regulation (e.g., licenses); etc. See also:

Native fauna. 136   Net manufacture. 286

Manufacture of poisons 278   Boats. 501

227 FISHING GEAR--description of fishing implements and equipment; miscellaneous gear used in fishing (e.g., rods, baskets, lures); etc. See also:

Manufacture of lines. 283   Manufacture of tackle. 391

Manufacture of nets 286

228 MARINE INDUSTRIES--commercial elaboration of the fishing industry; cultivation of fish and shellfish; nonfood marine industries (e.g., sponge collection, pearl diving, shell gathering); specialized equipment and apparatus; organization of labor and production; regulation; fish packing industry; scientific fisheries research; etc. See also:

Canning industry 255   Work in shell. 321

----

23 ANIMAL HUSBANDRY

23 ANIMAL HUSBANDRY--general statements dealing with several of the specialized aspects of animal husbandry indicated below. Information on unspecialized animal husbandry will be filed under 231. For the relative importance of various productive activities see 433.

231 DOMESTICATED ANIMALS--captive and tamed animals; domesticated insects (e.g., silkworms, bees); pets (e.g., dogs, cats); domestic animals; special treatment and uses of each; taming and training; care and feeding; grooming; slaughtering; associated beliefs and rituals; economic and social importance of animal husbandry; diseases; etc. See also:

Work in furs, hides, and skins	281	Names of animals	552
Work in bone and horn	321	Animals as wealth	556
Animal shelters	343	Ethnozoology	825
Use of animals in transportation	492		

232 APPLIED ANIMAL SCIENCE--practical and scientific knowledge about animal husbandry; veterinary science; specialized knowledge of animal nutrition and disease control; selective breeding of animals; artificial insemination; raising of hybrids; special elaborations (e.g., raising and breeding of race-horses); veterinary services and fees; etc. See also:

Horseracing	541	Zoological science	815

233 PASTORAL ACTIVITIES--large-scale herding of grazing animals (e.g., cattle, sheep, reindeer); ranges; driving and watering; branding; roundups; special equipment; specialized personnel and organization; etc. See also:

Nomadism	221	Fences and corrals	417

234 DAIRYING--milking; handling and processing of milk; manufacture of butter and cheese; dairy equipment; special care of dairy animals; creameries; specialized distribution of milk products; organization and regulation of the dairy industry; etc. See also:

Ice cream manufacture	254	Dairy machines	407
Diet	262	Milk inspections	744
Stables	343		

235 POULTRY RAISING--domesticated fowl of economic importance; care and treatment (e.g., feeding, shelter); hatching; egg production; special equipment (e.g., incubation); raising of birds for special purposes (e.g., for eggs, for feathers, for fighting); elaboration of a specialized poultry industry; etc. See also:

Falconry	223	Poultry shelters	343
Poultry breeding	232	Incubators	416
Diet	262	Cockfighting	541
Featherwork	287		

236 WOOL PRODUCTION--specialized raising of sheep and other animals for wool; dipping; shearing; combing and carding; special equipment and apparatus; personnel and organization; etc. See also:

Textile manufacture	28	Tools and apparatus	41

237 ANIMAL BY-PRODUCTS--uses of animal by-products (e.g., bone, teeth, horn, hoofs, claws, eggshells, hides, fur, hair, bristles, feathers, sinews, brains, entrails, urine, manure); processing of such materials not elsewhere described; etc. See also:

Use of manure in agriculture. 241
Work in skins and furs 281
Cordage made from animal by-products. . . . 283
Featherwork. 287
Ornament. 301
Work in bone and horn 321
Glue manufacture 381
Fertilizer industry 387
Amulets, fetishes, and charms . . . 751, 778, 789

24 AGRICULTURE

24 AGRICULTURE--general statements dealing with several of the specialized aspects of agriculture detailed below. General data on unspecialized agriculture will be filed under 241. Information on beliefs and practices associated with specialized cultivation will be filed in the specific category. For the relative importance of various productive activities see 433.

241 TILLAGE--plants cultivated and their relative importance; special treatment accorded each crop; intensity of cultivation (e.g., brand tillage); clearing of land; soil preparation (e.g., hoeing, plowing); use of fertilizers and irrigation; planting; care and protection of growing crops (e.g., weeding, fencing, scarecrows); tools and implements used; economic importance, and adequacy for needs, of agriculture; organization of labor and production; distribution of products; agricultural beliefs, taboos, and rituals; etc. See also:

Agricultural tools and appliances 41
Annual cycle of economic activities 221
Landuse 311
Irrigation systems 312
Granaries and barns 343
Fertilizer manufacture 387
Manufacture of agricultural machines 392
Agricultural machines 407
Fences 417
Ceremonial calendar 796
Ethnobotany 824

242 AGRICULTURAL SCIENCE--practical and scientific knowledge of plant breeding, soils, and parasites; related practices (e.g., seed selection, hybridization, crop rotation, spraying); agricultural experiment and extension work; organization and specialized personnel; etc. See also:

Conservation policy. 185
Veterinary science and stock breeding 232
Applied science 816
Ethnobotany. 824
Agricultural education 874

243 CEREAL AGRICULTURE--specialized cultivation of cereal crops (e.g., maize, millet, rice, wheat); techniques of planting and harvesting (e.g., transplantation, threshing); use of specialized tools, equipment, and machinery; organization of labor and production; etc. See also:

Milling industry 256
Harvesting and threshing machinery. 407

244 VEGETABLE PRODUCTION--gardening where differentiated from field agriculture; truck gardening; specialized production of particular root crops, leaf plants, or vegetable fruits (e.g., peanuts, potatoes, cabbage, beans, tomatoes, melons); special techniques and apparatus; organization of labor and production; etc. See also:

Preservation and storage 251   Canning industry 255

245 ARBORICULTURE--specialized cultivation of trees and shrubs for their fruits, nuts, berries, or other edible products (e.g., apple, breadfruit, coconut, cacao, coffee, orange, raspberry, tea, hops); special care and treatment of each (e.g., grafting, picking, drying, packing); viniculture; silviculture (e.g., raising of trees for wood pulp, soil anchor, screens, shade, decoration); organization of labor and production; etc. See also:

246 FORAGE CROPS--specialized production of crops for animal fodder (e.g., hay, alfalfa, vetch); techniques of planting and harvesting; use of specialized tools, equipment, and machinery; organization of labor and production; processing (e.g., bailing); storage of product (e.g., in stacks, silos, barns); etc. See also:

Animal husbandry 23   Barns and silos 343

247 FLORICULTURE--cultivation of flowering and ornamental plants, shrubs, and trees; flower gardens; greenhouses; special techniques, care, and equipment; business elaboration (e.g., florists, nurseries); etc. See also:

Residential grounds and landscape   Flower arrangement 353
   architecture 351   Parks and botanical gardens 367

248 TEXTILE AGRICULTURE--specialized cultivation of crops for their fibers (e.g., cotton, flax, hemp, jute); techniques of planting and harvesting; use of specialized tools and equipment; separation of fibers (e.g., ginning); organization of labor and production; etc. See also:

Textile manufactures 28   Description of cotton gins and other
Silk production 231   special machinery 407
Wool production 236

249 SPECIAL CROPS--specialized cultivation of plants not classifiable under the foregoing headings (e.g., cinchona, indigo, oil palm, opium poppy, rubber, sugarcane, tobacco); techniques of planting and harvesting; use of specialized tools and equipment; organization of labor and production; processing prior to shipment or industrial use (e.g., curing, refining, grading); etc. See also:

Manufacture and use of narcotics 27   Rubber industry 383
Confectionery industries 257   Dyes 386
Condiments 263

25 FOOD PROCESSING--general statements dealing with several aspects of the techniques by which foodstuffs are transformed from their original state into forms more suitable for preservation or consumption.

251 PRESERVATION AND STORAGE OF FOOD--techniques of food preservation (e.g., drying, smoking, pickling, refrigeration, home canning); use of preservatives and special equipment; accumulation and storage of supplies and reserves; etc. Data on culturally elaborated or commercialized techniques of preservation and storage should be filed under the more specialized categories below. See also:

Granaries 343   Warehousing 488

252 FOOD PREPARATION--processing of edible materials (e.g., grinding, cutting, mixing); cooking methods and techniques (e.g., broiling, roasting, baking, boiling, frying); use of special apparatus (e.g., mills, motors, earth ovens, stoves); use of cooking implements and utensils; recipes; associated beliefs and practices; etc. Data on culturally elaborated or commercialized techniques of food preparation should be filed under the more specialized categories below. See also:

Household implements and utensils 41   Meals 264
Slaughtering 231   Cookhouses 343
Manufacture of butter and cheese 234   Ovens and stoves 354
Condiments 263   Fire and fuel 372

253 MEAT PACKING INDUSTRY--special techniques of slaughtering; methods of preservation (e.g., drying, smoking, refrigeration); special equipment and apparatus; specialized personnel; organization and regulation of the meat packing industry; etc. See also:

Fish packing industry 228   Work in bone and horn 321
Nonindustrialized slaughtering 231   Description of stockyards and factories . . . 348
Utilization of by-products 237   Fertilizer manufacture 387
Work in hides and skins 281   Meat inspection 744

254 REFRIGERATION INDUSTRY--ice harvesting and manufacture; specialized production of refrigerated fruits and vegetables; ice cream manufacture; cold storage plants; technology and equipment; personnel and organization; etc. See also:

Refrigeration of marine products 228   Manufacture of refrigerators 394
Refrigeration of meat products 253   Description of refrigerators 416
Description of industrial plants 348   Refrigerated railway and truck transporta-
Cooling and air-conditioning systems 354   tion 494, 497

255 CANNING INDUSTRY--industrialized processing of meat, fish, and vegetable foods in air-tight containers (e.g., cans, jars, bottles); canneries, special factories, and their equipment; organization of labor and production; etc. See also:

Agricultural production 24
Marine industries 228
Manufacture of bottles and jars 323
Manufacture of canning machinery. 392
Description of food processing machinery. . . 402
Utensils 415

256 CEREAL INDUSTRY--industrialized processing of cereal products (e.g., flour, starch, breakfast foods); storage facilities (e.g., grain elevators); mills and bakeries; technology and special equipment; organization of labor and production; etc. See also:

Cereal agriculture 243
Beverage industries 274
Baking ovens 354
Manufacture of milling machinery. 392
Manufacture of bakery equipment 394
Milling machines 402

257 CONFECTIONERY INDUSTRIES--industrialized processing of sweet condiments and confections (e.g., sugar, honey, syrup, jam, candy, chewing gum); materials, techniques, and equipment; organization of labor and production; etc. See also:

Collection of honey 222
Cultivation of sugarcane 249
Condiments. 263

258 MISCELLANEOUS FOOD PROCESSING AND PACKING INDUSTRIES--specialized processing of foods and nutrients not classifiable under the foregoing categories (e.g., salt, dried and powdered foods, edible oils, vitamins); food packaging in paper or miscellaneous containers; special materials, techniques, and equipment; organization of labor and production; etc. See also:

Beverages and narcotics 27
Dairy industry 234
Salt gathering 317
Boxes and barrels 415

---

26 FOOD CONSUMPTION

26 FOOD CONSUMPTION--general statements covering various aspects pertaining directly to the eating of food.

261 GRATIFICATION AND CONTROL OF HUNGER--ideas about food and ingestion; eating sparingly or to excess; attitudes toward wasting food; special adjustments to hunger or famine; dieting; cultural elaboration of food appetites (e.g., geophagy, gum chewing, epicures); etc. See also:

Famine relief. 731
Religious fasting 785
Theory of digestion 827
Conception of the hunger drive 828
Food craving during pregnancy. 843
Infant feeding. 853
Food training of children 862

262 DIET--staple and other foods consumed; seasonal changes in diet; proportion of various foods in diet; group differences in diet (e.g., by age, sex, social class); discriminations between edible and harmful foods; food preferences and avoidances; food taboos; etc. See also:

Food processing 25   Religious taboos 784
Nutritional balance 146   Food taboos during pregnancy 843
Standard of living 511   Infant feeding 853

263 CONDIMENTS--kinds of condiments used in the preparation and consumption of food (e.g., salt, sugar, honey, spices); processing of savory herbs and spices; uses of condiments; etc. See also:

Use of seasoning in cooking 252   Salt manufacture 258
Manufacture of sugar and sweet confections . . 257

264 EATING--regularity of eating; informal eating (e.g., between meals, at work or play); meals (e.g., hours, number per day, participation, composition); techniques of eating; table manners; sequels to eating (e.g., disposal of waste and excess food, cleaning of utensils); associated beliefs and practices; etc. See also:

Eating implements and utensils 41   Feasts and entertaining at meals 574
Food preparation 252   Etiquette 576
Ablutions 515   Military mess arrangements 705

265 FOOD SERVICE INDUSTRIES--specialized eating establishments (e.g., restaurants, tea shops, lunchrooms); food catering services; organization and specialized personnel; regulation; etc. See also:

Food processing industries 25   Hotels and inns 485
Drinking establishments 275   Night clubs and cabarets 547
Restaurant buildings 347   Public health and sanitation 744
Food retail outlets 444

266 CANNIBALISM--prevalence of cannibalism; participants; victims (e.g., captives, felons, slaves, sacrificial victims); parts eaten; occasions; associated beliefs and practices; etc. See also:

Human sacrifice 782

---

27 DRINK, DRUGS, AND INDULGENCE

27 DRINK, DRUGS, AND INDULGENCE--general statements covering several aspects of the allaying of thirst and special appetitive cravings, with the manufacture of artificial means of satisfying them, and with the preparation of drugs for other purposes.

271 WATER AND THIRST--use of water for drinking; manifestations and control of thirst; ideas and practices related to the drinking of water; etc. See also:

Water supply . . . . 312 Libations 782
Municipal purification of water . . . . . . 364 Notions about water 823
Utensils . . . . 415 Conception of the thirst drive 828

272 NONALCOHOLIC BEVERAGES--drinking of nonalcoholic beverages (e.g., tea, coffee, lemonade, milk, blood); special techniques of preparation (e.g., boiling, percolating); consumption (e.g., quantities, occasions); food values and physiological effects; drinking etiquette; etc. See also:

Dairying. . . . . 234 Meals. 264
Cultivation of tea, coffee, and cacao. . . . 245 Utensils. 415

273 ALCOHOLIC BEVERAGES--types of alcoholic beverages used (e.g., beer, wine, spirits); techniques of preparation (e.g., brewing, distilling); apparatus (e.g., stills); consumption (e.g., users, quantities, occasions); drinking etiquette; craving for liquor; prevalence of drunkenness and behavior under intoxication; associated beliefs and practices; social and legal controls; etc. See also:

Industrialized manufacture of alcoholic   Sanctions against inebriation 689
  beverages . . . . 274 Alcoholism 733
Utensils . . . . 415 Religious orgies. 786

274 BEVERAGE INDUSTRIES--industrialized production of beverages (e.g., brewing, wine making, distilling, manufacture of soft drinks); specialized techniques and equipment; organization of labor and production; regulation; etc. See also:

Dairy industry . . . . 234 Industrial structures 348
Cereal agriculture . . . . 243 Manufacture of canning and bottling machines . 392
Vineyard production . . . . 245 Canning and bottling machines 402
Sugar manufacture . . . . 257 Brewing and distilling apparatus and utensils . . 415

275 DRINKING ESTABLISHMENTS--specialized dispensers of beverages; types of establishment (e.g., bars, taverns, soft-drink parlors); services and clientele; special equipment; organization; regulation (e.g., licensing, curfew); etc. See also:

Structures . . . . 34 Hotels and inns 485
Restaurants . . . . 265 Night clubs and cabarets 547
Retail beverage outlets 444

276 NARCOTICS AND STIMULANTS--drugs consumed for nontherapeutic purposes (e.g., tobacco, betel, coca, peyote); techniques of manufacture and preparation; methods of consumption (e.g., eating, chewing, smoking); special apparatus (e.g., cigarette holders, pipes, hypodermic needles); users; quantities consumed; physiological effects; behavior under narcosis and stimulation; associated beliefs and practices; social and legal controls; etc. See also:

Psychiatric aspects of drug addiction 158   Illicit narcotics traffic 548
Cultivation of narcotic plants 249   Treatment of drug addicts 733
Condiments 263   Notions about drug cravings 828
Palliation of labor with drugs 461

277 TOBACCO INDUSTRY--industrialized production of tobacco; specialized techniques and equipment; organization of labor and production; regulation; etc.
See also:

Growing of tobacco. 249   Description of tobacco processing machines. . 402
Industrial structures. 348   Government tobacco monopolies 655
Manufacture of tobacco manufacturing machines. 392

278 PHARMACEUTICALS--materia medica and pharmacology; manufacture of narcotics, drugs, and poisons; processing techniques; products; organization of labor and production; regulation; specialists (e.g., pharmacists); etc.
See also:

Use of poisons in hunting and fishing. 22   Use of medicines 757
Drugstores 444

———————————

28 LEATHER, TEXTILES, AND FABRICS

28 LEATHER, TEXTILES, AND FABRICS--general statements dealing with several aspects of the processing of raw materials to yield textile products and other flat goods such as leather and paper.

281 WORK IN SKINS--preparation of hides and furs (e.g., drying, scraping, tanning, tawing); materials and products; special apparatus; cutting and sewing of skins; specialization and organization; etc. See also:

Animal by-products 237   General tools. 412
Manufacture of garments 294

282 LEATHER INDUSTRY--industrialized processing of skins; specialized manufacture of leather goods other than wearing apparel (e.g., harness, leather utensils); special techniques and apparatus; organization of labor and production; etc. See also:

Shoe manufacture 295

283 CORDAGE--types of cordage made (e.g., thread, yarn, string, rope); materials used (e.g., bast fiber, cotton, wool, silk, sinew, hair); preparation of materials (e.g., soaking, retting); techniques of manufacture (e.g., twisting, spinning, braiding); special apparatus (e.g., spindle, spinning wheel); specialized personnel and organization; etc. See also:

Industrialized manufacture of cordage 288   Nautical rigging 501
Sewing 294   String figures 524

284 KNOTS AND LASHINGS--types of knots and their uses; splices; methods of lashing, hafting, and joining; etc. See also:

Weapons and tools   41   Surgical ligatures. 752
Knot records   211

285 MATS AND BASKETRY--techniques of manufacture (e.g., checkerwork, coiling, twilled work, twining, wickerwork, wrapped work); materials; products; uses of mats and baskets; personnel and organization; etc. See also:

Household appurtenances. 352   Utensils. 415

286 WOVEN FABRICS--textiles; weaving, knitting, and netting techniques; special apparatus (e.g., netting needle, loom); products and their uses; specialized personnel and organization; etc. See also:

Clothing.   29   Industrial production of textiles. 288
Spinning   283   Description of power looms 402

287 NONWOVEN FABRICS--manufacture of nontextile fabrics (e.g., barkcloth, felt, featherwork); materials; techniques; apparatus; personnel; etc. See also:

Nontextile uses of feathers   237   Plastics. 384

288 TEXTILE INDUSTRIES--industrialized production of textile products; cotton, woolen, silk, and rayon mills; cordage manufacture; specialized techniques and apparatus; economic importance of and self-sufficiency in textile manufactures; organization of labor and production; etc. See also:

Silk production.   231   Clothing manufacture. 294
Wool production   236   Manufacture of synthetic fabrics 384
Textile agriculture   248   Textile machinery 402

289 PAPER INDUSTRY--manufacture of paper; materials (e.g., wood pulp, rags); processing methods; special artifacts and apparatus used; organization of labor and production; special products; types of paper produced; etc. See also:

Writing and printing supplies   218   Pulp mills. 313
Food packaging.   258   Paper-making machinery 402

---

29 CLOTHING

29 CLOTHING--general statements covering several aspects of the manufacture, description, use, and care of wearing apparel. For adornment see 30.

291 NORMAL GARB--nude and covered parts of body; services of clothing (e.g., protection, vanity, modesty); standard costume; age and sex differences; seasonal variations; styles and fashions; description of individual garments; means of attachment and suspension (e.g., belt); etc. See also:

Cyclical trends in fashions. 178   Sexual modesty. 834
Sumptuary laws 434   Swaddling and infant attire 854

292 SPECIAL GARMENTS--clothing of special occasions (e.g., festive apparel, rain gear, bathing costumes); headgear and footwear not ordinarily worn; costumes associated with special statuses and activities; special methods of wearing garments; etc. See also:

Dance and dramatic costumes 53   Military uniforms 714
Personal or body armor 714   Ceremonial attire 796

293 PARAPHERNALIA--dress accessories (e.g., fans, special paraphernalia and regalia); protective apparatus (e.g., umbrellas, goggles); etc. See also:

Ornaments 301   Medals. 554
Eyeglasses 416   Hearing aids 732
Canes, crutches, and other aids to locomotion. . 481   Shamanistic paraphernalia 756
Riding gear 492   Amulets 751, 778
Athletic equipment 526   Ceremonial paraphernalia 796

294 CLOTHING MANUFACTURE--techniques of manufacture (e.g., cutting, fitting, sewing); special treatment of particular materials and products (e.g., shoe-making, hat manufacture); decoration (e.g., embroidery); use of special implements and apparatus (e.g., sewing machines); specialization (e.g., dress-makers, tailors, cobblers, hatters); etc. See also:

Leather and textile industries 28   Household sewing machines 404
Factory buildings 348   Decorative art 531

295 SPECIAL CLOTHING INDUSTRIES--industrialized production of shoes and hats; readymade garment industries; industrial manufacture of underwear, hose, shirts, gloves, and furs; specialized techniques and equipment; organization of labor and production; etc. See also:

Leather industry 282   Machines used in clothing production 402
Textile industries 288   Retail clothing shops 444
Manufacture of machines used in clothing
    production 392

296 GARMENT CARE -- methods of laundering clothes; repair techniques (e.g., darning, patching); special care and preservation of clothing (e.g., drying, snow removal, waterproofing, storage); organized services (e.g., laundries, dry-cleaning and pressing establishments, shoe-shining and repairing specialists); special techniques and apparatus; etc. See also:

Soap manufacture 388   Domestic laundry appliances 404
Commercial laundry and dry-cleaning
    machinery 402

30 ADORNMENT--general statements dealing with several aspects of methods of adorning the body other than by the wearing of clothing, and with the manufacture of the means of adornment.

301 ORNAMENT--types of ornament worn (e.g., necklaces, bracelets, rings, anklets, earrings, labrets, hair ornaments); mode of attachment or suspension; age, sex, and status differences; materials and manufacture; occasions of use; etc. See also:
Work in bone, horn, and shell 321

302 TOILET--shaving and depilation; hair styles (e.g., cutting, parting, arranging); care of the hair (e.g., washing, brushing); care of the nails (e.g., cutting, filing); body painting; use of cosmetics, ointments and perfumes; age, sex, and status differences in toilet; associated beliefs and practices; etc. See also:

Electrical appliances	403	Bathing and laving	515
Combs, brushes, etc.	412	Decorative art	531
Barbering tools	413	War paint	714
Elimination	514	Menstrual hygiene	841

303 MANUFACTURE OF TOILET ACCESSORIES--preparation of cosmetics, ointments, and perfumes; production of toilet articles (e.g., compacts); special apparatus; organization of labor and production; specialists; etc. See also:

Manufacture of paints, dyes, and pigments	386	Manufacture of razors, clippers, and tweezers.	391
Soap manufacture	388	Manufacture of electrical appliances	393

304 MUTILATION--scarification and tattooing; cranial deformations; tooth filing and removal; piercing of ears, nose, and lips; genital mutilation (e.g., castration, circumcision, clitoridectomy); age, sex, and status differences; special techniques and apparatus; associated beliefs; etc. See also:

Masochism	158	Self-torture	785
Mutilation of criminals	681	Eunuchs	839
Mayhem	683	Initiatory rites	852, 881
Mutilation of captives	727		

305 BEAUTY SPECIALISTS--barbers and hairdressers; manicurists; tattooers; specialized cosmetic services (e.g., beauty salons); special techniques (e.g., shampoos); special apparatus; organization and training; etc. See also:

Public baths	368	Electrical appliances	403

306 JEWELRY MANUFACTURE--cutting, polishing, and mounting of gems; specialized work in precious metals; lapidary art; manufacture of valuable ornaments and costume jewelry; specialized jewelers; etc. See also:

Nonprofessional manufacture of ornaments . . 301   Manufacture of silverware and gold plate . . 328

Work in ivory and mother-of-pearl 321   Lapidary tools 413

Smiths and their crafts 326

---

31 EXPLOITATIVE ACTIVITIES

31 EXPLOITATIVE ACTIVITIES--general statements dealing with several aspects of the extraction from nature of raw materials other than food. Transformation of raw materials into tools, structures, clothing, and other finished products is classified elsewhere.

311 LAND USE--completeness and efficiency with which the potentialities of the land and its resources are utilized; distribution of waste land, forests, pasture, tilled land, and areas of settlement and industrial use; diversification and specialization (e.g., monoculture); trends; etc. See also:

Natural resources 13   Conservation 185

Animal husbandry 23   Forestry 313

Agriculture 24   Productive capacity of the economy 433

Settlements 36

312 WATER SUPPLY--sources of water (e.g., springs, wells, rainwater catchment); waters with special properties (e.g., mineral water); waterworks (e.g., dams, reservoirs, settling basins); transportation of water (e.g., containers, pipes, aqueducts, canals); irrigation and drainage systems; construction, maintenance, and regulation of water supply systems; etc. See also:

Natural occurrence of water 133   Containers 415

Use of irrigation in agriculture 241   Water rights 423

Excavation 332   Canal navigation 502

Water purification 364   Bathing 515

Water power 376   Flood control 731

Pumps 406   Public health 744

Plumbing . . . . 336, 414   Beliefs about water 823

313 LUMBERING--kinds of timber exploited; gathering of firewood; logging operations (e.g., felling, trimming, hauling); techniques and apparatus used; sawmills and pulp mills; economic importance of lumbering; organization of labor and production; forestry science, practices, and policy; etc. See also:

Forest resources 137   Industrial structures 348

Conservation policies 185   Fuel 372

Silviculture 245   Lumbering machinery 402

Paper manufacture 289   Tools 412

Woodworking 322   Moving of heavy weights 483

Building supplies industries 339   State and national forests 659

314 FOREST PRODUCTS--exploitation of forests and other uncultivated areas for products other than timber or food (e.g., gums and resins, rubber, vegetable oils, dyestuffs, medicines, bark, textile fibers, peat); intermediate processing (e.g., refining of palm oil or rubber, production of charcoal); organization of labor and production; etc. See also:

Chemical industries	38	Materia medica	278
Collecting of edible materials	222	Ethnobotany	824

315 OIL AND GAS WELLS--exploration for oil and natural gas; methods of extraction (e.g., skimming, drilling); use of special apparatus; pipelines, pumping stations, and storage tanks; special precautions against fire and explosion; organization of labor and production; specialized personnel; regulation; etc. See also:

Natural resources	13	Petroleum refining	382
Heating and lighting appliances	354	Manufacture of drilling machinery	392
Urban fire protection	368	Drilling machinery	402
Fire and fuel	372		

316 MINING AND QUARRYING--minerals exploited (e.g., flint, coal, iron); methods of extraction; mining engineering; economic importance of mining and quarrying; organization of labor and production; etc. See also:

Metal industries	32	Mining machinery	402
Mineral resources	135	Digging tools	412
Stone industries	324	Mining schools	874
Explosives	389		

317 SPECIAL DEPOSITS--minerals sought (e.g., sand, salt, clay, ocher, sulphur, phosphates); methods of extraction; organization of labor and production; utilization of products; etc. See also:

Mineral resources	135	Property in exploitative sites with	
Salt manufacture	258	monopoly value	423

---

32 PROCESSING OF BASIC MATERIALS

32 PROCESSING OF BASIC MATERIALS--general statements covering several aspects of the technology of converting basic raw materials into finished or semi-finished products. Data on the acquisition of raw materials, descriptions of the finished products, and information on the manufacture of complex artifacts, will be classified elsewhere.

321 WORK IN BONE, HORN, AND SHELL--techniques of cutting, drilling, and polishing; treatment of special materials (e.g., ivory, mother-of-pearl, chitin); use of special implements and apparatus; bone, horn, and shell

products not elsewhere described; industrial elaborations (e.g., button manufacture); specialized personnel and organization; etc. See also:

Tools	41	Featherwork	287
Marine industries	228	Ornaments	301
Animal by-products	237		

322 WOODWORKING--methods of seasoning wood; techniques of shaping (e.g., cutting, planing, burning, warping); treatment of special materials (e.g., coconut, bamboo, gourds, bark); use of special apparatus; finishing techniques (e.g., oiling, lacquering); elaborated woodworking crafts (e.g., cooperage, cabinet making), manufacture of wooden and other furniture; specialized personnel and organization; wooden products not elsewhere described; etc. See also:

Lumbering and sawmills	313	Shipbuilding	396
Carpentry in building construction	335	Lathes and other woodworking machines	402
Description of furniture	352	Tools	412
Woodworking machine manufacture	392	Sculpture in wood	532

323 CERAMIC INDUSTRIES--manufacture of pottery and glass; preliminary processing of materials (e.g., cleaning, mixing); shaping (e.g., modeling, use of molds, coiling, blowing); firing; special apparatus (e.g., potter's wheels, kilns); methods of decoration (e.g., glazing, painting, incising); ceramic products not elsewhere described; specialization (e.g., potters, glass blowers); industrially elaborated ceramic manufactures (e.g., bottle making, porcelain manufacture); etc. See also:

Acquisition of raw materials	317	Utensils	415
Brick manufacture	339	Optical instruments	416
Interior decorating	353	Decorative designs and motifs	531

324 STONE INDUSTRY--methods of shaping stone (e.g., chipping, pecking, grinding); materials used; products not elsewhere described; special stone industries (e.g., carving of tombstones and monuments); specialized personnel and organization; etc. See also:

Work in gems	306	Monuments	349
Quarrying	316	Tools	412
Masonry	333	Moving of heavy weights	483
Cement manufacture	339		

325 METALLURGY--smelting and refining of ores; alloys; methods of casting; hot and cold forging; tempering; soldering; welding; special apparatus (e.g., bellows, anvil); practical and scientific metallurgical knowledge; etc. See also:

Capital goods industries	39	Industrialized elaboration of metallurgical	
Tools and weapons	41	processes	327, 328
Mining	316		

326 SMITHS AND THEIR CRAFTS--nonindustrialized specialization in metallurgical crafts; types of specialists (e.g., blacksmiths, coppersmiths, tinsmiths, silversmiths, goldsmiths, gunsmiths); special skills and services of each; products not elsewhere described; organization (e.g., guilds); social status

of smiths; etc. See also:

Tools, weapons, utensils, and appliances . . .   41   Industrial specialization in metallurgi-
Jewelers 306   cal processes 327, 328

327 IRON AND STEEL INDUSTRY--industrial production of iron and steel products
(e.g., pig iron, rails, sheet steel, wire); special plants (e.g., iron foundries,
blast furnaces, rolling mills); products and their uses; economic importance
of and self-sufficiency in iron and steel production; organization of labor and
production; etc. See also:

Industrial organization. 47   Structural steel work 334
Mining 316   Manufacture of industrial machines 392
Metallurgical science 325   Industrial machines 402

328 NONFERROUS METAL INDUSTRIES--industrialized processing of nonferrous
metals (e.g., aluminum, copper, tin, zinc, silver, gold, mercury); smelting,
refining, and ingot production; products and their uses; economic importance
of nonferrous metal industries; organization of labor and production; etc. See
also:

Jewelry manufacture 306   Aircraft industry 399
Mining 316   Coinage 436
Coppersmiths, tinsmiths, silversmiths, and
  goldsmiths 326

33 BUILDING AND CONSTRUCTION

33 BUILDING AND CONSTRUCTION--general statements on several topics
primarily concerned with the technological skills involved in assembling raw
or semi-finished materials to construct buildings and other structures, together with certain business and industrial activities directly related thereto.

331 CONSTRUCTION--civil and structural engineering; construction industries;
specialized builders, contractors, and wreckers; organization of labor and
production; etc. Data on construction not classifiable under succeeding categories will be filed here. See also:

Labor 46   Housing 342, 362
Business and industrial organization 47   Highway and railway construction 499
Military engineering and the construction of   Waterways improvements 503
  military installations. 71   Contracts 675
Architecture 341

332 EARTH MOVING--techniques of excavating, grading, and earth removal; use
of special implements and apparatus; specialized personnel and organization;
etc. See also:

Mining and quarrying 316   Manufacture of earth-moving machines . . . 392
Explosives 389   Earth-moving machines 406

Digging tools 412   Railway and highway construction 499
Weight moving 483   Dredging 503

333 MASONRY--laying of bricks and stones; use of mortar; mixing and laying of adobe and concrete; types of construction (e.g., foundations, floors, walls); structural principles (e.g., arch, dome); use of special implements and apparatus (e.g., trowel, hod, cement mixer); specialized personnel and organization; etc. See also:

Stone industry. 324   Tools 413
Brick and cement manufacture 339

334 STRUCTURAL STEEL WORK--erection and assembly of structural steel elements (e.g., girders, cables); joining techniques (e.g., welding, riveting); products (e.g., bridges, radio towers, skeleton framework of buildings); specialized personnel and organization; etc. See also:

Tools and apparatus. 41   Weight moving 483
Iron and steel industry 327   Bridges 491

335 CARPENTRY--special treatment of wooden materials in building construction; techniques of joining (e.g., by mortise and tenon, with nails or screws); structural devices (e.g., struts, king-post); specialized personnel and organization (e.g., carpenters' guilds or unions); etc. See also:

Nonstructural woodworking 322   Tools. 412
Shipbuilding 396   Hardware 414

336 PLUMBING--laying and fitting of water, gas, and sewer pipe; installation and repair of plumbing fixtures; implements and apparatus; steamfitting; specialized personnel and organization; etc. See also:

Water supply 312   Sewer systems 364
Oil and gas pipelines 315   Gas plants 382
Heating and lighting systems 354   Plumbing fixtures 414

337 ELECTRICAL INSTALLATION--wiring structures for electricity; installation of electrical fixtures and appliances; special equipment and apparatus; specialized personnel and organization; etc. See also:

Electric power. 377   Electrical appliances. 403
Electrical supplies industry 393

338 MISCELLANEOUS BUILDING TRADES--structural specialists not classifiable under the preceding categories (e.g., plasterers, roofers, painters, paperhangers, glaziers); special techniques, equipment, and services of each; organization; etc. See also:

Tools and hardware 41   Interior decoration 353
Coppersmiths and tinsmiths 326

339 BUILDING SUPPLIES INDUSTRIES--manufacture of building and construction supplies not elsewhere described (e.g., brick, cement); processors of building materials (e.g., mill work companies, brick yards); suppliers to builders and contractors; business organization of manufacturers, processors, and suppliers of building materials; etc. See also:

Lumbering	313	Manufacture of construction hardware	391
Stone industry	324	Manufacture of electrical supplies	393
Steel industry	327	Hardware	414
Paint manufacture	386	Retail marketing	443

---

34 STRUCTURES

34 STRUCTURES--general statements describing several types of structures detailed below. Only purely descriptive information on types of buildings and other structures, as well as data on materials and construction not classifiable under 33 will be filed here. The uses of each type of structure are described under appropriate headings elsewhere.

341 ARCHITECTURE--styles of domestic and nondomestic buildings; architectural theory and principles; practice of architecture (e.g., solicitation of business, planning, draftsmanship, supervision of construction, fees); specialization (e.g., architects, draftsmen); etc. See also:

Construction	33	Interior decoration	353
Landscape architecture	351	Decorative art	531

342 DWELLINGS--description of residential buildings; seasonal, local and status differences in dwelling types; durability and portability of dwellings; mode of construction; adequacy (e.g., for protection from elements, for security, for light and ventilation); typical number of occupants; ceremonies during and after construction; etc. See also:

Housebuilding specialists	33	Names of houses	552
Adequacy of housing	362	Household organization	592

343 OUTBUILDINGS--description of domestic nonresidential buildings (e.g., cookhouses, latrines, menstrual lodges, bathhouses, granaries, barns, stables); special characteristics of each; construction; etc. See also:

Stables and stalls	231	Latrines	514
Cookhouses	252	Bathhouses	515
Boathouses	504	Menstrual lodges	841

344 PUBLIC STRUCTURES--description of public buildings (e.g., municipal halls, courthouses, prisons and jails, postoffices, hospitals); special characteristics and facilities of each; mode of construction; etc. See also:

Building trades	33	Postal service	205
Municipal government	63	Hospital administration	743
Functioning of courts, jails, and prisons	69		

345 RECREATIONAL STRUCTURES--description of clubhouses, theaters, stadiums, gymnasiums; special characteristics and construction of each; etc. See also:

Entertainment 54   Drama 536
Inns, taverns, restaurants, etc. 347   Sodalities 575
Functioning of recreational facilities 529

346 RELIGIOUS AND EDUCATIONAL STRUCTURES--description of shrines, temples, churches, libraries, museums, schools, and other religious and educational structures; special characteristics of each; mode of construction; etc. See also:

Administration of schools and colleges 87   Administration of sacred places 778
Administration of libraries and museums . . . 217   Administration and functioning of churches . . 794

347 BUSINESS STRUCTURES--description of office buildings, retail stores, and other business structures; special characteristics of each; mode of construction; etc. See also:

Building trades 33   Retail marketing 443
Operation of restaurants 265   Operation of banks 453
Operation of bars and taverns 275   Operation of warehouses 488
Elevators. 406   Operation of garages and filling stations . . . 495

348 INDUSTRIAL STRUCTURES--description of factories and other manufacturing plants; special characteristics of each type; mode of construction; etc. See also:

Operation of food processing plants 25   Operation of textile industries. 288
Building trades 33   Operation of paper mills 289
Operation of chemical factories 38   Operation of clothing factories 294
Capital goods industries 39   Operation of sawmills and pulp mills. . . . 313
Operation of breweries and distilleries 274   Operation of iron foundries and steel mills . 327
Operation of tobacco factories. 277   Operation of munitions factories. 719

349 MISCELLANEOUS STRUCTURES--description of structures not classifiable above (e.g., monuments, radio towers, lighthouses, hangars, railway stations); special characteristics of each; mode of construction; etc. See also:

Radio and television 207   Adjuncts to navigation 502
Commemorative statues and monuments . . . 211   Airport facilities 508
Railway terminal facilities 498   Funerary monuments 764

---

35 EQUIPMENT AND MAINTENANCE OF BUILDINGS

35 EQUIPMENT AND MAINTENANCE OF BUILDINGS--general statements covering several aspects of the material equipment, care, and upkeep of dwellings and nonresidential buildings. For descriptions of other machines, appliances,

tools, utensils, hardware, and apparatus used in buildings see 40 and 41.

351 GROUNDS--house plots and building lots; courtyards; walls, fences, and gates; grading; gardens and ornamental plants; swimming pools; landscape architecture; upkeep of grounds; etc. See also:

Gardening 247   Description of fences and gates 417

352 FURNITURE--pegs, racks, shelves, and cupboards; description of furniture (e.g., chairs, tables, chests, beds, hammocks, head-rests); floor cover-ing (e.g., mats, rugs); special uses of furniture; etc. See also:

Mat making 285   Hardware 414
Furniture manufacture 322   Bedding 513

353 INTERIOR DECORATION AND ARRANGEMENT--painting, carving, and in-cising of walls and woodwork; screens and draperies; color schemes; furni-ture arrangement; use of pictures and prints; shrines and sacred objects; bric-a-brac and objets d'art; flower arrangement; specialization in interior decoration (e.g., interior decorators); storage of household items; etc. See also:

Storage of food 251   Decorative art 531
Storage of clothing 296

354 HEATING AND LIGHTING EQUIPMENT--systems for the lighting, heating, insulation, ventilating and air-conditioning of buildings; hearths and fire-places; special lighting equipment (e.g., candles, oil lamps, gas lights, electric lights); special heating appliances (e.g., wood, coal, oil, gas, and electric stoves and furnaces); air-conditioning installations; insulating mate-rials; etc. See also:

Heat, light, and power 37   Manufacture of candles 388
Cooking 252   Manufacture of heating and lighting appliances. 394
Electrical installations. 337   Refrigerators, incubators, and portable lights . . 416
Manufacture of fuel oil and illuminating gas . 382

355 MISCELLANEOUS BUILDING EQUIPMENT--description of building equipment not classifiable elsewhere (e.g., eaves and drains, fire extinguishers, dumb waiters); special uses of each; etc. See also:

Water supply 312   Elevators. 406
Installation of plumbing 336   Plumbing fixtures 414
Electrical appliances 403   Utensils 415
Household machines 404   Refrigerators 416

356 HOUSEKEEPING--upkeep of dwelling and outbuildings (e.g., painting, repairs); routine indoor chores (e.g., housecleaning, bed-making); use and care of household implements and appliances; etc. See also:

Household tools and appliances 41   Painters and paperhangers. 338
Food preparation 252   Household machines 404
Cleaning of cooking and eating utensils . . . 264   Daily routine 512
Laundering 296

357 DOMESTIC SERVICE--prevalence and functional differentiation of household servants (e.g., cooks, butlers, chambermaids, gardeners, chauffeurs, governesses); status and activities of each; arrangements for room and board; wages; hiring and firing; master-servant relationships; etc. See also:

Labor relations 466   Composition of household 592
Slavery 567

358 MAINTENANCE OF NONDOMESTIC BUILDINGS--upkeep and repair of public, business, industrial, religious, educational, and recreational buildings; maintenance activities (e.g., sweeping, window-cleaning, tending of furnaces); specialized caretakers (e.g., janitors, scrubwomen, chimney sweeps, watchmen); organization of maintenance activities; etc.

---

36 SETTLEMENTS

36 SETTLEMENTS--general statements covering several specific aspects of the physical configuration and material facilities of settlements ranging in size and complexity from a temporary camp to a great metropolis. See category 369 for characteristics of urban and rural life. The social and political organization of communities and municipalities is described under 62 and 63. Information on nonmunicipal public utilities, commercial facilities, etc., will be found elsewhere under appropriate headings (e.g., telephone and telegraph, 206; water supply, 312, etc.).

361 SETTLEMENT PATTERNS--location and distribution of settlements; physical types and descriptions of settlements and the incidence of each (e.g., temporary camp, settled hamlet or village, town, city, urban metropolis); degree of permanence or impermanence; settlement plan; urban ecology (e.g., residential, business, and industrial areas); satellite areas (e.g., suburbs); patterns of urban growth; zoning; city planning; etc. See also:

Demography 16   Land use 311
Place names . . . . . . , ... 103   Community organization 621
Social planning 185

362 HOUSING--adequacy of housing facilities (e.g., for physical protection, for comfort, for privacy); housing shortages and overcrowding; effects of poverty, war, and natural calamities; public and private housing and slum clearance programs; etc. See also:

Dwellings 342   Standard of living 511
Renting and leasing 427   Public welfare 657

363 STREETS AND TRAFFIC--type and plan of settlement paths and streets; paving, gutters, and sidewalks; type and amount of urban traffic (e.g., pedestrians, animals, carts, automobiles, trams); parking and traffic regulations;

street maintenance; etc. See also:

Street lighting 373   Highways 491

Routes 487

364 SANITARY FACILITIES--sewerage system; sewage disposal plants; collection and disposal of garbage and waste; street-cleaning services; purification of water; municipal sanitary facilities and regulations; etc. See also:

Elimination and personal hygiene 51   Plumbing 336, 414

Water supply 312   Army sanitary corps 708

Fertilizer industry 387   Public health 744

365 PUBLIC UTILITIES--availability of publicly and privately operated municipal utilities (e.g., water system, telephone facilities, bus and tram services, power and light systems); services rendered and the extent of their utilization; etc. See also:

Telephone service 206   Manufacture of illuminating gas 382

Water supply 312   Ownership and control of capital 471

Electric power plants 377   Cab, bus, and tram services 494

366 COMMERCIAL FACILITIES--availability and location of markets, retail shops, wholesale outlets, warehouses, office buildings, banks, restaurants, hotels, garages, and other business facilities; trading centers and trade areas; etc. See also:

Marketing 44   Hotels 485

Restaurants 265   Warehouses 488

Business buildings 347   Garages 495

Banks 453

367 PARKS--availability, location, use, and maintenance of municipal parks, playgrounds, and athletic fields; zoological and botanical gardens (e.g., location, support, operation, use); etc. See also:

Entertainment 54   Amusement parks and other recreational

Floriculture 247   facilities 529

Landscape architecture 351   State and national forests 659

368 MISCELLANEOUS URBAN FACILITIES--fire protection services (e.g., fire-fighting apparatus and equipment, specialized personnel); availability and location of piers, railway stations, airports, and bus terminals; availability and location of religious, educational, and recreational facilities (e.g., churches, temples, schools, libraries, museums, theaters, opera houses, art galleries, gymnasiums, public baths, clubhouses); etc. See also:

Description of structures 34   Manufacture of fire-fighting machinery . . . 392

Transportation . . . . 48, 49, 50   Functioning of recreational facilities 529

Entertainment 54   Police protection 625

369 URBAN AND RURAL LIFE--degree of differentiation of rural, small town, and urban modes of life; characteristics of each and contrasts between them;

effects of urbanization upon social institutions; trends in urban development; etc. See also:

Social stratification	56	Statistics on rural and urban population	162
Communities	62	Sociocultural trends	178

37 ENERGY AND POWER

37 ENERGY AND POWER--general statements dealing with several aspects of the utilization of the sources of energy in nature and with the transformation of such energies into industrial power. For the mechanical devices by which power is translated into work see 40. For human labor see 46.

371 POWER DEVELOPMENT--sources of energy utilized and not utilized; potential and developed power resources; public and private programs of power development; etc. For the utilization and development of specific power resources see also:

Urban public utilities	365	Ownership and control of capital	471
Productive capacity of the economy	433		

372 FIRE--generation of fire; techniques and apparatus (e.g., fire plow, fire drill, flint and steel, fire piston, matches); borrowing, preservation, and transportation of fire; tinder and kindling; fuels; uses of fire; beliefs about fire and associated practices; etc. See also:

Brand tillage	241	Firing of pottery	323
Cooking	252	Hearths, stoves, and lamps	354
Gathering of firewood	313	Fire protection	368
Production of charcoal	314	Manufacture of oil and gas	382
Coal mining	316	Conflagrations	731

373 LIGHT--sources of light; methods of producing light; practical and scientific knowledge about lighting; uses of light; outdoor lighting systems (e.g., street lighting); beliefs about light; etc. See also:

Signaling with lights	202	Portable lights	416
Photography	215	Theatrical lighting	536
Indoor lighting systems and appliances	354	Ideas about day and night	821
Manufacture of lighting appliances	394	Ideas about colors and shadows	822
Optical instruments	416		

374 HEAT--sources of heat; methods of producing and regulating heat; beliefs about heat and cold; practical and scientific knowledge about heat; uses of heat; etc. See also:

Chemical industries	38	Heating, insulation, and air-conditioning	
Cooking	252	systems and appliances	354
Refrigeration industry	254	Manufacture of heating appliances	394

Refrigerators and incubators 416   Ethnophysics 822

375 THERMAL POWER--generation of power for industrial purposes through the combustion of fuels; engines (e.g., heat, steam, internal combustion); fuels (e.g., wood, coal, oil, gas); thermal power plants; actual and potential output of thermal power; specialized personnel; organization of labor and production; etc. See also:

Power-operated machinery 40   Natural resources of coal and petroleum. . . 135
Railway, automobile, airplane, and marine   Coal mining 316
    engines 49,50   Production of fuel oil and illuminating gas . . 382

376 WATER POWER--generation of industrial power by harnessing the energy of flowing or falling water; hydraulic engines (e.g., rams, water wheels, turbines); special installations and facilities (e.g., tidal installations); actual and potential output of water power; specialized personnel (e.g., hydraulic engineers); organization of labor and production; etc. See also:

Water supply 312   Pumps and power-operated machinery. . . . 406
Hydroelectric plants 377

377 ELECTRIC POWER--conversion of other energies into electricity; electrical generators; electric power plants; special installations and apparatus; methods of storage and transmission; electrical engineering; actual and potential output of electric power; specialized personnel; organization of labor and production; regulation; etc. See also:

Telephone and telegraph 206   Municipal power and light systems 365
Radio 207   Manufacture of electrical equipment 393
Electrical installations in building construction. 337   Description of electrical machinery and
Heating and lighting appliances 354   appliances 403

378 ATOMIC ENERGY--generation of power through nuclear fission and fusion; materials used; special installations and apparatus; actual and potential output of atomic power; specialized personnel; organization of labor and production; regulation; etc. See also:

Atomic weapons 713   Development of nuclear physics 815

379 MISCELLANEOUS POWER PRODUCTION--special utilization of sources of power not classifiable under previous categories (e.g., human and animal energies, wind power, solar radiation); special apparatus (e.g., treadmills, windmills, rotor engines, solar radiation plants); specialization and organization; etc. See also:

Description of power machinery 40   Use of animals in travel and transportation. . 492
Human labor 46   Sailing vessels. 501

38 CHEMICAL INDUSTRIES--general statements dealing with several aspects of the processing of raw materials in a series of industries where the technology is primarily chemical rather than physical. For industrial structures see 348; for power see 37.

381 CHEMICAL ENGINEERING--industrial chemistry; research laboratories, equipment, and techniques; specialized personnel (e.g., technicians, engineers); special chemical industries not classifiable in the succeeding categories (e.g., adhesive manufacture) including products and their uses; etc. See also:

Military engineering 711   Alchemy. 822
Development of chemical science 815

382 PETROLEUM AND COAL PRODUCTS INDUSTRIES--refining and processing of petroleum; manufacture of coal products (e.g., illuminating gas, coal tar); use of special apparatus and machinery; processing techniques; products and their uses; economic importance of petroleum and coal products industries; organization of labor and production; etc. See also:

Oil and gas wells and pipelines 315   Refining machinery 402
Coal mines 316   Plumbing fixtures 414
Heating and lighting systems 354   Filling stations 495
Thermal power 375

383 RUBBER INDUSTRY--processing of natural rubber; refining techniques; methods of shaping and molding; products and their uses (e.g., rubber balls, syringes, automobile tires); organization of labor and production; synthetic rubber industry; etc. See also:

Agricultural production of rubber 249   Industrial machinery. 402
Rubber gathering 314

384 SYNTHETICS INDUSTRY--manufacture of plastics and other synthetic products; materials used; processing techniques and apparatus; products and their uses; organization of labor and production; etc. See also:

Manufacture of ceramics 323   Industrial machinery. 402

385 INDUSTRIAL CHEMICALS--production of acids, bases, and other industrial chemicals; materials used; processes of manufacture; special techniques and apparatus; products and their uses; organization of labor and production; etc. See also:

Manufacture of drugs and poisons 278

386 PAINT AND DYE MANUFACTURE--paints, dyes, and pigments; materials used in their manufacture; processing techniques; special equipment; products and their uses (e.g., aniline dyes, ink, art supplies); organization of labor and production; etc. See also:

Body painting 302   Interior decoration 353
Manufacture of cosmetics 303   House painting 338, 356
Forest products 314   Pictorial art 532
Special deposits 317

387 FERTILIZER INDUSTRY--manufacture of agricultural fertilizers; specialized techniques and equipment; materials and products; organization of labor and production; etc. See also:

Animal by-products 237   Sewage conversion plants 364
Use of fertilizers 241   Use of hydroelectric power in the
Exploitation of guano, nitrate, and   manufacture of nitrates 377
phosphate deposits 317

388 SOAP AND ALLIED PRODUCTS--manufacture of soap, detergents, and other oil and fat products (e.g., candles); materials used; specialized techniques and apparatus; products and their uses; organization of labor and production; etc. See also:

Edible oil production 258   Bathing and laving 515
Laundering 296

389 MANUFACTURE OF EXPLOSIVES--production of gunpowder, nitroglycerin, and other explosives; materials used; processing techniques and equipment; products and their uses (e.g., fireworks, dynamite, ammunition); manufacturing plants; organization of labor and production; etc. See also:

Mining 316   Military weapons 713
Atomic energy 378   Munitions industries 719

---

39 CAPITAL GOODS INDUSTRIES

39 CAPITAL GOODS INDUSTRIES--general statements dealing with several aspects of the manufacturing processes which produce tools and machines, and with their technological and economic organization. Descriptions of the specific artifacts used in or produced by these industries will be classified under other headings. For industrial structures see 348; for productive capacity of the economy see 433.

391 HARDWARE MANUFACTURE--production of agricultural, industrial, and other tools; manufacture of cooking and eating implements and utensils (e.g., cutlery, kitchen utensils); manufacture of construction hardware (e.g., nails, wire, bolts, pipe, fixtures); manufacture of fishing tackle; industrial specialization; organization of labor and production; etc. See also:

Wood, stone, metal, and ceramic industries . . . 32   Description of fishing gear 227
Building construction 33   Basketry 285
Description of tools, utensils, and apparatus . . . 41   Furniture manufacture 322

392 MACHINE INDUSTRIES--machine shops; industrial manufacture of all types of machines and complex mechanical appliances other than those operated by electricity and those employed in transportation, heating, lighting, and photography; industrial specialization; economic importance of and self-sufficiency in machine industries; organization of labor and production; etc. See also:

Power 37   Ordnance manufacture 719
Descriptions of specific machines 40

393 ELECTRICAL SUPPLIES INDUSTRY--construction of electric motors, generators, and transformers; manufacture of electrical equipment (e.g., wiring, insulation, connections, coils, batteries); production of electrical appliances; industrialization; manufacture of electronic equipment; organization of labor and production; etc. See also:

Use of telephone, telegraph, radio, and   Electric power 377
   television equipment 20   Description of electrical machinery
Electrical installations in building construction. 337   and equipment 403
Description of electrical heating and
   lighting appliances 354

394 MANUFACTURE OF HEATING AND LIGHTING APPLIANCES--manufacture of stoves, furnaces, bakery equipment, and other nonelectrical heating appliances; production of ice-making machinery; manufacture of heat-regulating appliances (e.g., incubators, refrigerators, air-conditioning apparatus); manufacture of lamps and other nonelectric lighting appliances; industrial specialization; organization of labor and production; etc. See also:

Heat, light, and power 37   Description of heating and lighting appliances. 354
Refrigeration industry 254   Description of incubators and refrigerators. . .416

395 MANUFACTURE OF OPTICAL AND PHOTOGRAPHIC EQUIPMENT--lens-grinding; manufacture of optical instruments and supplies; manufacture of still and motion-picture cameras and projectors; manufacture of photographic equipment and supplies (e.g., film, developing materials); industrial specialization; organization of labor and production; etc. See also:

Photography 215   Description of optical instruments
Glass manufacture 323   and photographic apparatus 416
                                               Motion-picture industry 546

396 SHIPBUILDING -- construction and repair of boats, ships, and underwater craft; manufacture of shipbuilding materials and equipment (e.g., marine motors, nautical gear); industrial specialization (e.g., shipyards); organization of labor and production; etc. See also:

Manufacture of cordage 283   Description of water craft 501
Woodworking 322   Water transport 505
Carpentry 335   Naval vessels 716

45

397 RAILWAY EQUIPMENT INDUSTRY--locomotive works; manufacture of rolling stock; production of railway equipment (e.g., rails, signaling devices, brakes); manufacture of special rail vehicles (e.g., trams); industrial specialization; organization of labor and production; etc. See also:

Iron and steel industry 327   Rail transportation 497
Description of railway vehicles 493

398 MANUFACTURE OF VEHICLES--wagon making; manufacture of bicycles and motorcycles; production of automobiles, trucks, and buses; manufacture of automobile parts and accessories (e.g., engines, bodies, upholstery, instruments); manufacture of automobile servicing equipment; industrial specialization; organization of labor and production (e.g., assembly lines); etc. See also:

Manufacture of automobile tires 383   Highway transportation 494
Manufacture of tractors 392   Motorized military equipment 715
Description of vehicles 493

399 AIRCRAFT INDUSTRY--construction of air and space craft; manufacture of airplane parts, accessories, and servicing equipment; industrial specialization; organization of labor and production; etc. See also:

Aluminum industry. 328   Air transportation 509
Description of aircraft 506   Military aircraft 717

---

40 MACHINES

40 MACHINES--general statements describing several distinct types of machines and complex appliances and with the mechanical knowledge embodied in them. Manufacture of machines is described under 392, their use under numerous functional headings.

401 MECHANICS--knowledge and utilization of simple machines (e.g., lever, wheel and axle, pulley, inclined plane, wedge, screw); elements utilized in the construction of complex machines (e.g., cam, ratchet, shaft, rack and pinion, chain, belt, ball and socket, valve, piston, governor, bearing); machine designing; mechanical engineering; etc. See also:

Civil engineering 331   Moving of heavy weights 483
Patents 424   Applied science. 816

402 INDUSTRIAL MACHINERY--power generating machines (e.g., steam engines, turbines, windmills); machine tools (e.g., lathes, planing and stamping machines); typesetting, printing, and bookbinding machines; mining, lumbering, and drilling machinery; stone crushers; pile drivers; milling and refining machinery; spinning and weaving machinery; canning, bottling, and packaging machinery; machines for processing leather, paper, chemicals, and other industrial materials; etc. See also:

Power . . . . 37 Description of hand looms 286
Transportation machines . . . . 49, 50 Hydraulic engines 376

403 ELECTRICAL MACHINES AND APPLIANCES--electric motors, generators, and transformers; machines and appliances operated by electric current (e.g., electric fans, electric razors); electrical supplies (e.g., wiring, insulation, connections, batteries); telephone, telegraph, radio, and television equipment and supplies; electrical engineering; etc. See also:

Telephone and telegraph . . . . 206 Generation of electric power 377
Radio and television . . . . 207 Manufacture of electric equipment 393
Electrical installations in building construction . 337 Electric trams and locomotives 493
Electric heating and lighting appliances . . . 354

404 HOUSEHOLD MACHINES AND APPLIANCES--grinding and mixing machines; sewing machines; laundry appliances (e.g., washing machines, wringers); dishwashing machines; sweeping appliances (e.g., carpet sweepers); etc. See also:

Use and care of household machines and Nonhousehold appliances 416
appliances. 356

405 WEIGHING, MEASURING, AND RECORDING MACHINES--scales; meters; thermostats; clocks and watches; calculating machines; computers; cash registers; phonographs; sound recorders; typewriters; etc. See also:

Writing . . . . 212 Mensurating tools 413
Sound records . . . . 216 Weights and measures 804

406 WEIGHT-MOVING MACHINERY--pumps; hoisting machines (e.g., cranes, jacks, elevators); earth-moving machines (e.g., bulldozers, dredges); other weight-moving machines (e.g., winches); etc. See also:

Earth removal . . . . 332 Vehicles 493
Moving of heavy weights . . . . 483 Dredging 503

407 AGRICULTURAL MACHINERY--farm tractors; machines used in animal husbandry (e.g., milking machines); ground breaking machines (e.g., plows, harrows); planting and cultivating machines; mowing machines and harvesters; sorting and packing machines; processing machines (e.g., cotton gins, threshing machines); etc. See also:

Animal husbandry . . . . 23 Manufacture of agricultural machinery 392
Agriculture . . . . 24 Agricultural tools 412

---

41 TOOLS AND APPLIANCES

41 TOOLS AND APPLIANCES--general statements describing several distinct types of artifacts employed in industrial activities and of the motor habits

involved in their use. The manufacture and industrial uses of the artifacts are treated under a variety of other headings, and are described below only in instances where there is no provision for their description elsewhere.

411 WEAPONS--striking and thrusting weapons (e.g., club, spear); missile weapons (e.g., boomerang, lance, harpoon, bola); complex projectile weapons (e.g., sling, bow and arrow, spearthrower, blowgun, firearms); other weapons employed in hunting, fowling, fishing, marine hunting, and animal husbandry; methods of gripping, striking, and hurling; arrow and dart poisons; etc. See also:

Manufacture of poisons	278	Decoration of weapons	531
Lashings and bindings	284	Specialized military weapons	713
Games with weapons	526	Shields	714

412 GENERAL TOOLS--cutting tools (e.g., knife, ax, adze, chisel, wedge, plane, scissors, saw, sickle); boring tools (e.g., awl, needle, drill, augur, bit, reamer); abrading tools (e.g., scraper, file, grindstone); striking tools (e.g., maul, hammer, pestle); eating utensils (e.g., knife, fork, spoon); digging tools (e.g., digging stick, spade, pick, hoe, shovel); gripping tools (e.g., tongs, tweezers, pincers, vise, grapnel, wrench); miscellaneous tools of general utility (e.g., broom, brush, fan, comb, rake, fork); parts and their assembly (e.g., blades, handles); See also:

Lashings	284	Hardware manufacture	391

413 SPECIAL TOOLS--writing instruments (e.g., pencil, pen, brush); artists' tools; surgical instruments; specialized tools of particular crafts (e.g., of jewelers, barbers, smiths, masons, weavers); mensurating tools (e.g., gauge, compass, calipers, measuring rod, square, level, quadrant); etc. See also:

Weighing and measuring machines	405	Oars and paddles	501

414 MISCELLANEOUS HARDWARE--nails and screws; nuts, bolts, and rivets; pins and clips; pothooks; hinges, latches, and locks; plumbing fixtures (e.g., pipe, hose, faucets); miscellaneous fixtures; etc. See also:

Machines and parts	40	Building supplies industries	339
Cordage	283	Hardware manufacture	391

415 UTENSILS--water containers (e.g., tanks, barrels); food and beverage containers (e.g., cans, bottles, jars); kitchen utensils (e.g., pans, dishes, kettles, bowls, ladles); containers made from special materials (e.g., gourds, baskets, earthen pots, leather bags, wooden boxes, paper cartons); chemical utensils (e.g., test tubes, flasks, retorts, vats); brewing and distilling apparatus; utensils with special functions (e.g., molds, funnels, sieves, drinking straws); etc. See also:

Drinking	27	Basket making	285
Household equipment	35	Cooperage	322

Ceramic industries.	323	Decorative art	531
Eating utensils	412	Measures	804

416 APPLIANCES--portable lights (e.g., torches, lanterns, flashlights); heat-regulating appliances (e.g., refrigerators, incubators); cameras; optical instruments (e.g., eyeglasses, microscope, telescope); appliances not elsewhere described; etc. See also:

Machines	40	Manufacture of optical and photo-	
Photography.	215	graphic equipment.	395
Umbrellas and goggles	293	Household appliances	404
Lighting, heating, and air-conditioning		Plumbing fixtures	414
appliances for buildings.	354	Hearing aids	732
Manufacture of incubators and refrigerators . .	394		

417 APPARATUS--supports (e.g., posts, frames, ladders, scaffolds); fences and gates; pens and corrals; birdcages; apparatus not elsewhere described; etc. See also:

Traps, snares, and fishing gear	22	Plumbing fixtures	414
Aids to locomotion and burden carrying	48	Riding gear.	492
Looms	286	Nautical rigging and gear	501
Furniture	352		

---

42 PROPERTY

42 PROPERTY--general statements dealing with several of the specific aspects of the property system. Material concerning the property system as a whole will be filed in 421. The term "property" is to be distinguished from wealth, material possessions, or any object of ownership. It is to be understood only in the strict technical sense of the jural relations of men with regard to some subject matter and governing the use and enjoyment of the latter. In precise usage, a "right" is correlated with a "duty" (if A has a right against B, B is under a corresponding duty toward A); a "privilege" is correlated with "no right" (if A has a privilege as against B, B has no right against A, instead of a duty); a "power" is correlated with "liability" (if A has a power as against B, B is under a liability that his jural relations may be changed by a voluntary act on the part of A). A "title" is a distinct constellation of rights, privileges, and powers with respect to some subject matter. A "type of ownership" refers to the social composition of the holders of a title, e.g., an individual, a partnership, a clan, a corporation, a state. A "property transaction" is an act which transfers a title to a new owner. A "property system" consists of every type of title, ownership, and property transaction recognized by a society with respect to all culturally defined classes of subject matter, and is not dependent upon the statistical frequency with which its constituent elements manifest themselves.

421 PROPERTY SYSTEM--principles of property law; rights, privileges, and powers commonly involved in property relations (e.g., rights that others shall not use or destroy, privileges of enjoyment, powers of alienation and of transmission after death); recognized types of titles or tenure; recognized types of ownership (e.g., individual, joint, corporate, collective, public); their relation to classes of subject matter (e.g., land, movables, slaves); their degree of integration; their legal and statistical importance; their association with kin and other social groups; etc. See also:

Law 67   Property arrangements upon
Ownership of productive capital 471   termination of marriage 586

422 PROPERTY IN MOVABLES--culturally defined categories of movables (e.g., food stores, personal clothing and ornaments, artifacts, domestic animals, ceremonial objects); recognized types of title or tenure; rights, privileges, and powers involved in each; relation of types of title to categories of movables; recognized types of ownership (e.g., individual, collective, corporate); legal and statistical distribution of types of ownership according to categories of movables, types of title, and classes of persons; records of ownership (e.g., property marks, registration); etc. See also:

Standard of living 511   Slavery 567
Accumulation of wealth 556   Offenses against property 685
Social classes 565

423 REAL PROPERTY--conception of the subject matter of real property (e.g., as that which produces food, as things that are fixed or immovable); culturally defined categories (e.g., land, trees, growing crops, buildings, water); types of land subject and not subject to property (e.g., sites with monopoly value, waste land); recognized types of title or estate (e.g., eminent domain, fee simple, life, leasehold, sufferance); rights, privileges, and powers involved in each (e.g., usufruct, reversionary claims, privileges of gift and sale, power of expropriation); recognized types of ownership (e.g., individual, collective, public); legal and statistical distribution of types of ownership according to categories of immovables, types of title or tenure, and classes of persons (e.g., exclusion of minors, of women, of slaves); general characteristics of the system of real property (e.g., private property, feudal tenure, collective property with periodic reallotments, communism); land reform; records of ownership (e.g., boundary marks, deeds); registration of titles; etc. See also:

Territories of kin and local groups 61,62   Serfdom 566
Land use 311   Taxation 651
Ownership of productive capital 471

424 INCORPOREAL PROPERTY--extent to which property is recognized in intangible things (e.g., names, titles, songs, dances, visions, recipes, rituals, inventions); culturally defined categories of intangibles; recognized types of title; rights, privileges, and powers involved in titles to each type of incorporeal property; recognized types of ownership (e.g., individual, collective,

corporate); distribution of types of ownership according to categories of intangibles, types of title, and classes of persons; records of ownership (e.g., registration of patents and copyrights); patent and copyright law; etc. See also:

Invention 176   Contractual rights 675

Corporate securities 473

425 ACQUISITION AND RELINQUISHMENT OF PROPERTY--recognized means by which property rights may be acquired (e.g., appropriation, forceful seizure, gift, purchase); creation of new property rights (e.g., by physical appropriation, by priority of claim, by expenditure of labor in manufacture); rituals and symbols of appropriation; recognized means by which property rights may be extinguished (e.g., destruction, abandonment, confiscation, gift, sale); rights, privileges, and powers of the finders and losers of objects of property; etc. See also:

Gifts 431   Judicial confiscation 681
Buying and selling 432   Theft 685
Marine salvage 502   War booty 721, 727
Taxation 651

426 BORROWING AND LENDING--bailment; rights, privileges, and powers of bailor and bailee; loans and debts; pawning rights, privileges, and powers of debtor and creditor; formalities in the arrangement and repayment of loans (e.g., witnesses, surety, sponsors); security; interest; notes and mortgages; specialization (e.g., pawn shops); bankruptcy (e.g., law, administration); etc. See also:

Credit 452   Debt slavery 567
Banking 453   Public finance 652
Corporate securities and receivership 473   Penalties for the nonpayment of debts 686

427 RENTING AND LEASING--extent to which real, movable, and incorporeal property may be leased or rented; leases and rents (e.g., negotiations, terms, formalities); modes of payment (e.g., money rent, share cropping); rights, privileges, and powers of lessor and lessee; eviction; prevalence of tenancy and of home and farm ownership; factors determining rental rates; regulation (e.g., rent controls); etc. See also:

Control and ownership of capital 471   Peonage and serfdom 566

428 INHERITANCE--forms of property and types of title subject and not subject to inheritance; disposition of noninherited property (e.g., destruction, abandonment, distribution by gift, reversion to a prior owner or his heirs); nondistribution (e.g., maintenance of estates intact within an extended family); preferred or natural heirs and relatives excluded from inheritance (e.g., children, siblings, spouses, parents); sex and age preferences (e.g., exclusion of females, primogeniture, ultimogeniture); persons who inherit in default of preferred heirs; types of ownership acquired by heirs; variant rules for different possessions and type of title; characterization of inheritance systems (e.g., as

matrilineal, patrilineal, testamentary); dower (e.g., special provision for widow or widower); testamentary disposition (e.g., wills, bequests, legacies); formalities (e.g., probate procedure); probate law; etc. See also:

Family	59	Inheritance taxes	651
Heirlooms	523	Probate courts	698
Rule of descent	611	Adjustments to death	768

429 ADMINISTRATION--guardianship (e.g., of minors, of widows, of defectives); rights, privileges, and powers of guardian and ward; trusts; rights, privileges, and powers of trustee and beneficiary; law of trusts; formalities; administration of estates; bankruptcy administration; specialization in administration (e.g., trust companies); regulation; etc. See also:

Role of heads of families and of kin and local groups as trustees for the property of their social groups	59, 61, 62	Embezzlement	685
		Care of defectives	732
		Philanthropic foundations	741
Receivership	473	Definition of minors	858
Levirate	587		
Agency	676		

---

43 EXCHANGE

43 EXCHANGE--general statements dealing with several aspects of the mechanisms of transferring economic goods and the titles to them, with the volume of such transactions, and with the determination of prices and economic values. For specialization in exchange see 44; for the transportation of goods see 48, 49, 50.

431 GIFT GIVING--alienation of property by gift; rights, privileges, and powers of donor and recipient; frequency, types, occasions, and purposes of gifts; social relationships within which gifts are given; formalities of giving and receiving; potlatches; reciprocal gift exchange (e.g., kula); role of gifts in the distribution of economic goods; etc. See also:

Status and mobility	55	Tribute giving	651
Property transactions in marriage	58	Bribery of officials	662
Acquisition and relinquishment of property	425	Almsgiving and charity	735
Bequests	428	Philanthropic foundations	741
Feasts	574	Sacrifice	782

432 BUYING AND SELLING--alienation of property by sale; rights, privileges, and powers of buyer and seller; law of sales; frequency of sales in comparison with gifts; cultural limitations on the sale of property; etc. See also:

Acquisition and relinquishment of property	425	Slavery	567
Types and formalities of exchange transactions	437	Bride-price	583
Merchants	441	Fraud	685
Salesmanship	446		

433 PRODUCTION AND SUPPLY--productive capacity of the economy (e.g., actual and potential productivity of agriculture and industry); relative importance of various productive activities; economic supply (e.g., production of surpluses available for distribution); overproduction and shortages; restrictions on production; general statements on different types of economic activity, See also:

Natural resources	13	Power development	371
Division of products in food-getting activities	22, 23, 24	Local and regional specialization in production	438
Capital goods industries	39	Business cycles	458
Annual economic cycle	221	Occupational specialization	463
Land use	311	Economic organization and structure	471

434 INCOME AND DEMAND--national, family, and individual income; distribution of income by sources (e.g., wages, interest, rent, profits); economic demand (e.g., potential demand, effective purchasing power); restrictions on demand (e.g., rationing, sumptuary laws); general statements on supply and demand. See also:

Interest	426	Standard of living	511
Rent	427	Income taxes	651
Saving and investment	454	Poverty	735
Wages and salaries	465		

435 PRICE AND VALUE--relation of economic values to other systems of value; factors determinative of price and value (e.g., abundance and scarcity, utility, cost of production, precedent); customary prices and conventional values; competitive prices; monopoly prices; price fixing and black market prices; price levels; prices of particular goods (e.g., in money, in purchasing power); etc. See also:

Social values	181	Competition and monopoly	477
Rent control	427	Bride-price	583
Inflation and deflation	458		

436 MEDIUM OF EXCHANGE--articles circulating in exchange at their intrinsic value as standard money (e.g., salt, cattle, grain, shells, metal bars or coins); forms of representative money (e.g., warehouse receipts, certificates of deposit of standard money); credit money (e.g., government notes, bank notes); token money (e.g., subsidiary coins, shell money, bead money); coinage and mints; right of issuance; counterfeiting; etc. See also:

Foreign exchange	457	Punishment of counterfeiting	687
Government issuance and manipulation of currency	652	Weights and measures	804

437 EXCHANGE TRANSACTIONS--types of exchange (e.g., barter, purchase of goods with money, exchange of services for goods); negotiations (e.g., higgling, auctioning); formalities; guarantees; trading expeditions; special trading relationships; etc. See also:

Marketing	44	Foreign exchange	457
Property transactions in marriage	58	Exchange of services	476
Gift exchange	431		

438 DOMESTIC TRADE--local and regional specialization in production within the society; (e.g., home and cottage industry, location of particular industries); division of labor between town and country; volume of trade within and between communities and regions; articles entering into domestic commerce; motivation (e.g., profit, prestige); patterns of internal commerce; etc. See also:

Agricultural specialization 24   Trade centers and areas. 366
Marketing 44   Urban and rural contrasts 369
Business and industrial organization 47   Trade routes 487
Land use 311

439 FOREIGN TRADE--intergroup specialization in production for export; articles entering into intergroup trade; volume of foreign trade (e.g., statistics of imports and exports); international trade agreements; smuggling; embargoes; etc. See also:

Productive capacity of the economy 433   Negotiation of trade agreements 648
Trading expeditions 437   Tariffs and tolls 651
Foreign exchange 457   Penalties for smuggling 687
Slave trade 567

---

44 MARKETING

44 MARKETING--general statements dealing with several aspects of the specialized elaboration and promotion of trade. For the mechanisms and volume of trade see 43; for its financing see 45; for business organization see 47.

441 MERCANTILE BUSINESS--extent of specialization in commerce; types and distribution of mercantile businesses; social status and special characteristics of merchants; business men's organizations (e.g., merchant guilds, trade associations, chambers of commerce); general characteristics of merchandising; special mercantile privileges and restrictions; etc. See also:

Urban commercial facilities. 366   Competition 477
Occupational specialization 463   Business schools 874
Craft guilds. 467

442 WHOLESALE MARKETING--degree of specialization in wholesale marketing; prevalent types of wholesale business; methods and techniques of wholesale merchandising; buying at wholesale (e.g., specialized buyers, conventions, wholesale lots, discounts); information on specific wholesale businesses; etc. See also:

Stock exchanges 455   Warehousing 488
Producers' cooperatives 474

443 RETAIL MARKETING--extent and variety of retail specialization; types of retail outlets (e.g., itinerant merchants, markets, bazaars, general stores, trading posts, specialty shops, chain stores, department stores, mail-order houses); pricing (e.g., fixed, variable); services to customers (e.g., deliveries); specialized personnel (e.g., sales clerks); etc. See also:

Business organization 47
Description of business structures 347
Upkeep of store buildings 358
Trading centers 366
Accounting methods 451
Extension of credit 452
Employer-employee relations 466

444 RETAIL BUSINESSES--special characteristics and business methods of particular types of retail outlets (e.g., pharmacists, grocers, furniture stores, dress shops); information on individual retail businesses; etc. See also:

Florists 247
Suppliers of building materials 339
Business structures 347
Filling stations 495
Distribution of art and recreational supplies. 549

445 SERVICE INDUSTRIES--degree of elaboration of retail businesses selling services rather than goods; types, distribution, and general characteristics of service industries; specific information on those not elsewhere described (e.g., consultants, rental services, repairing); etc. See also:

Building trades. 33
Financial services 45
Travel and transportation services . . . 48, 49, 50
Artists 53
Entertainers 54
Medical services 75
Veterinarians 232
Restaurants 265
Laundries 296
Beauty specialists 305
Business structures. 347
Landscape architects 351
Interior decorators 353
Domestic service 357
Employment agencies 464
Hotels. 485
Prostitution 548
Agency 676
Undertakers 767

446 SALES PROMOTION--methods employed by industrial and business enterprises to promote their products (e.g., salesmen, display of products, bargain offers, credit extension); market research; sales campaigns; specialists (e.g., sales managers, salesmen); etc. See also:

Credit system 452
Travel 484
Exhibits 543

447 ADVERTISING--uses and degree of elaboration of advertising; media (e.g., handbills, mail advertising, billboards, newspapers and periodicals, radio); special techniques and research; advertising programs; specialized personnel (e.g., counselors, copy writers); advertising agencies; regulation; etc. See also:

Fine arts 53
Newspapers and periodicals 204
Radio and television 207
Public opinion and polling techniques . . . 208

45 FINANCE--general statements dealing with several aspects of transactions in money and credit rather than in material goods.

451 ACCOUNTING--bookkeeping methods (e.g., double entry); principles and techniques of business accounting; preparation of financial statements (e.g., debits and credits, income and expenditures, profit and loss); methods of dealing with intangible factors (e.g., good will, depreciation); specialists (e.g., accountants, financial counselors); financial records; etc. See also:

Records 21   Mathematics 803
Government accounts 652

452 CREDIT--extension of credit by producers and middlemen; methods and terms; advances and discounts; bills of exchange; credit ratings and rating services; credit institutions other than banks (e.g., loan associations, finance companies); etc. See also:

Bankruptcy 426   Credit money 436
Interest, security, borrowing and lending   Cycles of expanding and contracting credit . 458
    transactions 426

453 BANKING--commercial banks; deposits and accounts; checks and drafts; bank loans and discounts; banking services and fees; clearing houses; specialized personnel; regulation; etc. See also:

Bank buildings 347   Loan associations 452
Pawn shops 426   Savings accounts 454
Trust services 429   Government banks 652
Bank notes 436   Embezzlement 685

454 SAVING AND INVESTMENT--saving; hoarding; safekeeping (e.g., safes, safe deposit boxes); savings in relation to income; funds available for investment; available and preferred forms of investment (e.g., in land, buildings, cattle, business and productive enterprises, corporate securities, government obligations); savings accounts, postal savings, and savings banks; underwriting and issuance of corporate securities; investment banking; specialized personnel (e.g., investment brokers); regulation; etc. See also:

Food preservation and storage. 251   Joint stock companies 473
Interest, loans, and mortgages 426   Accumulation of wealth 556
Income 434   Government finance 652
Fluctuations in investment capital. 458   Fraud 685

455 SPECULATION--speculative transactions (e.g., futures, margins, hedging); speculative trading and specialized personnel; stock and produce exchanges; speculative booms; etc. See also:

Gambling 525   Ideas about luck and chance 777

456 INSURANCE--distribution of risks through mutual aid; associations with insurance functions (e.g., lodges, mutual benefit societies); insurance organizations (e.g., private, mutual, governmental); types of insurance (e.g., life, health and casualty, fire, marine, old age); annuities; actuarial practice; insurance contracts; premiums; specialized personnel (e.g., adjustors, agents, salesmen); regulation; etc. See also:

Mutual aid 476   Contracts 675
Voluntary associations 575   Social insurance 745

457 FOREIGN EXCHANGE--international trade balances and their payment; role of invisible factors (e.g., tourist trade, immigrant remittances); international credits and loans; foreign exchange brokers and markets; exchange controls (e.g., pegged currencies, special trade restrictions); etc. See also:

Price levels 435   International relations 648
Money 436   Public finance 652
Foreign trade 439

458 BUSINESS CYCLES--periods of prosperity and depression; financial panics and recovery; cyclical expansion and contraction of credit; fluctuations in investment capital; inflation and deflation; etc. See also:

Social trends 178   Public finance and currency inflation. . . . 652
Speculative booms 455   Prevalence of periodic famines 731
Seasonal and cyclical unemployment 464

---

46 LABOR

46 LABOR--general statements dealing with several aspects of work habits, economic specialization, employment, and labor relations.

461 LABOR AND LEISURE--ideas of the value and dignity of labor; notions of pleasant and unpleasant tasks; distribution of labor and leisure time; incentives to labor (e.g., pride in craftsmanship, prestige, material rewards, compulsion); time and motion studies; intensity of effort; palliation of labor (e.g., with drugs, rhythm, music); work tempo (e.g., steady, intermittent);standards of productivity and production norms; laziness and malingering; rest periods; loafing and loitering; etc. See also:

Annual cycle of economic activities 221   Holidays 527
Unemployment 464   Slavery 567
Leisure-time activities 517   Social offenses 689

462 DIVISION OF LABOR BY SEX--activities customarily performed exclusively or predominantly by males or by females; activities forbidden to or despised by one sex; activities in which both sexes participate (e.g., jointly, alternatively); routine tasks and relative economic contribution of each sex; sex-limited

occupations and professions; etc. This category is designed primarily for summary statements about sex specialization; incidental information will frequently appear only under the headings for specific activities. See also:

Daily routine 512   Relations between husband and wife 593
Relative status of the sexes 562   Specialization by age 561, 857, 883, 887
Household division of labor 592

463 OCCUPATIONAL SPECIALIZATION--number of partially and fully specialized occupations; major occupational categories (e.g., learned and artistic professions, independent industrial and business entrepreneurs, managerial personnel, independent and tenant farmers, government officials, clerical and white-collar workers, skilled artisans, semi-skilled and unskilled industrial workers, farm laborers, domestic servants, slaves); general information about occupational specialization; vocational guidance; specific information on occupations not classifiable elsewhere; etc. This category is designed for summary statements about occupational specialization; in nearly all instances specific information will be classified elsewhere under a wide range of functional and occupational headings. See also:

Stratification of occupations by class and caste. .56   Status, role, and prestige 554
Occupational composition of the population . . 162   Vocational education 874

464 LABOR SUPPLY AND EMPLOYMENT--availability and scarcity of labor force; skilled and unskilled labor; incidence and types of unemployment (e.g., voluntary, intermittent, seasonal, cyclical, residual, technological); employment opportunities; labor mobility and turnover; employment agencies; regulation (e.g., age and sex restrictions); etc. See also:

Internal migration 166   Unemployment insurance. 745
Immigration 167   Unemployment relief 746
Business cycles 458

465 WAGES AND SALARIES--wage levels (e.g., real and money wages); range and variation by occupational categories; composition (e.g., proportion paid in money, in board and keep, in share of product); fees and percentages; determination of wages (e.g., by custom, negotiation; edict or legislation); payments (e.g., daily, weekly, monthly); regulation (e.g., minimum wage legislation); etc. See also:

Income and purchasing power. 434   Standard of living. 511

466 LABOR RELATIONS--respective rights, privileges, and powers of employers and employees; hiring and firing; tenure of employment; instruction and supervision; promotion and retirement; pension plans; working conditions (e.g., hours, hygienic conditions, safety provisions, recreational facilities); prevalence and types of forced labor; indentured labor; regulation (e.g., labor legislation); etc. See also:

Business and industrial organization 47   Slavery 567
Domestic servants. 357   Bride-service 583
Peonage and serfdom 566   Taxation through labor levies 651

Prison and penal labor 697   Social insurance 745
Military labor battalions 708   Vocational training 874

467 LABOR ORGANIZATION--existence of labor organizations (e.g., craft guilds, labor unions); prevalent types (e.g., craft, industrial, company, and government-sponsored unions); rules of admission; dues; status levels (e.g., apprentices, journeymen); officers (e.g., mode of selection, functions, powers); services to members; general political activities (e.g., affiliation with political parties, political action committees); relations with other labor organizations; with international organizations; government regulation of labor organization; etc. See also:

Building trades 33   Mutual benefit societies 456
Specific political behavior 66   Mutual aid 476
Merchant guilds 441

468 COLLECTIVE BARGAINING--negotiations between labor unions and employers; strikes and lockouts; strike-breaking and picketing; boycotts; labor agreements; arbitration; etc. See also:

Landlord-tenant negotiations 427   Political movements 668
Rioting 579   Contracts 675

---

47 BUSINESS AND INDUSTRIAL ORGANIZATION

47 BUSINESS AND INDUSTRIAL ORGANIZATION--general statements covering several types of business or industrial organizations. Specific types and modes of organization for the production and distribution of economic goods, with the characteristics of each, and with their relationship to the ownership and control of capital will be filed under the appropriate three digit category below.

471 OWNERSHIP AND CONTROL OF CAPITAL--major forms of productive capital (e.g., land, cattle, industrial plants); extent to which the instruments of production are individually, collectively, internationally and publicly owned; forms and elaboration of governmental control (e.g., nationalized industries); etc. Only generalized data will be filed here: for information on specific ownership and organization, see the more specialized categories below. See also:

Capital goods industries 39   Accumulation of wealth 556
Property 42   Social classes 565
Government enterprises and govern-   Political doctrines 668
   ment regulation 65   Ideas about economics and political
General statements on different types   systems 829
   of economic activity 433

472 INDIVIDUAL ENTERPRISE--business and industrial enterprises with owner management; specific characteristics and forms of organization (e.g.,

individual ownership and management, partnerships, family businesses);
opportunities for and justifications of individual enterprise; distribution of
profits between owners and employees; etc. See also:

Industrial enterprise . . . . 39 Local and regional specialization 438
Mercantile enterprises . . . . 44 Domestic trade 438
Bankruptcy . . . . 426 Employer-employee relations 466
Income . . . . 434 Accumulation of wealth 556

473 CORPORATE ORGANIZATION--business and industrial enterprises of a
corporate nature (e.g., joint stock companies, holding companies, international stock companies); incorporation; registration; corporate securities (e.g., bonds, preferred and common stocks); managerial structure and
functions (e.g., directors, officers, managers, foremen); rights, privileges,
and powers of stockholders and management; corporation law; reorganization
and receivership; etc. See also:

Incorporeal property . . . . 424 Monopolies and competition. 477
Investment in corporate securities . . . . . . 454 Agency 676
Labor relations . . . . 466 Philanthropic foundations 741

474 COOPERATIVE ORGANIZATION--producers' and consumers' cooperatives;
relationship between ownership, control, and management; organization
(e.g., Rochdale plan); services to members; collective farms; etc. See also:

Wholesale marketing . . . . 442 Cooperative work groups 476
Craft guilds 467

475 STATE ENTERPRISE--business and industrial enterprises under government
operation; method of finance; system of direction, supervision, and control;
managerial structure and functions; evidence bearing upon cost and efficiency
of operation; etc. See also:

Public schools . . . . 87 Governmental control in the absence of
Postal system 205   public ownership 656
Municipal public utilities . . . . 365 Political doctrines 668
Specific government enterprises . . . . . . 655 Social insurance 745

476 MUTUAL AID--cooperation in economic activities (e.g., mutual aid); exchange of services; cooperative work groups; material and social rewards of
cooperation; interaction and relative elaboration of cooperative and competitive activities; etc. See also:

Personality. . . . . 15 Interpersonal relations 57
Organization of labor and division of prod-   Cooperative relationships among kin . . 59, 60, 61
   ucts in food-getting and exploitative   Exchange of services for goods. 437
   activities . . . . 22, 23, 24, 31 Mutual benefit societies 456

477 COMPETITION--incidence of competition between economic enterprises of
the same and of different organizational types; manifestations of competition
(e.g., price-cutting); methods of restricting competition (e.g., price

agreements, monopolistic arrangements); characteristics of competitive and monopolistic enterprises; regulation (e.g., "trust-busting"); etc. See also:

Competitive and monopoly prices . . . . . . 435 Ingroup antagonisms 578
Sales promotion . . . . 446 Government monopolies 655
Competitive sports 526

_____

48 TRAVEL AND TRANSPORTATION

48 TRAVEL AND TRANSPORTATION--general statements dealing with several aspects of travel and transportation. For data on the major facilities for travel and transportation by land, sea, and air see 49 and 50; for military transport see 71; for communications see 20.

481 LOCOMOTION--walking and running; gaits; speed and distances covered; artificial aids (e.g., canes, crutches, stilts, snowshoes, skis, skates); special modes of locomotion (e.g., crawling, jumping, climbing, swimming, diving); etc. See also:

Couriers . . . . 202 Exercise 526
Ladders . . . . 417 Figure skating 535
Riding . . . . 492 Therapeutic apparatus 758
Postures . . . . 516 Transmission of skills 868

482 BURDEN CARRYING--methods of carrying burdens (e.g., on head, shoulders, back); gear (e.g., head pad, tumpline, carrying pole, pack basket); specialists in burden carrying (e.g., porters, coolies); uses (e.g., on safari); etc. See also:

Water carrying . . . . 312 Transport of corpse to place of disposal . . . 764
Gathering of firewood . . . . 313 Methods of carrying infants 854
Litters 493

483 WEIGHT MOVING--application of human energy in the transportation of heavy weights (e.g., logs, heavy stones, carcasses of large animals); mechanical aids and cooperative techniques employed; use of weight-moving machinery; lifting or raising of heavy objects (e.g., in loading vessels, erection of megaliths); etc. See also:

Building and construction . . . . 33 Weight-moving machines. 406
Logging . . . . 313 Vehicles 493
Knowledge of rollers, pulleys, and inclined
 planes 401

484 TRAVEL--volume, frequency, range, and occasions of travel; trips and expeditions (e.g., tourist travel, exploring expeditions); routine of travel (e.g., marching, caravans, camping); commuting; etc. See also:

Means of travel . . . . 49, 50   Traveling salesmen 446
Internal migration 166   Vacation resorts 529
Immigration 167   Guest friendship 572
Seasonal migrations 221   Visiting and hospitality 574
Hunting trips 224   Government-supported exploration 654
Trading expeditions 437   Military expeditions 726
Itinerant merchants 443   Pilgrimages 788

485 TRAVEL SERVICES--accommodations (e.g., hotels, inns, guest houses); information and travelers' aid services; guides; ticket and travel agencies; organizations of and for travelers (e.g., automobile clubs); etc. See also:

Restaurants 265   Highway services 495
Foreign exchange 457

486 REGULATION OF TRAVEL--restrictions on travel; permits and passports; examinations and inspections; registration; safe-conduct; etc. See also:

Immigration regulations 167   Police 625
Traffic regulations . . . . 363, 494   Diplomatic immunity 648

487 ROUTES--footpaths and trails (e.g., character, distribution); sea and air lanes; trade and caravan routes; marking of routes (e.g., blazes, signposts); route maps and charts; etc. See also:

Maps and place names 10   Railways 496
Topography 133   Aids to navigation 502
Streets 363   Map making 823
Highways 491

488 WAREHOUSING--operation and regulation of warehouses; services (e.g., storage, preservation, stockpiling, care of goods in transit); organization and personnel; charges; etc. See also:

Storage and preservation of food 251   Warehouse receipts as money 436
Warehouse buildings 347

489 TRANSPORTATION--extent of transportation; carrying capacity and volume of traffic by types of transport; transportation systems and their integration; regulation of transportation (e.g., permits, customs inspections); etc. See also:

Land transport 49   Foreign trade 439
Water and air transport 50   Tariffs and tolls 651
Postal service 205   Government ownership and control 471, 655
Articles entering into domestic commerce . . 438   Military supply and transport services 705

---

49 LAND TRANSPORT

49 LAND TRANSPORT--general statements dealing with several of the specialized means and facilities for land travel and transportation. For general information on travel and transportation see 48.

491 HIGHWAYS--number, location, and distribution of roads; character (e.g., straight, meandering); surfacing and drainage; adjuncts (e.g., culverts, bridges, causeways, tunnels, fords, ferries); highway maintenance (e.g., responsibility, techniques, special apparatus, personnel); etc. See also:

Urban streets 363   Use of roads. 494
Routes, footpaths, and trails 487   Ferry boats 501

492 ANIMAL TRANSPORT--use of pack, draft, and riding animals; gear (e.g., saddle, bridle, stirrup, yoke, harness); loads; methods of guiding and riding; etc. See also:

Animal husbandry 23   Horse racing 541
Carrier birds and animals 202   Cavalry 704

493 VEHICLES--burden vehicles (e.g., litter, sedan chair); drag vehicles (e.g., sledge, travois); wheeled vehicles (e.g., cart, wagon, wheelbarrow, bicycle, motorcycle, automobile, tram, railway rolling stock); motive power; structure and capacity; mode of operation; gear; etc. This category is designed for descriptive data only; uses of vehicles will be found in separate categories. See also;

Manufacture of vehicles 398   Military vehicles 715

494 HIGHWAY TRANSPORT--use of highways for travel and transportation; animal and vehicular traffic; private and public transport systems (e.g., carting, stagecoaches, cab services, trucking, tramways, bus lines); organization; specialized personnel (e.g., drivers, carters, tram and bus conductors); fares and tolls; regulation (e.g., licenses, traffic rules); highway patrols; etc. See also:

Urban transportation facilities 36   Incidence of highway accidents 164, 165

495 AUXILIARY HIGHWAY SERVICES--post and relay stations; livery stables; garages and repair shops; filling stations; organization and personnel; services; etc. See also:

Restaurants 265   Miscellaneous retail businesses 444
Business structures 347   Hotels 485
Petroleum industry 382   Bus terminals 498

496 RAILWAYS--number, location, and distribution of railways; tracks and roadbeds; bridges, trestles, and tunnels; sidings and switches; signaling and control systems; maintenance of roadbeds and rolling stock; etc. See also:

Signaling 202   Tram lines 494
Manufacture of railway equipment 397   Railway construction 499
Description of rolling stock 493   Military trains 715

497 RAIL TRANSPORT--freight and passenger services and accommodations; make-up and operation of trains; schedules; fares and freight charges; traffic control; special services (e.g., railway express, refrigerated freight service); organization and specialized personnel; regulation; etc. See also:

Postal system 205   Corporate organization 473
Labor unions 467   Government ownership and control 471, 655

498 TERMINAL FACILITIES--bus, tram, railway terminals; passenger services at railway and bus stations; freight yards; terminal repair facilities; freight and fuel storage facilities; etc. See also:

Description of terminal structures 349   Port facilities 504
Warehousing 488

499 HIGHWAY AND RAILWAY CONSTRUCTION--surveying of route; grading; construction of culverts, bridges, trestles, and tunnels; laying of ties and rails or of highway surface; organization of labor and production; etc. See also:

Specialization in construction 33   Corporate financing 454, 473
Labor 46   Public finance 652
Weight-moving machinery 406   Surveying 804

---

50 WATER AND AIR TRANSPORT

50 WATER AND AIR TRANSPORT--general statements dealing with several aspects of the means and facilities for travel and transportation by water and air. For general information on travel and transportation see 48.

501 BOATS--types of water craft (e.g., rafts, skin and plank boats, bark and dugout canoes, motor boats, sailing vessels, steamships); specialized craft (e.g., ferries, tugs, canal boats, tankers); mode of propulsion (e.g., poling, towing, paddling, rowing, sailing, power propulsion); rigging; machinery; gear (e.g., oars, paddles, rudders, anchors); seating, eating, and sleeping accommodations; etc. This category is designed for descriptive data only. See also:

Power 37   Water transport 505
Cordage 283   Boat names 552
Shipbuilding 396   Naval vessels 716

502 NAVIGATION--direction of water craft (e.g., steering, tacking, piloting); watches; laying of courses (e.g., by landmarks, compass); fixing of positions (e.g., by sounding, celestial observations); adjuncts to navigation (e.g., buoys, lighthouses); adaptations to special situations (e.g., docking, running of rapids, portaging, ice-breaking, canal navigation); maritime customs and regulations; shipwrecks; salvage; etc. See also:

Description of lighthouses 349   Boat racing 526
Optical instruments 416   Admiralty courts 698
Sea lanes and charts 487   Military use of radar and loran 718

503 WATERWAYS IMPROVEMENTS--description and building of canals; dredging of rivers and harbors; construction of piers and breakwaters; etc. See also:

Water supply	312	Pile drivers	402
Logging	313	Dredges	406
Development of water power	376	Public finance	652

504 PORT FACILITIES--boathouses; piers and docks; facilities for mooring, loading, and unloading; storage facilities; supply services (e.g., ship chandlers, fueling stations); facilities for repair and overhaul; use of natural harbors; etc. See also:

Construction	33	Warehousing	488
Ship repairs	396	Trucking	494
Cranes	406	Rail terminals	498
Weight moving	483		

505 WATER TRANSPORT--number, types, and distribution of shipping services; passenger and freight capacity and traffic; sailing schedules; fares and freight charges; booking arrangements; specialized personnel (e.g., line and engineer officers, crews, longshoremen, traffic agents); organization (e.g., shipping companies); regulation; etc. See also:

Marine insurance	456	Corporate organization	473
Labor unions	467	Government subsidies	654

506 AIRCRAFT--types of air and space craft (e.g., balloons, dirigibles, gliders, airplanes); mode of propulsion; machinery and instruments; landing gear; freight and passenger accommodations; etc. See also:

Power	37	Kites	524
Carrier birds	202	Rocket weapons	713
Manufacture of aircraft	399	Military aircraft	717
Air transport	509		

507 AVIATION--aeronautic and astronautic science; operation of aircraft (e.g., takeoff, banking, instrument flying, landing); laying of courses; fixing of positions; adjuncts to aerial navigation (e.g., beacons, radio beams, radar tracking stations); regulations governing flying; etc. See also:

Radio	207	Navigation	502
Air lanes and charts	487	Aviation personnel	509

508 AIRPORT FACILITIES--air fields; loading, unloading, and fueling facilities; facilities for repair and overhaul; freight and passenger facilities at airports and air terminals; etc. See also:

Description of hangars and other structures	349	Military airfields	712
Urban airport facilities	368		

509 AIR TRANSPORT--number and distribution of airlines; passenger and freight capacity and traffic; mode of conveyance to and from airports; flight schedules; fares and freight charges; booking arrangements; specialized personnel (e.g., pilots, navigators, radio operators, stewardesses, ground crews, sales force); private and public operation; mail subsidies; government regulation; etc. See also:

Postal system	205	Military air transport services	705
Government aid	654		

51 LIVING STANDARDS AND ROUTINES--general statements concerned with several aspects of economic and esthetic standards, and with some of the routine habits of life. For standards of etiquette and ethics see 57. For routine habits concerned with eating see 264, with drinking see 27, with sex see 83, with adornment see 30, with recreation see 52, with religion see 78, with labor see 46, with housekeeping see 356, with language see 19, with locomotion see 481.

511 STANDARD OF LIVING--ideal standards and actual levels of quantity and quality in regard to shelter, clothing, food, and other consumers' goods; extent to which actual levels fall below the minimal requirements for normal, healthy living; results of statistical studies (e.g., of family budgets); cultural standards of indulgence and luxuries in excess of minimal biological requirements; etc. See also:

Health and welfare	74	Leisure-time activities	517
Nutrition	146	Gradations in wealth	556
Population policy	168	Social classes	565
Diet	262	Ownership of dwelling	592
Housing	362	Taxation	651
Prevalence of home ownership and tenancy	427	Poverty	735
Income and purchasing power	434	Educational statistics	871
Wages and salaries	465		

512 DAILY ROUTINE--succession of activities throughout a typical day; time of arising and retiring; hours of work and relaxation; daily chores; longer rhythms (e.g., weekly, monthly); etc. See also:

Annual cycle of economic activities	221	Distribution of labor and leisure	461
Mealtimes	264	Holidays	527
Housecleaning	356		

513 SLEEPING--hours of sleeping; postures in sleeping; segregation in sleeping (e.g., by age, by sex); bedding; ideas about sleep and sleepiness; naps and siestas; etc. See also:

Beds	352	Sexual intercourse	833
Dream interpretation	787	Sleeping habits of children	857
Conceptions of fatigue and dreams	828		

514 ELIMINATION--postures in urination and defecation; conception of appropriate times and places for elimination; spitting; disposal of excreta; toilet facilities and fixtures; associated ideas and practices (e.g., modesty, scatalogic rites); etc. See also:

Diseases	164	Exuvial magic	754
Description of outdoor latrines	343	Use of cathartics	757
Sewage disposal	364	Ideas about elimination	827
Anal humor	522	Toilet training of children	863
Public health and sanitation	744		

515 PERSONAL HYGIENE--frequency and methods of bathing and laving; use of washing and bathing facilities; use of soap and other cleansers; use of towels; conception and idealization of cleanliness; miscellaneous hygienic practices (e.g., brushing of teeth, washing of hair, removal of body lice); etc. See also:

Bathing apparel	292	Ritual uncleanness and purification	783
Laundering and cleaning	296	Sexual hygiene	833
Hairdressing and cosmetics	302	Sexual modesty	834
Bathhouses	343	Menstrual hygiene	841
Soap manufacture	388	Cleanliness training of children	863
Bathing resorts	529		

516 POSTURES--bodily positions assumed in standing (e.g., with feet apart, on one leg, leaning against a support, slumping); relaxed postures (e.g., sitting, squatting, kneeling); recumbent postures (e.g., reclining on elbow); occasions for assuming particular postures; ideas about correct postures; motor habits not elsewhere described; etc. See also:

Motor habits in the use of artifacts	41	Dance postures	535
Nervous habits	157	Dramatic postures	536
Gestures	201	Etiquette	576
Furniture	352	Military drill	702
Gaits	481	Genuflection	782
Positions in sleeping	513	Positions in sexual intercourse	833
Positions in elimination	514		

517 LEISURE TIME ACTIVITIES--standards of amusement, recreation, and artistic appreciation; distribution of leisure time between active and passive, between social and individualistic, and between culturally preferred and less preferred pursuits; esthetic ideals and principles; canons of taste; levels of appreciation and "culture"; etc. See also:

Recreation	52	Distribution of labor and leisure	461
Artistic expression	53	Social classes	565
Entertainment	54	Visiting	574
Education	87	Religious activities	78, 796

---

52 RECREATION

52 RECREATION--general statements dealing with several different forms of recreation involving active participation. For those mainly involving spectatorship see 54.

521 CONVERSATION--loquacity and reserve; boasting and shyness; conversational patterns (e.g., idle chatter, rambling discourse, discussion, argument); occasions and places; participants; typical subjects (e.g., weather, news, gossip, politics); privileged and unprivileged communications; etc. See also:

Interpersonal relations 57
Stylistics 195
Verbal news dissemination and rumor 203
Drinking establishments 275
Idling and loitering 461

Oratory 537
Story telling 538
Debates 544
Lying 577
Gossip and intentional silence as a means of
    social control 626

522 HUMOR--conception of humor; sources of amusement (e.g., mishaps); types of humor (e.g., wit, puns, practical jokes); expressions of amusement (e.g., smiling, laughter); droll stories; coarse humor (e.g., anal, pornographic); humorists (e.g., wits, jesters, comedians); special elaborations of humor (e.g., comic strips); etc. See also:

Humor in the fine arts 53
Humor in entertainment 54
Patterned expressions of emotion 201
Clowns 536

Joking relationships between kinsmen 602
Ridicule as a means of social control 626
Ideas about laughing and smiling 827
Obscenity and pornography 831

523 HOBBIES--individual pastimes (e.g., reading); elaboration of economic and technological pursuits into hobbies (e.g., animal breeding, bookbinding, cookery, embroidery, woodworking); construction of models; collectors' hobbies (e.g., philately, coins, antiques, first editions); heirlooms; etc. See also:

Hunting and fishing 22
Artistic hobbies 53
Personality traits 157
Museum and library collections 217

Commercial breeding of animals 232
Gardening 247
Special dealers 549
Club activities 575

524 GAMES--playthings (e.g., dolls, blocks, mechanical toys); games of dexterity (e.g., string figures, tops, juggling, kite flying, billiards); problem games (e.g., riddles, charades, puzzles); games of calculation (e.g., chess, checkers, card games); special childrens' games; occasions for playing games; participants and spectators; special equipment; rules; organizers and sponsors of games (e.g., cliques, clubs, churches, communities, business organizations); etc. See also:

Childhood activities 857

525 GAMBLING--laying of wagers on games, athletic contests, and spectacles; betting; lotteries; special gambling devices (e.g., roulette wheels); calculation of odds (e.g., bookmakers, parimutuel machines); informal gambling; gaming houses and their operation; gambling as a method of finance (e.g., government lotteries, church bingo games, hospital sweepstakes, club slot machines); specialists (e.g., gamblers, croupiers); prevalence of and attitudes toward gambling; restrictions and regulations; etc. See also:

Debts 426
Speculation 455
Horse racing 541

Illicit gambling establishments 548
Conception and manipulation of luck
   and chance 777

526 ATHLETIC SPORTS--forms of exercise (e.g., hiking, swimming, skating, skiing, riding, mountain climbing, calisthenics, gymnastics); sports of pursuit (e.g., hide-and-seek, paper chases); individual contests (e.g., foot races, jumping, weight lifting, boxing, wrestling, archery, hoop and dart game, javelin throwing, trap shooting, bowling, tennis, golf); team contests (e.g., tug-of-war, boat races, lacrosse, hockey, football, baseball, basketball, polo); occasions; participants and spectators; special equipment; rules; associated ideas (e.g., sportsmanship, amateur status, value of physical fitness); organizers and sponsors of sports (e.g., clubs, schools, business organizations, promoters); etc. See also:

Fishing and hunting	22	Racing and fighting with animals	541
Recreational structures	345	Commercialized sports	542
Locomotion	481	Manufacture and distribution of sporting goods	549
Athletic clubs	529	Military training	702

527 REST DAYS AND HOLIDAYS--days reserved for rest from labor; conceptualization (e.g., as harvest celebrations, as patriotic or commemorative occasions, as reserved by religious taboos); secular festivals (e.g., harvest, housewarming, patriotic); birthdays and anniversaries; holiday activities (e.g., feasting, drinking, visiting, games, pageants); etc. For ceremonies associated with specific economic activities see elsewhere under specialized categories (e.g., agricultural ceremonies, see 24). See also:

Potlatches	431	Feasting	574
Distribution of labor and leisure	461	Victory celebrations	727
Leisure time activities	517	Taboos	784
Pageants	541	Religious festivals	796

528 VACATIONS--extended leave from labor; incidence, duration, and cultural justifications; vacation activities (e.g., rest, recreation, travel, visiting, frequenting of resorts); etc. See also:

Travel	484	Military leave	701
Visiting	574	Invalidism	734
Honeymoons	585	Pilgrimages	788

529 RECREATIONAL FACILITIES--vacation resorts (e.g., spas, mountain retreats, winter sports facilities, beach resorts, state and national parks); bridge, chess, riding, and rifle clubs and their facilities; athletic and country clubs; amusement parks; enterprises catering to games and sports (e.g., pool rooms, bowling alleys, shooting galleries, gymnasiums, skating rinks); special equipment, organization, operation and specialized personnel; etc. See also:

Urban parks and recreational facilities	36	Hotels and tourist services	485
Facilities catering to entertainment	54	Manufacture and distribution of recreational	
Recreational structures	345	equipment	549
		Social clubs	575

53 FINE ARTS--general statements dealing with several aspects of the creation and interpretation of art. For art as a source of entertainment see 54, for esthetic ideals and canons of taste see 517, for art forms associated with ceremonials see 796.

531 DECORATIVE ART--types of artifacts decorated and not decorated; decorative techniques (e.g., carving, engraving, painting, inlay, embroidery); use of color and relief; designs and patterns (e.g., naturalistic, geometric); decorative symbols and their meanings; elaborated styles; associated beliefs and practices; specialists; etc. See also:

Textiles	28	Tattooing	304
Clothing	29	Architecture	341
Tools, utensils, and appliances	41	Interior decoration	353
Chirography	212	Manufacture of paints and dyes	386
Ornament	301	Esthetics	517
Face and body decoration	302		

532 REPRESENTATIVE ART--techniques in painting and sculpture (e.g., drawing or painting on flat surfaces, incising in relief, modeling or carving in the round); materials and implements used; subjects (e.g., still life, landscapes, human beings, abstractions); use of color; composition; appreciation of form and perspective; styles (e.g., naturalistic, idealistic, symbolic, abstract); special products (e.g., etchings, bas-reliefs, masks); specialized fields (e.g., portraiture, commercial art, religious sculpture); artists and sculptors; etc. See also:

Commemorative statues	211	Advertising	447
Photography	215	Art supplies industry	549
Art galleries	217	Idols and images	778
Lapidary art	306	Ideas about form and color	822
Paints and pigments	386		

533 MUSIC--musical form and structure (e.g., scale, pitch, tone, tempo, rhythm); melody; harmony; vocal music (e.g., singing, humming, chanting); instrumental music (e.g., accompaniment, solo playing, orchestras); occasions for music; song styles (e.g., work songs, drinking songs, dance songs, war songs, love songs, lullabies, sacred music, dirges and laments); musical training and appreciation; composition of music; specialization (e.g., composers, minstrels, musicologists, musicians); organization (e.g., choirs, bands, orchestras); etc. See also:

Property in songs	424	Musical texts	539
Palliation of labor with music	461	Musical performances on the stage	545

534 MUSICAL INSTRUMENTS--idiophones (e.g., clappers, gongs, rattles); membranophones (e.g., drums); cordophones (e.g., zithers, lutes, harps); aerophones (e.g., flutes, pipes, trumpets); special instruments (e.g., bullroarers); complex mechanical instruments (e.g., piano, organ); care and repair of musical instruments; etc. See also:

Drum signaling	202	Sound recordings	216
Radio	207	Musical supplies industry	549

535 DANCING--dance styles (e.g., imitative, pantomimic, symbolic, stylized); technique (e.g., movements of the head, trunk, and limbs); gestures, postures, and their symbolism; solo, pair, and group dancing; choreographic patterns; extemporization and formalization; rhythm; musical accompaniment; occasions for dancing and associated dance forms (e.g., war dances, shamanistic dances, ballroom dancing, tap dancing); participants and spectators; dancing places (e.g., dance halls); dance costumes and paraphernalia; emotional expression in dancing; training in dancing; specialized dancers and dance leaders; choreographic arts allied to dancing (e.g., figure skating); etc. See also:

Gestures	201	Dance performances on the stage	545
Postures	516	Night clubs	547
Skating	526		

536 DRAMA--compositions for dramatic representation; types (e.g., tragedy, comedy, farce); themes (e.g., from myth, history, everyday life); treatment (e.g., realistic, stylized); conventional limitations on dramatic composition; characters and parts; impersonation; acting techniques (e.g., gestures, postures, emotional expression); costumes and paraphernalia; make-up; staging (e.g., scenery, lighting, props, musical accompaniment); acts, scenes, choruses, and interludes; specialists (e.g., playwrights, actors, stagehands, directors); relation of drama to dancing, mythology, magic, and ritual; special types of plays (e.g., puppet shows, shadow plays, musical comedies); special roles (e.g., clowns); etc. See also:

Gestures	201	Humor	522
Patterned expressions of emotion	201	Masks	532
Radio and television	207	Pageants and circuses	541
Cosmetics	302	Stage productions	545
Theater buildings	345	Motion pictures	546
Postures	516	Religious ceremonial	796

537 ORATORY--rhetorical style; patterned forms of oratory (e.g., narration, debating, exhortation); techniques of declamation (e.g., exaggeration, repetition, figures of speech); gestures and postures in orating; training in public speaking; occasions for oratory; etc. See also:

Stylistics	195	Parliamentary debates	646
Gestures	201	Electioneering	666
Postures	516	Arguments in court	695
Boasting	521	Pronouncing of spells	789
Lectures and debates	544	Preaching	793

538 LITERATURE--literary styles; poetry (e.g., epic, lyric); verse forms (e.g., couplets, stanzas); poetic techniques (e.g., meter, rhyme, alliteration); prose forms (e.g., tales, sagas, proverbs, fiction, short stories, essays);

narrative plot and structure; literary subjects and themes; characters (e.g., animals, men, gods); treatment (e.g., realism, fantasy, allegory, satire); composition; literary conventions; recitation and narration (e.g., occasions, audiences); specialists (e.g., poets, prose authors, story tellers, ghost writers); etc. This category is reserved for generalized descriptions of literatur For literary texts, and analyses and commentaries related to specific literary works see 539. See also:

Stylistics	195	Riddles	524
News stories and magazine articles	204	Lectures	544
Books and their publication	214	Mythology	773
Esthetic ideals and canons of taste	517	Sacred literature	779
Wit and humor	522	Humanistic studies	814

539 LITERARY TEXTS--texts, translations, and abstracts of folktales, myths, songs, and other individual literary products; critical analyses and commentaries thereupon; etc.

---

54 ENTERTAINMENT

54 ENTERTAINMENT--general statements dealing primarily with the enjoyment of recreational and artistic activities on the part of spectators rather than participants, and especially with the more commercialized aspects of such activities.

541 SPECTACLES -- patriotic celebrations; parades; fireworks displays; military reviews; secular pageants; carnivals, circuses, and rodeos; animal racing and fighting (e.g., horse and dog races, bull baiting, cockfighting); gladiatorial combats; public hangings; organization of spectacles; financing (e.g., by profits, voluntary contributions, subsidies); admissions (e.g., gratis, by ticket); specialists (e.g., organizers, performers); etc. See also:

Breeding of racehorses	232	Clowns	522, 536
Animal transport	492	Religious spectacles	796
Attendant gambling	525		

542 COMMERCIALIZED SPORTS--commercially organized athletic events (e.g., boxing and wrestling matches, ball games, racing events); sponsors (e.g., political units, educational institutions, business entrepreneurs); special facilities (e.g., stadiums, ball fields); promotional activities; seating arrangements and distribution of tickets; specialists (e.g., professional and amateur athletes, coaches, promoters); offering of rewards (e.g., prizes, cups); championships and records; international contests (e.g., Olympic games, test matches); behavior of spectators; etc. See also:

Recreational structures	345	Amateur sport	526
Sales promotion	446		

543 EXHIBITIONS--international expositions; local and regional fairs; animal-judging contests (e.g., horse and dog shows); handicraft displays; automobile and flower shows; art exhibitions; special exhibits (e.g., by libraries and museums); offering of prizes and awards; organization of exhibitions; mode of finance (e.g., by sale of tickets, sale of articles on display, voluntary contributions); specialized organizers and dealers; etc. See also:

Libraries, art galleries, and museums 217   Markets 443
Zoological and botanical gardens 367   Sales promotion 446
Auctioning 437   Advertising 447

544 PUBLIC LECTURES--lectures on literary and artistic subjects; illustrated travelogues; public debates; addresses on current events; forums on public issues; lectures on scientific and scholarly subjects; speeches at banquets; public appearances of a non-theatrical nature by artists and musicians; lecture tours and circuits; organization and promotion of lectures; finance (e.g., from endowed funds, by sale of tickets); etc. See also:

Education 87   Political campaigns 666
Oratory 537

545 MUSICAL AND THEATRICAL PRODUCTIONS--public concerts; operatic productions; performances by dance troupes (e.g., ballets); burlesque and vaudeville; production of musical comedies and plays; stock companies, amateur musicals and theatricals; metropolitan show business (e.g., selection of a play, backers, producers, casting, try-outs, staging, rehearsals, promotion, advance sales, first nights, reviews, runs, motion picture rights, royalties, returns on investment, road companies); promotion of other musical and dramatic productions; etc. See also:

Fine arts 53   Theatrical supplies industry. 549

546 MOTION PICTURE INDUSTRY--production, distribution, and exhibition of motion pictures; script writing; casting; locations and sets; filming; special equipment and techniques (e.g., technicolor, sound); products (e.g., film plays, animated cartoons, educational and documentary films); system of distribution (e.g., chains, block booking, runs); motion picture theaters and their operation; specialists (e.g., producers, script writers, actors, cameramen, distributors, operators); economic organization of the industry; regulation; etc. See also:

Fine arts 53   Cameras. 416
Photography. 215   Visual aids in education 876
Sound recording 216

547 NIGHT CLUBS AND CABARETS--enterprises providing food, liquor, music, and dancing in various combinations (e.g., supper clubs, jukebox cafés, cabarets, roadhouses); types of entertainment offered; patronage; organization and specialization; regulation; etc. See also:

Restaurants 265   Music. 533
Bars and saloons 275   Dancing 535

548 ORGANIZED VICE--prostitutes and houses of prostitution; recruiting of prostitutes; business methods; auxiliary specialists (e.g., procurers, madams, pimps); organized homosexuality; illicit narcotics trade (e.g., drug peddlers, opium dens); underworld gambling establishments; illicit liquor business (e.g., rumrunning, bootlegging, speakeasies); organization of underworld activities; political protection and graft; racketeering; etc. See also:

Use of narcotics and liquor	27	Crime	674
Political corruption	66	Public health	744
Sex	83	Religious prostitution	786
Gambling	525		

549 ART AND RECREATIONAL SUPPLIES INDUSTRIES--distribution of equipment and accessories used in recreation, entertainment, and the fine arts (e.g., sporting goods, stamps and philatelic equipment, books, art supplies, musical instruments, theatrical and motion picture equipment); manufacture of special equipment and supplies (e.g., toys, sporting goods, musical instruments, art and theatrical supplies); business methods and specialization; etc. See also:

Marketing	44	Publishing	214
Business and industrial organization	47	Manufacture of paints and pigments	386
Recreation	52	Manufacture of photographic equipment and	
Fine arts	53	supplies	395

---

55 INDIVIDUATION AND MOBILITY

55 INDIVIDUATION AND MOBILITY--general statements covering several aspects of individuation and mobility; status, names, and naming. The term "status" is here used to connote the position occupied by an individual in any repetitive social relationship. The behavior exhibited by the occupant of a status is his "role," i.e., his enactment of his part in the relationship. Societies tend to rank certain statuses as higher and lower, and within a status to rank the roles of different individuals in terms of how adequately they measure up to the cultural expectations for that status. The "prestige" of any individual reflects both the level of the various statuses that he occupies and the social estimate of his roles in each. Some statuses are ascribed and not achievable, being gained either automatically or not at all. An individual can enhance his prestige through his own effort only by improving the performance of his roles or by moving into achievable statuses of higher social standing. By "mobility" is meant the means by which these objectives are accomplished.

551 PERSONAL NAMES--proper names of individuals (e.g., number and variety, meanings, circumstances of use); sex and status differences, special name usages (e.g., nicknames, aliases, teknonymy); name taboos and avoidances; etc. See also:

Incorporeal property 424   Kinship terms 601
Naming 553   Names as souls 774
Titles 554

552 NAMES OF ANIMALS AND THINGS--proper names of individual animals,
   houses, boats, and other objects; meanings; bestowal and use; etc. See also:
   Names of kin groups 61   Property in names 424
   Place names 103   Names of supernatural beings 776
   Vocabulary 192

553 NAMING--bestowal of names in infancy; name givers and namesakes; naming
   ceremonies; exchange of names; reciprocal relationships created by naming
   or name exchange; assumption of new names (e.g., occasions, ceremonial);
   posthumous assumption of names; reasons for name changing; bestowal and
   assumption of honorific names and titles; etc. See also:
   Personal names 551   Godparents and godchildren 608
   Titles 554   Ceremonies during infancy 852

554 STATUS, ROLE, AND PRESTIGE--relative prevalence of ascribed and achievable statuses; statuses adapted to particular personality types; general comments on the social ranking of statuses and roles; types of roles and achievable
   statuses which bring the largest rewards in prestige; individuals typifying the
   foregoing (e.g., celebrities, national heroes); symbolic tokens of the achievement of prestige (e.g., medals, titles, insignia, praise songs, special privileges); general statements on the various avenues of mobility (e.g., technological skill, wealth, shrewdness, valor, piety, wisdom); etc. See also:
   Social stratification 56   Occupational specialization 463
   Relation between individual roles and   Ethical ideals 577
      culturally defined statuses 156   Military virtues and prestige 703
   Ethos 181

555 TALENT MOBILITY--extent to which prestige can be gained by mastering or
   excelling in some complex or difficult cultural activity (e.g., religious ritual,
   fine arts, scholarship, war, technology, business); talents and skills most
   highly rewarded in prestige (e.g., directly rather than indirectly through the
   material remuneration they may bring); frequency with which such channels of
   mobility are chosen; desirable statuses achievable thereby; symbolic tokens
   of success; specific techniques (e.g., counting coup, writing a bestseller,
   making a scientific discovery, winning an Olympic race); etc. See also:
   Education 87   Preferment of war veterans 729
   Occupational specialization 463

556 ACCUMULATION OF WEALTH--extent to which prestige can be gained through
   amassing wealth; means used to accumulate wealth or degree of skill involved;
   principal objects of wealth (e.g., money, cattle, slaves, land); relative importance of sheer accumulation, of display, of generosity in distribution;
   prominence of wealth accumulation as a mobility mechanism; desirable statuses
   achievable thereby; symbolic tokens of success; specific techniques (e.g.,

75

conspicuous consumption, potlatching, endowing a college, buying a title); etc. See also:

Property. 42   Individual enterprise 472
Potlatches. 431   Wealth in relation to social classes 565
Saving and investment 454   Hospitality 574

557 MANIPULATIVE MOBILITY--extent to which desirable statuses and the prestige they bring can be achieved by opportunistic manipulation of social relationships (e.g., cultivation of persons in authority, political machinations, exploitation of friends and relatives, backslapping, marriages of convenience); prominence and relative effectiveness of manipulative techniques as compared with acquisition of skills and wealth; desirable statuses achievable thereby (e.g., political preferment); etc. See also:

Interpersonal relations 57   Traits of leadership. 157
Political behavior 66

558 DOWNWARD MOBILITY--possibility and incidence of serious loss of prestige; extent to which such loss involves actual descent to less desirable statuses or merely a less favorable estimate of role enactment in the same statuses; major factors in downward mobility (e.g., loss of wealth, misalliance, cowardice, impiety, crime); special examples (e.g., losing face, losing caste); etc. See also:

Breaches of etiquette and ethics 57   Crime and sin 674
Social control. 626   Poverty. 735

---

56 SOCIAL STRATIFICATION

56 SOCIAL STRATIFICATION--general statements covering several aspects of the major differentiations in social status that are commonly hierarchically graded or stratified. For occupational differentiation see 463; for differentiation in political statuses see 62, 63, and 64.

561 AGE STRATIFICATION--recognized age levels and their differentiation (e.g., age terms); generalized information on rites of passage from level to level; organized age-grades (e.g., composition, admission, advancement, symbols of membership, activities); relations between age levels and age groups; division of labor by age; etc. See also:

Status and activities of children 85   Sodalities 575
Status and activities of adolescents, adults,
    and the aged 88

562 SEX STATUS--rights, privileges, powers, duties, and disabilities of each sex (e.g., legal, domestic, economic, political, ceremonial); special exceptions for each sex; general statements bearing upon the status inferiority or superiority of women; special elaborations (e.g., chivalry, notions of the

uncleanness of women); explanations of sex differences; etc. See also:

Marriage 58
Status and activities of children 85
Division of labor by sex 462
Franchise 641

Cloistering of women 837
Transvestitism 838
Menstrual isolation 841

563 ETHNIC STRATIFICATION--alien and immigrant subgroups; racial and national minorities; cultural differences between and characteristics of ethnic and minority groups; social and political status of ethnic subgroups; race prejudice and discrimination; assimilation and irredentism; extent of intermarriage; race crossing and amalgamation; racial hybrids and their status; etc. See also:

Racial affinities 144
Ethic composition of the population 162
Immigration 167
Acculturation 177
Degree of subcultural differentiation 184
Ethnocentrism 186

Ingroup antagonisms 578
Naturalization 641
Reservations 657
Religious persecutions 798
Race theories 829

564 CASTES--presence or absence of stratified groups between which mobility is theoretically impossible; number, distribution, and ranking of castes and subcastes; basis of differentiation (e.g., race, occupation, religion); insignia and stigmata of caste; prerogatives and disabilities; organization and activities; relations between castes; special marriage regulations (e.g., endogamy, hypergamy); extent of intermarriage; special outcaste groups; etc. See also:

Subcaste as a kin group 61
Occupational specialization 463

Individual mobility as between castes 554
Sects 795

565 CLASSES--presence or absence of stratified groups between which mobility is to at least some extent possible; number and ranking of social classes; composition and distribution; basis of differentiation (e.g., wealth, occupation, ascribed status, conquest); class consciousness; degree of class organization; integration of cliques with classes; class prerogatives and disabilities; insignia and stigmata of classes; relations between classes; extent of intermarriage; status and affiliation of children of interclass marriages; special social classes (e.g., royalty, nobles and commoners, bourgeois and proletariat); etc. See also:

Mobility 55
Political statuses 62, 63, 64, 66
Occupational specialization 463
Standards of living 511

Cliques 573
Revolutionary movements 669
Poverty 735

566 SERFDOM AND PEONAGE--presence or absence of a semi-servile class bound to the land; prerogatives, disabilities, and stigmata of serfs in a feudal society; characteristics of peonage in nonfeudal societies; etc. See also:

Land tenure 423
Tenancy 427

Forced labor. 466

567 SLAVERY--presence or absence of a servile class of chattel slaves; number of slaves and proportion in the population; activities of slaves; methods of control; treatment; stigmata; rights and privileges of slaves (e.g., to hold property, to marry, to contract debts); rights, privileges, and powers of masters (e.g., to kill, to sell, to hire out); enslavement (e.g., of war captives, for debt, for crime); slave trade; permanency of servile status (e.g., hereditary, for life); redemption (e.g., manumission, adoption, purchase of freedom, escape, asylum); intermarriage between slaves and freemen; status of children of mixed marriages; etc. See also:

Enslavement of criminals 681   Prisoners of war 727
Slave raids 721

---

57 INTERPERSONAL RELATIONS

57 INTERPERSONAL RELATIONS--general statements dealing with several specific aspects of interpersonal relations. Society is a structure of interpersonal relationships, i.e., sets of reciprocally adjusted habitual responses between pairs of interacting individuals. These tend widely to become culturally defined or standardized in terms of polar statuses. A social group arises whenever a number of specific individuals are linked, each to every other, by relationships of the same general types, e.g., friendship, kinship, or coresidence. Groups likewise reveal a marked tendency to become culturally standardized. The categories below are concerned with the general characteristics of interpersonal relationships and social groups, with some of their more voluntary forms, and with the unifying standards and disruptive influences typical of social relationships and groups in general.

571 SOCIAL RELATIONSHIPS AND GROUPS--incidence of types of social relationships (e.g., face-to-face, stereotyped); social interaction (e.g., interaction rates); categories of social groups (e.g., primary, secondary); general observations on the nature, structure and interrelations of social groups not classifiable elsewhere (e.g., intelligentsia, Philistines, secular cult groups, elites, etc.); sociometric data; evidence bearing upon the dynamics of group formation; general statements on decision-making within social groups; etc. Information on specific interest groups, kin groups, political and religious groups, etc. will be filed elsewhere under specialized categories. See also:

Personality 15   Age-grades 561
Property relationships 42   Ingroup antagonisms 578
Economic organization. 47   Kin relationships 602
Family organization 59   Community organization 621
Political organization . . . . 63, 64   Contractual relationships 675
Ecclesiastical organization 79   Children's play groups 857

572 FRIENDSHIPS--conceptualization of friendship; informal friendships and their development; formal friendships (e.g., best friends, guest friendship);

reciprocal obligations of friends; etc. See also:

Economic partnerships 472   Relationships with nonrelatives 609

Economic cooperation 476

Blood brotherhood and other artificial kin

   relationships 608

573 CLIQUES--groups of intimate friends; basis of association; organization and leadership; attitude toward outsiders; clique activities; special types of cliques (e.g., gangs); etc. See also:

Leadership traits. 157   Neighborliness 621

Age-grades. 561   Children's cliques and gangs 857

Integration of cliques with class structure . . . 565   Adolescent gangs 883

574 VISITING AND HOSPITALITY--extent and occasions of visiting; social relationships characterized by reciprocal visiting; reception and entertainment of visitors; informal and formal hospitality; offering of food and drink; feasts and parties; etc. See also:

Drinking 27   Travel. 484

Recreation 52   Banquet speeches 544

Eating 264   Wedding feasts 585

Gift giving 431   Mortuary feasts 765

575 SODALITIES--prevalence of clubs, fraternities, and comparable voluntary associations; types (e.g., lodges, secret societies, men's clubs, women's clubs); organization, characteristics, and activities of each type (e.g., intersodality relationships; origin accounts, paraphernalia, etc.); selection of members; initiation; meetings; special rituals; etc. See also:

Medicine societies 75   Age-grades 561

Clubhouses 345   Military societies 701

Mutual-benefit societies 456   Veterans' organizations 729

Craft guilds and labor unions. 467   Cult groups 794

Athletic clubs 529   Initiation at puberty 881

576 ETIQUETTE--greetings and salutations; obeisances; compliments; concept of courtesy; general patterns of etiquette in eating, drinking, smoking, visiting, and travel; deference to status superiors; noblesse oblige; breaches of etiquette and the resulting social sanctions; etc. See also:

Drinking etiquette. 27   Intentional impoliteness. 578

Patterned behavior toward kinsmen. 60   Informal social control 626

Sexual etiquette. 83   Court etiquette 644

Table manners 264   Diplomacy 648

Postures 516   Propitiation 782

Polite conversation 521   Religious ritual 788

Sportsmanship 526   Training of children in etiquette 867

Chivalry 562   Treatment of the aged 888

577 ETHICS--abstract ethical ideals (e.g., truth, righteousness, justice); ideals of individual virtue (e.g., honesty, loyalty, industry, courage, temperance,

tolerance, filial piety); notions of right and wrong; conception of conscience and character; incidence and causes of, and attitudes toward breaches of ethics (e.g., lying, cowardice, flouting of kinship obligations); conflicts between ideal values and practical considerations; etc. See also:

Personality	15	Punishment of social offenses	689
Law	67	Military virtues	703
Ethos	181	Professional ethics	693, 759
Industry and sloth	461	Philosophical systems of ethics	812
Esthetic ideals	517	Ethnopsychological concepts of	
Organized vice	548	character	828
Informal social control	626	Chastity	831
Civic virtues	641	Sexual modesty	834
Crime and sin	673	Inculcation of ethics	867

578 INGROUP ANTAGONISMS--prevalence and importance of antagonisms within the society; sources (e.g., economic deprivation, sexual rivalry, political repression, ethnic and religious cleavages, rigor of socialization or social control); expression in individual behavior (e.g., snobbishness, intentional impoliteness, ridicule, insults, vituperation); prevalence, causes and forms of quarrels; participants (e.g., husband and wife, business competitors, rival claimants to property); manifestations (e.g., verbal exchanges, fist fights, duels); reaction of onlookers; repression and control of aggression; etc. See also:

Social stratification	56	Informal justice	627, 628
Family antagonisms	59	Torts and crimes	673
Ethnocentrism	186	Slander	683
Economic competition	477	Litigation	691
Wit and practical jokes	522	Sorcery	754
Rivalry in sports	526	Cursing	789
Lying	577	Religious persecution	798
Avoidance relationships	602	Quarreling and fighting by children	857
Moiety rivalries	616	Control of aggression in children	865
Social control and gossip	626		

579 BRAWLS, RIOTS, AND BANDITRY--prevalence and causes of brawls; types (e.g., drinking brawls, gang fights); running amok; incidence and types of riots (e.g., bread riots, race riots, political riots); methods of control; manifestations of mob psychology; incidence of organized violence (e.g., banditry piracy); etc. See also:

Political corruption	66	Revolutions	669
Strikes	468	Punishment of disorderly conduct	689
Organized vice	548	Martial law	722
Police	625	Warfare	726
Social control	626	Petty delinquency	738
Lynching	627	Children's gangs	857
Feuds	628		

58 MARRIAGE--general statements dealing with several specific aspects of marriage. Marriage is a socially sanctioned relationship between a man and a woman involving economic cooperation and residential and sexual cohabitation. The culturally patterned norms of this relationship regularly specify who may and may not enter into it, how it may be established and terminated, and what each partner may and may not do within it. As a relationship, marriage is to be distinguished sharply from the family, the social group within which it is typically embedded.

581 BASIS OF MARRIAGE--theories of the origin, purpose, sanctity, and permanency of marriage; conception of the marriage bond and of the status of matrimony; economic, sexual, and romantic factors in marriage; incentives to marriage; qualities desired in a spouse (e.g., beauty, wealth, industry, skill); relation of marriage to the family; etc. See also:

Family organization 59   Marriages of convenience 557
Sex 83

582 REGULATION OF MARRIAGE--minimum and average age at marriage for each sex; postponement of marriage (e.g., for economic reasons, to enable an elder sibling to marry first); marriage laws and regulations; physical and mental bars to marriage; endogamous and exogamous restrictions; primary marriage preference and practice (e.g., with a cross-cousin, hypergamy); explanations and rationalizations of marriage restrictions; tests of marriageability (e.g., of skill, prowess, fertility); etc. See also:

Marriages between members   Sex and marital offenses 684
  of different social strata 56   Incest taboos and privileged sex
Kin group exogamy 61   relationships 835
Preferred secondary marriages 587   Premarital sexuality 836
Polygamous marriages 595   Puberty ordeals 881
Local exogamy and endogamy 621   Definition of majority 884

583 MODE OF MARRIAGE--wife-capture (e.g., actual, ceremonial); marriage by exchange (e.g., of sisters); wife-purchase; marriage by payment of consideration (e.g., substantial bride-price, token bride-price, dowry); bride-service (e.g., premarital, postmarital); marriage by gift exchange; marriage by formal or informal initiation of common residence; temporary and trial marriage; elopement (e.g., motives, subsequent adjustments); prevalence and prestige of each mode; relation to rules of residence; conceptualization of bride-price or dowry (e.g., as purchase price, as compensation for loss of services, as guarantee of marriage stability); content and mode of payment of consideration; contributors and recipients; etc. See also:

Gift giving 431   Residence rules 591
Differential modes in secondary marriages . . 587

584 ARRANGING A MARRIAGE--marriage preliminaries; courtship (e.g., opportunities, methods); initiation of negotiations (e.g., by youth, by girl, by

parents of either); conduct of negotiations (e.g., by parents, through a go-between); marriage brokers; proposal of marriage; methods and consequences of rejection; requirement of consent (e.g., of youth, of girl, of parents, of chief); betrothal (e.g., conceptualization, announcement, ceremonial, symbols, duration); status and behavior of betrothed persons; infant betrothal (e.g., prevalence, procedure, nullification); breaking an engagement (e.g., reasons, procedure, consequences); adjustment to death of betrothed (e.g., substitution of a sibling); etc. See also:

Sex status	562	Sexual overtures	832
Contractual relationships	675	Adolescent activities	883

585 NUPTIALS--wedding (e.g., preferred time and place, ceremonial, persons attending and officiating); symbolic rites; means of assuring publicity and legality (e.g., banns, licenses); civil and ecclesiastical weddings; variations dependent upon status; associated property transactions (e.g., transfer of gifts, of bride-price); homecoming of bridal couple; consummation (e.g., immediate or deferred, private or public); defloration rites (e.g., jus primae noctis); concern for virginity of bride (e.g., exhibiting tokens); postwedding events (e.g., honeymoon, exchange of visits); status and activities of newly married persons; etc. See also:

Marital sexuality	83	Residence in marriage	591

586 TERMINATION OF MARRIAGE--methods (e.g., desertion, separation, annulment, divorce); prevalence of each; reasons (e.g., cruelty, infidelity, laziness, sterility); initiative and rights of each sex; procedure; residence readjustments; allocation of children (e.g., to mother, to father, to parent least at fault, division by age or sex); property arrangements (e.g., return of bride-price, alimony); subsequent relations of divorced spouses; social attitudes toward separation and divorce; etc. See also:

Sex status	562	Termination of marriage following the death	
Sex and marital offenses	684	of one spouse	768
Dependency	736	Adultery	837
		Barrenness and sterility	842

587 SECONDARY MARRIAGES--remarriage of widowed and divorced persons; differential rules governing secondary marriages (e.g., preference for relative of first spouse, reduction in bride-price, curtailing of ceremonial); levirate and sororate unions (e.g., prevalence, preferences, procedure); etc. See also:

Status and activities of widows and widowers	589	Polygamous unions	595

588 IRREGULAR UNIONS--marriages in violation of incest taboos, exogamous rules, caste restrictions, or prohibitions of bigamy; common-law marriages; marriages to gods, to deceased persons, to trees, to persons of the same sex; frequency of irregular unions; social reactions; etc. See also:

Incestuous, premarital, adulterous, and		Castes	564
homosexual liaisons	83	Exogamous restrictions	61, 582

589 CELIBACY--prevalence of bachelors and spinsters; reasons for celibacy; status and activities of unmarried, widowed, and divorced celibates; etc. See also:

Religious celibates	79	Chastity	831
Care of widows	736	Premarital adulthood	885
Mourning	765		

---

59 FAMILY

59 FAMILY--general statements dealing with several specific aspects of the family. The family is a social group consisting of two or more adults of different sex who are married to one another, and of one or more children, own or adopted, of the married parents. It is to be distinguished alike from marriage, the social relationship uniting the parents of opposite sex, and from the household, the social group occupying a dwelling or other domicile. Hence, strictly speaking, a married but childless couple or a widowed or divorced parent with children may form a household but not a family.

591 RESIDENCE--prevailing rule governing the place of residence of a married couple (e.g., matrilocal, avunculocal, patrilocal, neolocal); existence of combined rules (e.g., alternating, bilocal, matri-patrilocal); occurrence of alternative rules under special circumstances; extent to which marriage normally involves the removal of bride or groom to another community (e.g., local exogamy, local endogamy); residence changes by children or unmarried adults (e.g., removal to home of grandparents or maternal uncle); residence changes made late in married life; evidence bearing upon former or current changes in residence rules; etc. See also:

Dwellings	342	Residence readjustments after divorce	586
Settlement patterns	361	Organization of the community	621
Bride-service	583	Residence changes by widows and widowers	768
Postmarital visits	585		

592 HOUSEHOLD--typical composition (e.g., nuclear or polygamous family, joint or extended family, clan); range, types, and incidence of variations; extent of inclusion of servants, retainers, and dependent relatives (e.g., aged grandparents, parents-in-law); physical seat (e.g., a single small or large dwelling, a cluster of adjacent huts, a compound); functions and cooperative activities of the household unit as such (i.e., irrespective of variations in family composition); locus of authority; rule of succession; mechanism for adjusting disputes within the household; ownership of dwelling, food stores, and household possessions; etc. Functions associated with particular forms of the family rather than with the household as such will be found in separate categories. See also:

Property	42	Cooperative labor	476
Type of dwelling	342	Slaves	567
Servants	357	Care of aged	737, 888

593 FAMILY RELATIONSHIPS--patterns of behavior between spouses, between parents and children, between siblings; rights, privileges, and powers of husband, wife, father, mother, son, daughter, brother, and sister; family law; emotional attachments; evidences of ambivalence; etc. See also:

Kinship terminology and patterned behavior between secondary and remoter relatives . . .	60	Division of labor by sex	462
Marital sexuality	83	Sex status	562
Care, status, activities of children	85	Quarrels	578
Socialization	86	Conception of marriage	581
Personality traits	157	Incest taboos	835
		Theory of paternity	842

594 NUCLEAR FAMILY--degree of emphasis on the social group consisting of a married couple and their children; exclusiveness with which this group is associated with economic, sexual, reproductive, child-rearing, and educational functions; other family functions (e.g., religious, recreational); domicile (e.g., single dwelling, apartment); family authority (e.g., matripotestal, patripotestal); family possessions; etc. See also:

Reproduction	84	Family budgets	511
Education	87	Primary groups	571
Size of families	162	Collective liability	672
Inheritance	428	Child care	855

595 POLYGAMY--relative prevalence of monogamy, polygyny, polyandry, and group marriage; patterning of plural marriages (e.g., prohibited on principle, unpatterned and exceptional, disfavored for economic reasons, confined to persons of wealth or high status, preferential); numerical limitations; prevalence of and preferences for sororal polygyny and fraternal polyandry; distinctive procedures for secondary polygamous marriages; concubinage; organization and activities of polygynous families; relations between co-spouses (e.g., economic cooperation, supremacy of first wife); residential arrangements (e.g., common dwelling, separate quarters for each plural spouse); sexual adjustment (e.g., jealousy, sexual rotation); relations between half siblings and between stepparents and stepchildren in polygamous families; etc. See also:

Levirate and sororate marriages	587	Cicisbeism	837

596 EXTENDED FAMILIES--incidence of extended families; prevailing type or types (e.g., matrilocal, avunculocal, patrilocal, and bilocal extended families, fraternal joint families); size and composition; domicile (e.g., compound, single large dwelling); locus of authority; rule of succession (e.g., matrilineal, patrilineal, succession by a younger sibling); collective or individual ownership of dwelling, land, food stores, and household equipment; economic cooperation; routine activities; collective responsibility; cohesive and fissive tendencies; etc. See also:

Property and inheritance 42   Clans 618
Kin relationships 602   Collective liability 672
Lineages 613   Ancestor worship 769

597 ADOPTION--extent to which children are adopted or exchanged; motives and procedure; status of adopted children; reciprocal relations of adoptive parents and adopted children; relations between adoptive siblings; special types of adoption (e.g., adoption of adults, posthumous adoption; ceremonial adoption); etc. See also:

Guardianship 429   Care of orphans 736
Adoption of slaves 567   Fosterage 853
Artificial kin relationships 608   Status of children 858
Adoption of captives 727

---

60 KINSHIP

60 KINSHIP--general statements dealing with several specific aspects of the general characteristics and component terminology of kinship systems and with the specific patterns of behavior prevailing between kinsmen who do not belong to the same nuclear or polygamous family. For kin relationships within these types of family structure see 593.

601 KINSHIP TERMINOLOGY--lists and application of kinship terms; genealogical kinship charts; use of kinship terms relative to personal names and teknonymy; differentiation of vocative and referential forms; morphological typology (e.g., elementary, derivative, and descriptive terms); number of elementary terms; incidence of denotative and classificatory terms; classificatory distinctions observed and overridden (e.g., generation, sex, affinity, collaterality, bifurcation, polarity, relative age, speaker's sex, decedence); classification of avuncular and nepotic terms (e.g., bifurcate collateral, bifurcate merging, lineal, generation); classification of cousin terminology (e.g., Eskimo, Hawaiian, Iroquois, Crow, Sudanese, Omaha); correlation between terminology and patterns of behavior; historical and functional interpretations of kinship systems; etc. See also:

Dynastic genealogies 173   Personal names and teknonymy 551
Linguistic relationships 197

602 KIN RELATIONSHIPS--conception of kinship; cultural definition of kinship statuses; kinship symbolism and its extensions (e.g., to kings, to gods); interpenetration of kinship with other aspects of culture (e.g., nepotism); analyses of patterned kinship behavior; incidence and interpretations of stereotyped patterns (e.g., joking, respect, avoidance); categories of kin not classifiable elsewhere (e.g., patrikin and matrikin, general affinal relatives) and relationships among them; etc. Data on relationships between specific secondary and tertiary relatives will be found in separate categories. See also:

Kin groups   61
Functional integration 182
Mutual aid. 476
Visiting and hospitality 574
Ingroup antagonisms 578
Marriage restrictions 582
Patterned behavior between primary relatives . 593
Kin relationships within polygamous families . 595

Political nepotism 661
Mortuary functions of kinsmen. 764
Sex prohibitions and permissions between
   kinsmen 835
Changes in social relationships upon birth
   of child 851
Instruction of children in kinship behavior. . . . 867

603 GRANDPARENTS AND GRANDCHILDREN--patterns of behavior between grandparents and grandchildren; respective rights, privileges, and powers of the relatives involved; relationships between great uncles and aunts and grand nephews and nieces; etc. See also:

Activities and status of the aged 88

604 AVUNCULAR AND NEPOTIC RELATIVES--patterns of behavior between paternal and maternal uncles and aunts and fraternal and sororal nephews and nieces; respective rights, privileges, and powers of the relatives involved; special elaborations (e.g., avunculate, amitate); relationships with the spouses of avuncular and nepotic relatives; etc. See also:

Avunculocal residence 591

605 COUSINS--patterns of behavior between cousins; distinctions between types of cousins (e.g., first and second cousins, cross and parallel cousins); respective rights, privileges, and powers of the relatives involved; etc. See also:

Preferential cross-cousin marriage 582   Privileged sex relationships 835

606 PARENTS-IN-LAW AND CHILDREN-IN-LAW--patterns of behavior between fathers- and mothers-in-law and sons- and daughters-in-law; respective rights, privileges, and powers of the relatives involved; special elaborations (e.g., mother-in-law avoidance); etc. See also:

Ingroup antagonisms 578   Rule of residence. 591
Mode of marriage 583   Relationships between parents of a
                                                        married couple 602

607 SIBLINGS-IN-LAW--patterns of behavior between brothers-in-law, between sisters-in-law, and between brothers- and sisters-in-law; respective rights, privileges, and powers of the relatives involved; relationships with the spouses of siblings-in-law; etc. See also:

Levirate and sororate marriages 587   Privileged sex relationships 835

608 ARTIFICIAL KIN RELATIONSHIPS--creation of kinship ties by artificial means (e.g., blood brotherhood); establishment of kinship through ceremonial sponsorship (e.g., godparents and godchildren); kinship terms employed by artificial kinsmen; reciprocal relations and stereotyped behavior patterns exhibited; etc. See also:

Relations between guardian and ward 429   Friendship 572
Naming ceremonies 553   Adoption 597

609 BEHAVIOR TOWARD NONRELATIVES--cultural definition of nonrelatives; relationships and associated behavior defined by absence of kinship ties; behavior toward strangers and aliens; etc. See also:

Interpersonal relationships.	57	Behavior toward ethnic subgroups	563
Behavior toward individual observers	123	International relations	648
Ethnocentrism	186		

61 KIN GROUPS

61 KIN GROUPS--general statements dealing with several specific types of kin groups. In every society, individuals maintain interpersonal relationships, characterized by particular kinship terms and culturally patterned behavior, with each type of relative recognized by the prevailing kinship system. In addition, an individual is normally affiliated with one or more kin groups, each consisting of some, but not all, of his relatives. By "descent" is meant a cultural rule defining the types of relatives with whom an individual is affiliated in a kin group. It need not, and commonly does not, imply that these relatives are more closely akin to him than are those who do not belong to the same group. The major types of kin groups are defined at the beginning of the appropriate categories below.

611 RULE OF DESCENT--unilinear rules (e.g., matrilineal, patrilineal); ambilineal descent (i.e., in each successive generation descent is traced through either parent); bilateral descent (i.e., absence of unilinear emphasis); double descent (i.e., concurrent matrilineal and patrilineal descent); anomalous rules (e.g., sex-linked descent); special exceptions (e.g., ambil-anak or matrilineal descent for one generation in default of direct male heirs); degree of correspondence or divergence between the rule of descent and the recognition of kinship; evidences of former or recent transitions in the rule of descent; etc. See also:

Descent of children in marriages between persons of different castes or social classes	56	Rules of residence.	591
		Succession to chiefship in the community.	622
Rules of succession to authority in the family or household	59	Succession to executive positions in the state	63,643
		Theory of paternity	842
Inheritance rules	428	Social placement of infants.	851
Allocation of the children of divorced parents.	586		

612 KINDREDS AND RAMAGES--presence of bilateral kin groups embracing the near relatives of an individual (i.e., kindreds); ambilineal kin groups consisting of persons tracing descent from a common ancestor (i.e., ramages); composition; reciprocal relations of members; bearing upon the regulation of marriage (e.g., exogamy, agamy); group functions; relations between kindreds or ramages; etc. See also:

Marriage restrictions	582	Demes	621
Bilocal extended families	596		

613 LINEAGES--presence of unilinear kin groups consisting of persons who can trace actual descent from a common ancestor; affiliation (e.g., matrilineal, patrilineal); regulation of marriage (e.g., exogamy, agamy, endogamy);

distinguishing characteristics (e.g., names, insignia, totemism, food taboos); traditions; organization; headship and succession; prerogatives and obligations of members (e.g., mutual aid, blood vengeance); solidarity and group responsibility; common property; relationship to extended families and clans; unilinear kin groups intermediate between lineages and sibs; relations between lineages (e.g., subsibs); etc. See also:

Property	42	Blood vengeance	628
Mutual aid	476	Totemism	771
Marriage restrictions	582	Taboos	784
Extended families	596		

614 SIBS--presence of unilinear kin groups of traditional, but not actually traceable, common descent; number and distribution; affiliation (e.g., matrilineal, patrilineal); regulation of marriage (e.g., exogamy, agamy, endogamy); distinguishing characteristics (e.g., names, insignia, totemism, food taboos); origin and traditions; organization; headship and succession; prerogatives and obligations of members; solidarity and group responsibility; common property and cult; relationship to clans; unilinear kin groups intermediate between sibs and phratries; relations between sibs; etc. See also:

Property	42	Totemism	779
Mutual aid	476	Taboos	784
Marriage restrictions	582		
Blood vengeance	628		

615 PHRATRIES--presence of one or more unilinear kin groups, each of which embraces two or more sibs; affiliation (e.g., matrilineal, patrilineal); regulation of marriage (e.g., exogamy, agamy, endogamy); distinguishing characteristics; origin and traditions; organization; prerogatives and obligations of members; relations between phratries; etc. See also:

Marriage restrictions	582	Totemism	779

616 MOIETIES--presence of a unilinear dichotomy, each half of which consists of one or more sibs, which may or may not be organized into phratries; affiliation (e.g., matrilineal, patrilineal); regulation of marriage (e.g., exogamy, agamy, endogamy); distinguishing characteristics (e.g., names, totemism); origin and traditions; prerogatives and obligations of members, rivalrous behavior (e.g., inter-moiety games); pseudo-moieties (e.g., social dichotomies not based on unilinear descent); relations between moieties; etc. See also:

Economic competition	477	Marriage restrictions	582
Athletic competition	526	Totemism	779
Ingroup antagonisms	578		

617 BILINEAR KIN GROUPS--presence of kin groups consisting of persons united by double descent in the presence of moiety exogamy (e.g., sections, subsections, other "marriage classes"); number (e.g., two-class, four-class, six-class, and eight-class systems); regulation of marriage (e.g., restriction of eligibility to members of a single group); distinguishing characteristics

88

(e.g., names); reciprocal relationships of members; correlation of kinship terms with group membership; characteristics of irregular marriages; relations between bilinear kin groups; etc. See also:

Marriage restrictions 582   Kinship terms 601
Irregular marriages 588

618 CLANS--presence of localized kin groups consisting of unilinearly related persons of one sex and their spouses and young children but not including their outmarrying siblings of opposite sex; structural type (e.g., matri-clans, patri-clans, avuncu-clans, amita-clans); size (e.g., clan-barrios, clan-communities); number and distribution; subdivision (e.g., into subclans, extended families); organization; headship and succession; functions (e.g., economic, political); reciprocal relations between members; cohesive and fissive tendencies; land holdings; relations between clans; etc. Only data on clan-barrios will normally be filed under this category. See also:

Property. 42   Description and analysis of clan-
Mutual aid 476   communities. 621

619 TRIBE AND NATION--presence or absence of groups larger than the community to which people think they "belong" in an extended kinship sense; basis of identification (e.g., common name, common language, contiguous territory, common culture, tradition of common descent); intratribal intercourse and communication (e.g., trade, intermarriage); degree of development of nationalistic aspirations; etc. See also:

Tribal or national political organization . . . 64   Intertribal or international relationships. 648
Affiliation with a culture area or subarea . . . 101   Nationalistic movements 668
Ethnocentrism 186   Ideas about race 829
Intercommunity relationships 628

62 COMMUNITY

62 COMMUNITY--general statements dealing with several aspects of the community and the officials who govern it. The term "community" connotes the maximal group of persons who normally reside together in face-to-face association. Since a community can rarely embrace many more than 1000 individuals, in societies with larger urban aggregates the term will be confined to subdivisions of towns or cities which approach communities in size and face-to-face character, e.g., wards, precincts, or residential neighborhoods. In societies lacking political integration above the level of the community information on government will ordinarily be filed in this section rather than under 63, 64, or 65. In addition to political data on the community, this section includes information on social control, police, and informal justice irrespective of the level of political integration. Data on law offenses and sanctions will be filed in 67, 68 and 69 respectively whenever formal legal and judicial institutions are found even at the community level. Data

on political behavior will be filed in 66.

621 COMMUNITY STRUCTURE--physical type (e.g., migratory band, settled village, neighborhood of scattered households, aggregation of hamlets, ward or other local subdivision of a town); kinship structure (e.g., clan-community, endogamous or exogamous deme, segmented community of associated clan-barrios, unsegmented but homogeneous community, heterogeneous community); socio-political and economic structure and organization; local subdivisions of the community; community population (e.g., mean, range); area of territory exploited (e.g., mean, range); distinguishing characteristics (e.g., name, local dialect, local culture); tendency toward local endogamy or exogamy; cohesive and fissive tendencies; neighborliness; local pride; etc. See also:

Physical characteristics and facilities of		Town and city government	63
settlements	36	Place names	103
Social stratification	56	Real property	423
Interpersonal relations	57	Clans	618

622 HEADMEN--existence of community chiefs or headmen; qualifications; mode of selection (e.g., by seniority, informal acceptance, election, matrilineal or patrilineal succession); functions and activities; domestic establishment; special status and functions of headman's relatives; authority; prerogatives; etc. See also:

Headmen of kin groups	61	Leadership traits	157
Chiefs of territorial divisions	63	Chief executive of the state	643

623 COUNCILS--existence of advisory or deliberative bodies within the community (e.g., 'council of elders, assembly of adult males); membership; mode of selection; organization; functions (e.g., advisory, judicial, legislative); conduct of sessions; powers and prerogatives; etc. See also:

Councils of territorial divisions	63	Legislative and deliberative bodies of the state . . 646

624 LOCAL OFFICIALS--specialized offices within the community (e.g., war chief, fire chief, talking chief, recorder of deeds, surveyor, herald, chief priest); qualifications, mode of selection, functions, activities, and prerogatives of each type of official; etc. See also:

Officials of territorial divisions	63	State bureaucracy	647
Military organization	70	Priesthood	793

625 POLICE--specialized law-enforcement organs within the community and higher political units; personnel (e.g., qualifications, appointment, training, organization, promotion, retirement); equipment (e.g., uniform, insignia, arms); functions (e.g., crime prevention and detection, quelling disturbances, traffic control); specialization (e.g., patrolmen, detectives, vice squad); powers (e.g., arrest, detention, summary justice); degree of civilian control; special police organizations (e.g., state police, secret police); private police (e.g., bodyguards, watchmen, industrial police, private detectives); etc. See also:

Fire protection	368	Political graft	667
Examination of travelers	486	Legal and judicial personnel	693
Highway patrols	494	Methods of crime detection	694
Organized vice	548	Jails and prisons	697
Riots	579	Military police	708
Government pensions	657		

626 SOCIAL CONTROL--incentives to conformity (e.g., expectation of rewards, reciprocity, fear of social and supernatural sanctions, conscience); means of inducing conformity (e.g., example, precept, praise, rewards, warnings, threats); pressure of public opinion; informal mechanisms of social control (e.g., criticism, ridicule, gossip, cursing, sorcery, intentional silence, ostracism); incidence and effectiveness of such sanctions as compared with the application of physical force; etc. See also:

Socialization	86	Reactions to breaches of etiquette	576
Social norms	183	Breaches of ethics	577
Public opinion	208	Ingroup antagonisms	578
Wit and humor	522	Sorcery	754
Status and prestige	554	Supernatural sanctions for violations of	
Loss of face	558	taboos and other offenses	784
Primary groups	571	Cursing	789

627 INFORMAL INGROUP JUSTICE--unformalized mechanisms for adjusting grievances and applying sanctions within the community; private retaliation (e.g., lynching, tarring and feathering, feuding); negotiation and compromise; informal hearings before the headman or local council; etc. Data on justice will be filed under 69 rather than under this category whenever formal judicial institutions are found even at the community level. See also:

Liability	67	Offenses and punishments	68

628 INTER-COMMUNITY RELATIONS--traditional friendships and rivalries between communities; establishing, maintaining, and breaking relations; blood vengeance; feuds; negotiation and composition (e.g., payment of wergild); mediation and arbitration; etc. See also:

Formal justice	69	Gang wars	579
War	72	International law	648

---

63 TERRITORIAL ORGANIZATION

63 TERRITORIAL ORGANIZATION--general statements dealing with several distinct levels of political territorial organization. Statements dealing with territorial hierarchy will be filed in 631. Material on political institutions of administrative or territorial units intermediate in size or functional scope between the community and the state, the sovereign or maximal political unit will be filed in the three digit categories below. It will be used only for societies of some political complexity, not for those in which communities are politically independent or for those with petty states embracing only a single district or a small city with its environs. The individual categories represent increasing levels of size and complexity, but since these are not universally comparable they must be considered subject to modification in order to adapt them to the actual territorial units of particular societies.

631 TERRITORIAL HIERARCHY--territorial structure of the state; the various levels of territorial and administrative organization within the state and their reconciliation with the categories below; hierarchy of political officials; integration with larger political units (e.g., Ukraine within the USSR); general nature of the territorial hierarchy (e.g., feudal, administrative, federal); degree of local differentiation in structural forms (e.g., federal districts, free cities, territories, colonies); etc. See also:
Identification of the cultural group in relation
to culture areas and neighboring societies.   101

632 TOWNS--political organization of municipalities (e.g., towns, townships, boroughs, parishes) embracing a number of communities; governmental personnel (e.g., executive, advisory, administrative, legislative); mode of selection (e.g., appointment, election, hereditary succession); jurisdiction, authority, prerogatives, functions, and activities associated with each position; etc. See also:
Physical characteristics and facilities
of settlements.   36

633 CITIES--political organization of urban aggregates larger than towns (e.g., cities, metropolitan districts); governmental personnel (e.g., executive, advisory, administrative, legislative); mode of selection (e.g., appointment, election, hereditary succession); jurisdiction, authority, prerogatives, functions, and activities associated with each position; etc. See also:
Settlements and urban and rural contrasts . . 36   Political machines. 667

634 DISTRICTS--political organization of moderately extensive territories embracing a number of settlements or municipalities (e.g., a subtribe, an English or American county, a French department); governmental personnel (e.g., executive, advisory, administrative, legislative); mode of selection (e.g., appointment, election, hereditary succession); jurisdiction, authority, prerogatives, functions, and activities associated with each position; etc.

635 PROVINCES--political organization of extended regions embracing a number of districts (e.g., a Persian satrapy, a Roman or Inca province, an American state); governmental personnel (e.g., executive, advisory, administrative, legislative); mode of selection (e.g., appointment, election, hereditary succession); jurisdiction, authority, prerogatives, functions, and activities associated with each position; etc. See also:
Tribe and nation. 619

636 DEPENDENCIES--political organization of dependent regions not organized as provinces (e.g., a colony, a protectorate, a dependent territory); governmental personnel (e.g., executive, advisory, administrative, legislative); mode of selection (e.g., appointment, election, hereditary succession); jurisdiction, authority, prerogatives, functions, and activities associated with each position. Information on relations of dependency with colonial powers will be filed in category 648. See also:

Culture contact 177   Administration of dependent ethnic groups. . . 657
Ministers of colonial affairs. 645   Military government 727

---

64 STATE

64 STATE--general statements dealing with various aspects of the description of governmental institutions at the highest level of political integration, i.e., at the level where ultimate sovereignty resides, whether this be a district of a few communities under a paramount chief or a great empire embracing many nationalities. Material on societies revealing a level of political integration higher than that of the community will be filed here. For political organization on the community level see 62; for political organization of groups intermediate between the community and the state see 63.

641 CITIZENSHIP--conception of the relationship of the individual to the state; territorial versus gentile affiliation; distinctions between citizens and residents, and between different categories of citizens; rights, duties, privileges, powers, and liabilities of the citizen or subject (e.g. civil liberties, franchise, liability to military service); acquisition of citizenship (e.g., naturalization); loss of citizenship (e.g., through serious crime); notions of civic virtues; etc. See also:

Social stratification 56   Public service 663
Justice 69   Voting 666
Immigration 167   Treason 687
Symbolic representations of nationalism   Military service 701
    and patriotism 186   Social insurance 745
Forced or indentured labor 466   Ideas about political behavior 829
Taxation. 651   Legal majority 884

642 CONSTITUTION--prevailing system governing the distribution of political power and authority; extent of agreement or disagreement between formal constitutional provisions and actual practice; rights, privileges, and powers assigned or delegated to each organ of government, including the power to alter their distribution; centralization and diffusion of power; constitutional principles (e.g., separation of powers); temporary relaxations or extensions of political authority (e.g., interregnums, war powers); form of the state (e.g., empire, union, federal republic, U.N. trusteeships, colony protectorate); form of rule

(e.g., autocratic, oligarchic, aristocratic, theocratic, democratic); type of constitution (e.g., written, unwritten); framing and amending of constitutions; constitutional law; etc. See also:

Family authority	59	Hierarchy of political officials	631
Authority within kin groups	61	Political parties	665
Authority in the community	62	Judicial authority	692
Law	67	Political theory	829

643 CHIEF EXECUTIVE--type of executive (e.g., paramount chief, king, president); plural executives (e.g., peace chief and war leader, king and chief priest, constitutional monarch and prime minister, triumvirate, executive council); authority (e.g., supreme, nominal, dependent upon personal qualities); prestige (e.g., sanctity of person, divine descent); functions (e.g., administrative, judicial, military, religious); prerogatives; symbols of office; mode of selection (e.g., by election, seniority, matrilineal or patrilineal succession); qualifications (e.g., age, sex, rank, wealth, prowess, piety); installation; termination of tenure (e.g., deposition, expiration of term, killing of divine king); etc. See also:

Executives and rule of succession in the family	59	Executives and succession in the community	622
Executives and succession in kin groups	61	Mortuary rites	764, 766
Dynastic lists and genealogies	173		

644 EXECUTIVE HOUSEHOLD--executive residence and domestic establishment; guards, servants, and retainers; court personnel (e.g., number, characteristics, mode of selection, activities, prerogatives); court etiquette and ceremonial; special status and functions of executive's relatives; etc. See also:

Public buildings	344	Royalty as a social class	565
Manipulative mobility	557	Palace intrigue	662

645 CABINET--ministers and informal advisers to the chief executive; constitutionally elaborated cabinets; specialized cabinet functions (e.g., foreign affairs, war, finance, justice, internal and colonial administration, postal affairs, agriculture, industry, transportation, commerce, education); selection of ministers; authority, activities, and prerogatives of each; relation to parliament and political parties; cabinet meetings; etc. See also:

Government activities	65	Political behavior	66

646 PARLIAMENT--presence of deliberative or legislative bodies; type (e.g., council of headmen, popular assembly, oligarchical junta, elective legislature); number of houses (e.g., unicameral legislature, bicameral congress, three estates); membership qualifications; selection (e.g., appointment, election, succession); principle of representation; tenure (e.g., life, term, until deposed or recalled); powers and prerogatives; functions (e.g., advisory, legislative); organization; procedure (e.g., introduction, debating, passage of bills); special legislative provisions (e.g., executive veto, judicial review, popular referendum); etc. See also:

Comparable bodies in subordinate political divisions	63	Comparable bodies in the community	623
		Electoral process	666
		Statute law	671

647 ADMINISTRATIVE AGENCIES--special bureaus, institutions, boards, and commissions charged with conducting the activities of the state; responsibility (e.g., to chief executive, to cabinet officers, to parliament); organization, personnel, and authority of each agency; civil service; bureaucracy and its characteristics; public administration; etc. See also:

Comparable agencies in subordinate
    political divisions 63
Activities of these agencies 65
Government officials as an occupational class. . 463
Comparable agencies in the community 624
Administrative law 671

648 INTERNATIONAL RELATIONS--traditional friendships and rivalries with other states; relations between sovereign and dependent powers; determination of foreign policy (e.g., influence of domestic affairs); establishing, maintaining, and breaking diplomatic relations; foreign services (e.g., consular, diplomatic); specialized personnel (e.g., ambassadors, chargés d'affaires, military attachés, consuls); prerogatives (e.g., diplomatic immunity); activities of consuls and diplomats; transmission of intelligence and diplomatic messages; negotiation of treaties, military alliances, foreign aid programs and trade agreements; economic sanctions (e.g., embargoes); adherence to international conventions; international law; peaceful settlement of disputes between states (e.g., arbitration, special peace tribunals); relations with international political organizations (e.g., United Nations); international power politics; peacetime espionage; etc. See also:

War 72
Codes and ciphers 202
Foreign trade 439
Travel 484
International sports 542
Behavior toward strangers and aliens. 609
Informal intergroup justice 628
Dependencies 636
Punishment of espionage 687

---

65 GOVERNMENT ACTIVITIES

65 GOVERNMENT ACTIVITIES--general statements dealing with several aspects of the administrative activities of all governmental agencies usually above the level of the small local community.

651 TAXATION AND PUBLIC INCOME--sources of public income (e.g., gifts and bribes, tribute, license fees, ground rents, profits from public enterprises, fines, confiscations, tolls, taxes); types of taxes (e.g., taxes in kind, labor levies, poll taxes, property taxes, stamp taxes, excise taxes, customs duties, income taxes, inheritance taxes); importance of and revenue from each type; differentiation by administrative level; principles of taxation; tax law; mode of fixing and collecting taxes; specialized personnel (e.g., tax collectors, tax consultants); tax exemptions; etc. See also:

Property and inheritance 42
Gift giving 431
Income 434
Foreign trade 439
Forced labor 466

Government lotteries 525   Fines 681
Government monopolies 655

652 PUBLIC FINANCE--government budgets and financial estimates; statistics of public revenues and expenditures; government accounts; appropriations and financial legislation; disposition of surplus revenues; methods of meeting deficits (e.g., borrowing, currency inflation, debt repudiation); fiscal policies (e.g., use of public finance to influence foreign trade or employment); public debt and debt service; issuance and manipulation of currency; relations of the treasury with private banks; government banks; etc. See also:

Borrowing and lending 426   Accounting. 451
Money 436   Banking 453

653 PUBLIC WORKS--government construction of dams, reservoirs, canals, ship channels, railways, highways, sewers, and public buildings; method of accomplishment (e.g., by labor drafts, by contract with private entrepreneurs); public works policies (e.g., to relieve unemployment, to increase public revenues); maintenance of public works; etc. See also:

Cultural goals. 185   Forced labor 466
Water supply 312   Highway and railway construction 499
Construction contractors 331   River and harbor improvements 503
Public buildings 344   Political graft 667
Sewers 364   Public works programs to relieve unemployment . 746

654 RESEARCH AND DEVELOPMENT--government-supported research in applied science (e.g., agriculture, fisheries, mining, forestry, nutrition, medicine); public extension and demonstration services; government subsidies to weak or essential industries (e.g., airlines, shipping, agriculture); exploration; coast, geodetic, and geological surveys; meteorological research and weather stations; etc. See also:

Mining and forestry. 31   Agricultural science. 242
Water and air transport 50   Exploring expeditions 484
Cultural goals 185   Military research 711
Marine industries. 228   Public Health 744

655 GOVERNMENT ENTERPRISES--government monopolies (e.g., salt, tobacco); enterprises operated by the state or its political subdivisions (e.g., postal system, telephone and telegraph services, railways, power plants, banks); organization and mode of operation of each; types of government enterprise; etc. See also:

Social planning 185   Government property 421
Postal system 205   Banks 453
Telephone and telegraph 206   Government ownership and control of capital. . 471
Salt manufacture 258   Economics of state enterprise 475
Tobacco manufacture 277   Monopolies 477
Municipal power and light facilities 365   Railways 496
Power development 371

656 GOVERNMENT REGULATION--policies underlying government regulation of private enterprises and activities; general aspects of supervision, restriction, and enforcement; specific instances of government regulation not classifiable elsewhere; etc. See also:

Government regulation of hunting and fishing . . . 22
Government regulation of food processing 25
Government regulation of the manufacture and distribution of liquor and drugs 27
Government regulation of banking and finance . . 45
Government regulation of business and industry . . 47
Government regulation of travel and transportation 48
Government regulation of immigration 167
Conservation policies 185
Government regulation of radio 207
Government regulation of dairying 234
Rationing 434
Price controls 435
Government regulation of wages 465
Government regulation of marriage 582
Wartime regulations 722
Government regulation of medical personnel . . 759
Government regulation of weights and measures . 804

657 PUBLIC WELFARE--pensions and welfare services for government employees; government care and administration of dependent ethnic groups (e.g., reservations); extent of public support of social work, welfare, relief, social insurance, and public health; etc. See also:

Social problems 73
Government housing programs 362
Public parks and playgrounds 367
Administration of dependent territories 636
Public health 744
Social insurance 745
Public assistance 746

658 PUBLIC EDUCATION--extent of direct and indirect public support to education; government sponsorship and support of the fine arts, pure science, libraries, and museums; etc. See also:

Fine arts 53
Science 81
Education 87
Libraries and museums 217
Musical and theatrical productions 545

659 MISCELLANEOUS GOVERNMENT ACTIVITIES--governmental activities not classifiable elsewhere (e.g., census taking, government support of national and state forests; of established churches); expenditures on public safety (e.g., military establishment, police, fire protection, disaster relief); etc. See also:

Census data 16
Army, navy, and air forces 70
Fire protection 368
State and national parks 529
Police 625
Disaster relief 731
Established churches 795

---

66 POLITICAL BEHAVIOR

66 POLITICAL BEHAVIOR--general statements dealing with several specific types of political behavior. Since informal mechanisms of social control do not operate effectively above the level of the community, all government at higher levels depends upon the authority and power to supplement such mechanisms with organized force. Hence political behavior, as opposed to other forms of social behavior, is characterized by the exercise or manipulation of such power, or the striving for it, as a means of accomplishing goals by force or the threat thereof. For ethnopolitical theory see 829.

661 EXPLOITATION--exercise of their power by holders of political office to further personal goals, whether materialistic, psychological, or ideological; perquisites of office (e.g., exceptional income and material comforts, special sexual or marital privileges, unusual honors or deference); use of office for self-aggrandizement (e.g., exhibitionism, extortion of bribes, protection of vice, acceptance of commissions for services rendered); employment of power to force others to conform to personal ethical or religious convictions; suppression of rivals (e.g., purges); oppression of opponents; nepotism; protection of vested interests; etc. See also:
Organized vice 548   Religious persecution. 798
Political machines. 667

662 POLITICAL INTRIGUE--use of the techniques of manipulative mobility to wrest favors from the holders of power or to obtain political preferment; flattery and ingratiation; use of bribery; deals; palace intrigue; opportunism; "playing politics"; etc. See also:
Manipulative mobility. 557   Punishment of bribery 687

663 PUBLIC SERVICE--use of nonexploitative methods to retain a political office or secure a higher one; exercise of economy, suppression of corruption and vice, exhibition of administrative skill, statesmanship, and comparable methods of gaining and keeping mass support as a bulwark against opposing political forces; appealing to the intelligence and conscience of the public; etc. See also:
Reform movements 185   Civic virtues 641

664 PRESSURE POLITICS--exertion of organized pressure on holders of political office to use their power to further group goals; pressure groups; lobbying; organized manifestations of group solidarity (e.g., mass demonstrations, letter-writing campaigns); use of publicity channels and propaganda techniques; adoption of labor tactics (e.g., picketing); etc. See also:
Public opinion. 208   Social control 626
Collective bargaining 468

665 POLITICAL PARTIES--organization for the purpose of acquiring and retaining political power; political factions; organized political parties (e.g., number, composition, leadership, objectives); party organization (e.g., national, regional, and local committees); methods of recruiting and rewarding members (e.g., spoils system); nomination procedure (e.g., caucuses, primaries, conventions, slates); special organization during electoral campaigns; integration of political parties with the structure of the state and its subdivisions; etc.

666 ELECTIONS--voting; informal methods of selecting public officials; organized electoral systems (e.g., election districts, registration of voters, requirements for nomination, polling places, balloting, precautions against fraud); election campaigns (e.g., fund raising, campaign platforms, speaking tours, use of publicity and propaganda); voting behavior and its determinants; electoral intimidation and fraud; methods of minority control (e.g., gerrymandering, rotten-borough system, poll taxes); etc. See also:

Nonelectoral methods of filling
  political offices 62, 63, 64
Molding of public opinion. 208
Oratory. 537
Franchise 641
Punishment of electoral fraud 687

667 POLITICAL MACHINES--special organizations for the control of elections and office and the distribution of spoils; personal and party machines; rewards to members and controlled voters (e.g., jobs, contracts, favors, police protection, petty graft); mechanisms of mobility within the machine (e.g., ward heeling, getting out the vote); relations with the underworld; extent of political corruption; attempts at reform; etc. See also:

Police 625
City government 633

668 POLITICAL MOVEMENTS--mass movements for substantial political change; types (e.g., messianic, nativistic, nationalistic, radical, revolutionary, reactionary); organization (e.g., into political parties, underground cells); leadership; doctrines, policies, and programs (e.g., socialism, communism, fascism); overt activities (e.g., passive resistance, propaganda, pressure politics, mass demonstrations, fomenting of labor disturbances); covert activities (e.g., infiltration, circulation of disparaging rumors, secret distribution of inflammatory literature, "front" organizations); proportion of population affected; etc. See also:

Social trends 178
Reform movements 185
Propaganda 208
Collective bargaining 468
Socialism 471
Development of nationalism 619
Temperance movements 733
Sociopolitical theories 829

669 REVOLUTION--attempts to seize political power by violent means; types (e.g., palace revolts, fifth columns, insurrections, class uprisings, civil wars); causes and objectives; rationalizations; participants; tactics (e.g., seizure of leading opponents, of military strongholds, of strategic urban utilities); counter-revolutionary tactics and movements; results of success and failure; etc. See also:

History and culture change 17
Social stratification 56
War 72
Cultural goals 185
Ingroup antagonisms 578
Riots 579
Punishment of treason 687

67 LAW--general statements dealing with several aspects of customary or imposed norms of behavior for violations of which sanctions may be enforced by some agent or agency of the politically organized community or state, and not alone through informal mechanisms of social control.

671 LEGAL NORMS--extent of differentiation of social norms enforceable by some organ of politically constituted society from those enforced only by informal social control; conception of law (e.g., as precedent, as a body of absolute or relative principles); comparative prevalence of customary or common law and of "made" laws (e.g., edicts, decrees, ordinances, statutes, constitutions, binding judicial or administrative decisions, imposed taboos, divine revelations); lawgivers; law codes; legal categories (e.g., civil and criminal law); legal rules and administrative law; jurisprudence; uniform and multiple systems of law; etc. See also:

Justice	69	Informal justice	627
Innovation	176	Civil rights	641
Customary norms	183	Constitutional law	642
Property law	421	Government regulation	656
Family law	593	Martial law	722
Informal social control	626		

672 LIABILITY--conception of the liability of individuals and groups for breaches of legal norms; extension of liability to others (e.g., parents, spouse, sibmates); exemptions from legal responsibility (e.g., minors, insane persons, chiefs); recognition of extenuating or aggravating circumstances (e.g., youth or old age, sex or class status of aggressor or victim, accident, self-defense, intent, negligence, recidivism); liability of animals or inanimate objects (e.g., "the ox that gored"); etc. See also:

Collective responsibility of families	59	Sanctions	681
Collective responsibility of kin groups	61	Moral accountability	812
Responsibility of a principal for acts of his agent	676	Status of minors	858

673 WRONGS--general definitions of acts which violate legal norms; major categories of breaches (e.g., crimes, torts, violations of contract, sins); recognized gradations in the gravity of offenses (e.g., malum prohibitum and malum in se, misdemeanors and felonies, venial and deadly sins); etc. See also:

Specific offenses and their sanctions	68	Breaches of ethics	577
Sex perversions	83	Taboo	784
Breaches of etiquette	576		

674 CRIME--prevalence and incidence of crime; common and rare offenses; crime statistics (e.g., number of reported violations, arrests, and convictions for various offenses); types of offenders (e.g., juvenile delinquents, criminal castes; narcotic addicts, professional criminals); motives in crime (e.g., greed, frustration, sexual jealousy); contributory social factors (e.g., poverty, oppression); criminology; etc. See also:

Socialization . . . . 86 Crime prevention 625
Neuroses and psychoses . . . . 158 Sanctions 681
Organized vice . . . . 548 Litigation of civil cases 691
Ingroup antagonisms . . . . 578 Juvenile delinquency 738
Banditry and piracy . . . . 579 Suicide 762

675 CONTRACTS--conception of contractual relations; agreements, bargains, promises, and their enforceability; consideration; rights, privileges, and powers of contracting parties; procedure in the conclusion of contracts (e.g., presence of witnesses); terms and stipulations; types of contracts (e.g., legal forms, oral agreements, covenants); etc. See also:

Builders and contractors . . . . 331 Social relationships 571
Loans . . . . 426 Marriage contracts 584
Leases . . . . 427 Treaties and alliances 648
Sales . . . . 432 Penalties for breaches of contract 686
Insurance contracts . . . . 456 Religious vows 782
Labor relations 466

676 AGENCY--conception of the delegation of authority; implications and limitations; rights, privileges, and powers of principal and agent; responsibility of a principal for the acts of his agent; intrusting and revocation; commissions and fees of agents; types of agents (e.g., factors); etc. See also:

Public carriers . . . . 49, 50 Labor relations 466
Messengers . . . . 202 Corporation law 473
Domestic servants . . . . 357 Marriage brokers 584
Trust administration . . . . 429 Government agencies 647
Salesmen . . . . 446 Attorneys at law 693
Investment brokers . . . . 454 Private welfare agencies 747

---

68 OFFENSES AND SANCTIONS

68 OFFENSES AND SANCTIONS--general statements covering several distinct definitions, in legal or other form, of specific actionable or punishable offenses and for data on the general and specific incidence of punitive sanctions. For criminal behavior see 674.

681 SANCTIONS--incidence and distribution of the major types of sanctions; capital punishment (e.g., hanging, decapitation, strangling, burning, dismembering); corporal punishment (e.g., flogging, mutilation, torture); property sanctions (e.g., damages, fines, confiscation); public humiliation (e.g., ridicule, pillory); deprivation of civil rights (e.g., enslavement, outlawry, imprisonment); theory of sanctions; systematization of sanctions (e.g., wergild, criminal codes); purpose of sanctions (e.g., compensation, punishment, prevention); penology; recipient of fines, damages, confiscated property (e.g., state,

injured party); etc. See also:

Formal justice 69   Informal justice 627
Social control 626   Prisons and penal labor 697

682 OFFENSES AGAINST LIFE--definitions of and sanctions for homicide (e.g., murder, manslaughter); punishments for attempted homicide and attempted suicide; penalties for abortion and infanticide; etc. See also:

Euthanasia 73   Headhunting 721, 727
Accidents . . . . 164, 165   Suicide 762
Cannibalism 266   Abortion and infanticide 847
Blood feuds . . . . 627, 628   Killing the aged 888
Liability in instances of accident or self defense. 672

683 OFFENSES AGAINST THE PERSON--definitions of and sanctions for acts of physical and verbal aggression (e.g., assault, battery, mayhem, slander, libel); penalties for sorcery; etc. See also:

Quarrels 578   Sorcery 754
Gossip 626

684 SEX AND MARITAL OFFENSES--definitions of and penalties for sex offenses (e.g., fornication, seduction, adultery, prostitution, incest, miscegenation, rape, sodomy, bestiality); punishments for marital and family offenses (e.g., nonsupport, desertion, neglect of children); etc. See also:

Marriage 58   Miscegenation 563
Sex 83   Illegitimacy 848
Prostitution 548

685 PROPERTY OFFENSES--definitions of and penalties for stealing (e.g., theft, poaching, robbery, burglary, fraud, embezzlement); definitions of and punishment for property damage (e.g., trespass, arson, malicious mischief); etc. See also:

Property 42   Banditry 579

686 NONFULFILLMENT OF OBLIGATIONS--penalties for breach of contract and nonpayment of debts; definition of and sanctions for criminal negligence; etc. See also:

Borrowing and lending 426   Enforcement of contracts and debts 696
Contracts 675

687 OFFENSES AGAINST THE STATE--definitions of and punishments for political offenses (e.g., treason, espionage, illegal entry, conspiracy, lese majesty, electoral fraud, malfeasance in office); penalties for military offenses (e.g., insubordination, cowardice, desertion, mutiny); definitions of and punishments for judicial offenses (e.g., giving or receiving bribes, perjury, subornation, barratry, contempt of court); penalties for monetary or fiscal offenses (e.g., counterfeiting, falsification of records or documents, smuggling, tax evasion); etc. See also:

Money	436	Revolution	669
Smuggling.	439	Court procedure.	695
International law.	648	Courts-martial	698
Taxation	651	Military discipline	703

688 RELIGIOUS OFFENSES--definitions of and punishments for blasphemy and impiety; penalties for specific sins of omission and commission (e.g., ritual
offenses, violation of taboos); etc. See also:

Fear of supernatural sanctions	626	Expiation	783
General definition of sin	673	Taboos	784

689 SOCIAL OFFENSES--definitions of and punishments for quarrelsomeness, dis-
orderly conduct, and commission of nuisances; penalties for drunkenness and
abnormal behavior; patterned punishments for lying and other breaches of
ethics; punishments for indolence and noncooperation; etc. See also:

Living standards and routines	51	Breaches of etiquette	576
Neuroses and psychoses.	158	Breaches of ethics	577
Behavior under intoxication.	273	Ingroup antagonisms	578
Laziness and loafing	461	Social control	626
Mutual aid	476		

---

69 JUSTICE

69 JUSTICE--general statements dealing with several aspects of the formal procedures and the authorized agents of the community or state through which
violations of legal norms are determined and sanctions imposed. For social
control and informal mechanisms of justice see 62.

691 LITIGATION--incidence of civil actions; statistics of civil cases; causes and
types of litigation; abuses (e.g., barratry, ambulance chasing); etc. See also:

Ingroup aggression	578	Incidence of criminal actions and criminal	
Informal justice	627	behavior.	674
Torts	673		

692 JUDICIAL AUTHORITY--extent to which the settlement of disputes, redress of
injuries, and application of sanctions is withdrawn from the parties concerned
and vested in some constituted authority; degree of identification or separation
of judicial and executive authority; specialized judges and courts; judicial system (e.g., courts of original and appellate jurisdiction, courts of law and
equity, civil and criminal courts); jurisdiction of each type of court; judicial
powers and prerogatives; etc. See also:

Judicial authority of executive and		Constitution	642
administrative officials.	63, 64	Legal norms	671
Concept of justice	577	Special courts	698
Informal justice within the community	627		

693 LEGAL AND JUDICIAL PERSONNEL--specialized law-enforcement personnel other than police (e.g., sheriffs, bailiffs, constables, posses, coroners); attorneys at law (e.g., counselors, barristers); bar associations; justices of the peace; court officials (e.g., judges, prosecuting attorneys, public defenders, clerks, court reporters); grand and petit jurors; parole and probation officers; executioners; qualifications, selection, functions, and prerogatives of each; payment (e.g., fees, commissions, salaries); legal ethics; etc. See also:

Police 625   Legal education 874

694 INITIATION OF JUDICIAL PROCEEDINGS--complaints and accusations; methods of detection; bringing suit; indictments (e.g., by grand jury); warrants and summonses; arrests and detention; bail; writs (e.g., of habeas corpus); pleas and demurrers; etc. See also:

Police 625   Litigation 691

695 TRIAL PROCEDURE--types of court procedure (e.g., summary, criminal, civil, appellate); arraignment; testimony (e.g., witnesses, rules of evidence); arguments and summations; special tests (e.g., oaths, ordeals, torture, judicial duels); judicial decisions (e.g., by judge, jury, arbitration); judgments and sentences; appeals; etc. See also:

Court records 217   Judicial abuses and their punishment 687
Courthouses 344   Martial law 722
Oratory 537
Informal judicial procedure at the com-
  munity level 627

696 EXECUTION OF JUSTICE--manner in which judgments and sentences are executed (e.g., self-help, execution by special officials); enforcement of contracts and debts; writs (e.g., of execution, attachment, replevin); probation; evasions of justice (e.g., procedural loopholes, bribery, flight, asylum); etc. See also:

Bankruptcy administration 429   Blood vengeance 628
Public executions 541   Sanctions 681
Lynch law   627   Places of asylum 778

697 PRISONS AND JAILS--places of imprisonment and detention; precautions against escape; personnel (e.g., jailers, wardens, chaplains, guards); differential treatment of inmates (e.g., women, trusties); organization of penal institutions; prison rules and routines; rewards and punishments for behavior; terms; paroles and pardons; prison labor; penal labor camps; special prisons (e.g., prisons for political offenders, military prisons); etc. See also:

Prison buildings 344   Prisoners of war 727
Forced labor 466   Reformatories 738
Penology 681   Insane asylums 743

698 SPECIAL COURTS--courts with special functions (e.g., courts-martial, claims courts, probate courts, juvenile courts, admiralty courts); arbitration tribunals; commissions with judicial authority; special personnel, jurisdiction, powers, and procedure of each type; etc. See also:

Probate procedure 428   International courts 648
Marine customs and regulations 502   Military discipline 703

---

70 ARMED FORCES

70 ARMED FORCES--general statements covering several distinct aspects of specialized military organization. Generalized data on unspecialized military organization will be filed under 701, except for aspects sufficiently elaborated in the particular society to merit special treatment under one of the succeeding categories.

701 MILITARY ORGANIZATION--purpose of military organization (e.g., defense, internal police, prestige); composition of the armed forces in peace and war; standing army and navy (e.g., size, disposition, state of preparedness); eligibility and liability for military service (e.g., age and sex qualifications); status of warriors (e.g., prerogatives, disabilities); military leaders (e.g., qualifications, mode of selection, authority, functions); extent of differentiation of military from political organization; coordination of armed forces (e.g., of a war party, an army, a complex military establishment); hierarchical organization (e.g., gradations in rank, chain of command); system of payment, promotion, and retirement; furloughs and leave; special organizations (e.g., military societies); etc. See also:

Prestige and mobility 55   Military technology and equipment 71
Political organization . . . . 62, 63, 64   Leadership traits 157

702 RECRUITMENT AND TRAINING--induction into the armed forces (e.g., voluntary enlistment, conscription); screening (e.g., tests of fitness, medical examinations); training (e.g., instruction, drill, practice with weapons, tactical maneuvers); special elaborations (e.g., recruiting stations, manuals of arms); etc. See also:

Athletics 526   Training camps 712
Military reviews 541   Military schools and colleges 874
Citizenship 641

703 DISCIPLINE AND MORALE--military virtues (e.g., courage, obedience); punitive and summary judicial powers of military leaders; military rewards (e.g., medals, badges, special privileges); level of morale in the armed forces; integrating and demoralizing factors; special techniques of instilling morale; etc. See also:

Symbolic tokens of prestige 554   Military offenses and sanctions 687
Ethical ideals 577   Courts-martial 698
Ingroup antagonisms 578   Prerogatives of veterans 729

704 GROUND COMBAT FORCES--specific organization of the army; high command; specialized combat branches (e.g., infantry, cavalry, artillery, tank corps); combat units (e.g., squads, companies, battalions, regiments, divisions); composition, organization, and special functions of each; specialized combat forces (e.g., scouts, marines, anti-aircraft defense units); etc. See also:

Land transport 49   Tactics 725
Military technology and equipment 71

705 SUPPLY AND COMMISSARIAT--special organization of supply services (e.g., quartermaster corps, naval and air transport services); system of procurement and distribution; rations and their issuance; mess arrangements; specialized personnel (e.g., cooks, stewards, supply officers); etc. See also:

Food consumption 26   Logistics 724

706 NAVY--specific organization of the navy; high command; combat units (e.g., scouting and task forces); organization of a ship (e.g., command, complement, line and engineering specialization, communications personnel); fleet auxiliaries; organization of ports, yards, depots, and other shore establishments; special naval forces (e.g., coast guard, submarine service); etc. See also:

Ships, navigation, and water transport 50   Naval strategy and tactics 72
Naval vessels, ordnance, and equipment . . . 71   Marine corps 704

707 AIR FORCES--organization of air forces; high command; combat and administrative units (e.g., strategic and tactical forces, wings, groups, squadrons); organization of personnel; organization of ground services; etc. See also:

Air transport 509   Military aircraft 717
Military air transport services 705   Tactical air operations 725

708 AUXILIARY CORPS--organization and functions of specialized noncombat services (e.g., medical and sanitary corps, army engineers, labor battalions, signal corps, intelligence services, military police); other specialized personnel (e.g., paymasters, chaplains, judge advocates, military government officers, specialists in communications and psychological warfare); etc. See also:

Communication 20   Supply and commissary services 705
Medicine 75   Military engineering 711
Police 625   Military government 727
Peacetime espionage 648   Public health 744
Courts-martial 698

71 MILITARY TECHNOLOGY--general statements on several aspects of technology peculiar to war. Technological processes and products used similarly in war and in industry are described under appropriate headings elsewhere.

711 MILITARY ENGINEERING--scientific knowledge of military technology; research and experimentation in applied military science; development and testing of new weapons and equipment; specialized techniques of army engineers; etc. See also:

Civil engineering	331	Navy engineering personnel	706
Chemical engineering	381	Army engineers	708
Mechanical engineering	401		

712 MILITARY INSTALLATIONS--defensive fortifications; harbor and coast defenses (e.g., coast artillery emplacements, antisubmarine nets); radar and antiaircraft installations; military camps and posts; arsenals; naval stations and bases; military airfields; missile bases; construction, maintenance, and distribution of military installations; etc. See also:

Construction trades	33	Antiaircraft defense units	704
Settlements	36	Organization of coast guard and naval	
Civilian airport facilities	508	shore stations	706

713 ORDNANCE--specialized military weapons; description of complex weapons (e.g., small arms, artillery, poison gas, flamethrowers, torpedoes, mines, bombs, rockets); description of accessory equipment (e.g., cavalry gear, gun mounts and carriages, armor, range finders, ammunition); ordnance stocks; etc. See also:

Atomic energy	378	Riding gear	492
Unspecialized weapons	411	Ordnance manufacture	719

714 UNIFORM AND ACCOUTERMENT--military garb (e.g., hair style, body armor, body painting, amulets and charms, uniform); description of personal equipment (e.g., canteen, haversack, helmet, gas mask, first-aid kit, shields); distinctions (e.g., according to rank, between different corps and services, between parade and field uniforms and equipment); etc. See also:

Clothing and accessories	29	Military medals and badges	703
Adornment	30		

715 MILITARY VEHICLES--description of specialized military vehicles (e.g., armored trains, tanks, jeeps, amphibious vehicles); number, mode of operation, and special uses of each; etc. See also:

Automobile industry	398	Military materiel other than vehicles	713
Nonmilitary vehicles	493		

716 NAVAL VESSELS--description of specialized naval vessels (e.g., war canoes, carriers, destroyers, submarines, mine layers, landing craft); motive power,

speed, armament, special equipment, and functions of each; fleet statistics (e.g., number and disposition of units); etc. See also:

Shipbuilding 396   Ship complements. 706
Other than naval craft 501   Naval ordnance 713

717 MILITARY AIRCRAFT--description of specialized military air and space craft; motive power, speed, armament, and special equipment of each type; special adaptations (e.g., catapults, carrier arresting gear); number and disposition of military aircraft; etc. See also:

Aircraft industry. 399   Organization of air force. 707
Nonmilitary aircraft 506

718 SPECIAL MILITARY EQUIPMENT--description of communications devices specialized for military use (e.g., field telephones, portable radio equipment, semaphore and blinker systems); special navigation and detection devices and equipment (e.g., radar, loran, special electronic gear); etc. See also:

Description of nonmilitary signalling,tele-   Manufacture of electrical equipment 393
     phone, telegraph, radio, and radar equipment. 20   Army signal corps 708
Photography 215

719 MUNITIONS INDUSTRIES--industries specializing in the manufacture of ordnance and other military supplies and equipment; ownership and operation; organization of labor and production; regulation; degree of economic self-sufficiency in munitions manufacture; etc. See also:

Capital goods industries 39   Manufacture of explosives 389
Gunsmiths 326

---

72 WAR

72 WAR--general statements dealing with several aspects of the conduct and results of contests between independent political units involving the use of organized military force. For ingroup violence see 578; for revolution and civil war see 669.

721 INSTIGATION OF WAR--frequency of war (e.g., common, rare, unknown); military preparedness; scale, severity, and duration of wars; small-scale military operations (e.g., raids for slaves or cattle, headhunting, privateering); conception of war (e.g., as glorious, as holy, as wrong but inevitable, as less debilitating than peace); prevalent motives for waging war (e.g., vengeance, self-defense, aggrandizement, prestige); predominance of offensive or defensive warfare; material gains through war (e.g., booty, trophies, slaves, women, mercantile advantages, territory); decision as to war (e.g., deliberations, negotiations); methods of initiating hostilities (e.g., challenges, declarations of war, attacks without warning); etc. See also:

Ethnocentrism 186
Cannibalism 266
Prestige. 554
Riots, piracy and banditry 579
Feuds 628
International relations 648
Revolution 669

722 WARTIME ADJUSTMENTS--emergency adjustments (e.g., martial law); war-
time restrictions; disposition and behavior of noncombatants (e.g., removal
to place of security, mobilization for war industries, observance of special
taboos); means of maintaining civilian morale; civilian defense activities;
economic readjustments to war; etc. See also:
Rationing 434
Price controls 435
Wartime extensions of political authority . . . 642
Public finance 652
Government regulation 656
Conscription 702

723 STRATEGY--principles of military, naval, and aerial strategy; nontechno-
logical aspects of military science; planning of wars and campaigns; coordination of military forces; planned use of propaganda and psychological
warfare; economic warfare; etc. See also:
Public opinion 208
Negotiation of alliances 648

724 LOGISTICS--wartime procurement of military supplies; logistic planning; or-
ganization of land, sea, and air transport; expediting of supplies; depots, dumps,
and supply trains; etc. See also:
Land transport 49
Water and air transport 50
Military vehicles, naval vessels, and
military aircraft 71
Organized commissariat and supply services . 705

725 TACTICS--specialized tactics of ground, air, and naval forces; combined
tactics; offensive tactical maneuvers; defensive tactics (e.g., trench warfare,
use of underground installations); special tactics (e.g., parachute attacks,
landing operations, raids in depth, tactics of resistance movements); etc.
See also:
Revolutionary tactics 669
Unspecialized tactics 726

726 WARFARE--wartime mobilization; departure of troops (e.g., public ceremonies, rituals for securing supernatural aid, exhortations to bravery); military expeditions (e.g., marching, scouts, protection of flanks and rear, camping, mounting of guards, foraging, billeting); types of combat (e.g., skir-
mishes, surprise attacks, assaults, pitched battles, siege operations); joining
battle (e.g., choice of time and place, ritual preliminaries and precautions);
deploying and coordination of forces; special characteristics of naval and air
combat; military conventions and rules of war (e.g., flag of truce); personal
encounters (e.g., duels between champions); termination of combat (e.g.,
after first casualty, after desperate last stand); tactical withdrawals; flight
and pursuit; surrender; etc. See also:
Religious practices 78
War songs 533
International law. 648
Organization of army or war party 701

727 AFTERMATH OF COMBAT--number and nature of casualties; treatment of own casualties (e.g., retrieving and disposal of dead, care of wounded); treatment of enemy casualties (e.g., despoiling, mutilation, killing); taking of trophies; treatment of captives and prisoners (e.g., slaughter, torture, mutilation, release, exchange, holding for ransom, adoption, enslavement, sacrifice); punishment of enemy leaders; military occupation and military government; homecoming after war (e.g., return trip, reception of returning warriors); home reactions to victory and defeat; victory celebrations (e.g., dances, feasts, memorials); demobilization; resumption of normal life; reconstruction of war damage; etc. See also:

Commemorative statues and monuments . . . . . 211 Slavery 567
Cannibalism 266   Colonial administration 636
Mutilation 304   Prisons 697
War dances 535   Mortuary practices 764

728 PEACEMAKING--truce and peace negotiations; peace conferences; terms (e.g., tribute, indemnities, cession of territory, demilitarization); ratification of peace terms; consolidation of annexed territory; transplantation of conquered populations; etc. See also:

Migrations . . . . 166, 167 Naturalization 641
Colonial administration   636   International relations 648

729 WAR VETERANS--status and activities of military veterans; special prerogatives (e.g., political and economic preferment); military pensions and soldiers' bonuses; special institutions (e.g., old soldiers' homes, veterans' hospitals); veterans' organizations; reunions; etc. See also:

Prestige and mobility . . . . 55 Veterans administration 647
Patriotic holidays and anniversaries . . . . . 527 Public welfare 657
Sodalities . . . . 575 Hospitals 743

73 SOCIAL PROBLEMS

73 SOCIAL PROBLEMS--general statements dealing with several distinct types of major social problems and with the incidence, treatment, and care accorded each major type. See 74, for coordinated welfare programs and highly institutionalized methods of care and relief.

731 DISASTERS--prevalence and major types of disasters (e.g., earthquakes, epidemics, conflagrations, typhoons, tornadoes, floods, droughts, famines, insect plagues); explanations and rationalizations; incidence of disastrous accidents (e.g., train wrecks); reactions to disasters; organization of relief (e.g., private, public); role of special relief agencies (e.g., Red Cross); emergency measures; reconstruction; preventive measures (e.g., flood control); etc. See also:

Relief agencies 74   Adjustments to famine 261
Cyclonic storms. 132   Water supply 312
Areas of volcanic and seismic activity 133   Municipal fire-fighting services 368
Occurrence of epidemics 164   Reconstruction of war damage 727

732 DEFECTIVES--incidence of serious physical defects (e.g., blindness, deaf-mutism, crippling infirmities and deformities, feeblemindedness); interpretation of deformities and defects; care and treatment of defectives (e.g., neglect, persecution, euthanasia, home care, charity, institutionalization); organization, operation, and financial support of special institutions for defectives; adjustments to defects (e.g., seeing-eye dogs, prosthetic devices, hearing aids); sterilization of defectives; etc. See also:

Incidence of insanity 158   Begging. 735
Sign language 201   Care of the insane 758
Guardianship 429   Interpretations of physical abnormalities. . . 826
Aids to locomotion. 481   Infanticide 847
Care of war veterans 729   Care of aged 737, 888

733 ALCOHOLISM AND DRUG ADDICTION--incidence of excessive or chronic use of alcohol or narcotics; social problems arising therefrom (e.g., poverty, delinquency, broken homes); care and treatment of alcoholics and drug addicts (e.g., neglect, attempts at restraint and cure); special institutions for the treatment and cure of alcoholics and addicts; temperance movements; etc. See also:

Use of alcoholic beverages and narcotics 27   Organized vice 548
Psychiatric aspects of alcoholism and drug   Political movements. 668
     addiction 158   Relief of dependents 736

734 INVALIDISM--chronic illness and invalidism (e.g., mental illness, tuberculosis. multiple sclerosis); prolonged convalescence after illness; treatment and care (e.g., hospitalization, neglect, euthanasia, nursing, diet, rest); home care and institutionalization; sanatoriums, mental institutions, convalescent homes; economic problems arising from chronic illness; relief of the chronically ill and their families (e.g., charity, public relief); etc. See also:

Malnutrition 146   Hospitals and clinics 743
Morbidity 164   Social insurance 745
Insurance 456   General data on medical care 758

735 POVERTY--prevalence and definition of poverty; causes (e.g., low income, unemployment, sickness, alcoholism, improvidence, indolence); social attitudes toward poverty; begging and beggars; poor relief (e.g., almsgiving, private charity, public relief); special institutions for the poor (e.g., almshouses); support of institutions (e.g., municipal, ecclesiastical, private endowment); etc. See also:

Social stratification 56   Housing 362
Social insurance, public assistance, and   Gift giving 431
     private welfare agencies 74   Income 434

111

Laziness 461   Standards and levels of living 511

Wages 465

736 DEPENDENCY--incidence of dependency (e.g., orphans, widows, deserted and divorced wives, families of defectives and alcoholics, families of invalids and criminals); attitudes toward dependency; care and support of dependents (e.g., adoption, support by relatives, private charity, public relief); special institutions for dependents (e.g., orphanages); etc. See also:

Social insurance, public assistance, and   Status of widows   589
    private welfare agencies   74   Adoption   597
Insurance 456   Treatment of motherless infants   846
Levirate   587

737 OLD AGE DEPENDENCY--incidence of dependency for the aged of both sexes; care and support of the aged (e.g., support by relatives, private charity, public relief, institutionalization); special institutions for the aged (e.g., old people's homes); support of institutions (e.g., private, municipal, fraternal, ecclesiastical); etc. See also:

Age distribution of the population 162   Pensions and social insurance 745
Savings 454   Public assistance   746
Annuities 456   Status and treatment of the aged   888

738 DELINQUENCY--incidence of petty delinquency (e.g., hoodlumism and vandalism, inveterate gambling, sex delinquency, nonsupport); prevalence, causes, and types of juvenile delinquency; attitudes toward and methods of dealing with petty and juvenile delinquents; special institutions (e.g., reformatories, houses of correction); etc. See also:

Drunkenness 273   Social offenses and their sanctions 689
Laziness 461   Prisons.   697
Gambling 525   Juvenile courts   698
Prostitution 548   Premarital sex relations   836
Brawls 579   Children's gangs   857
Crime 674   Adolescent problems   883

---

74 HEALTH AND WELFARE

74 HEALTH AND WELFARE--general statements covering several aspects of the more highly institutionalized adjustments to social problems and disease.

741 PHILANTHROPIC FOUNDATIONS--private endowments for relief of distress, social welfare, health, and education; church endowments for philanthropic and educational purposes; corporate foundations for the promotion of health, welfare, science, and education; special philanthropic organizations (e.g., community trusts); organization, administration, and policies of foundations; finance (e.g., gifts, investments, tax exemption); fund-raising methods;

distribution of funds; etc. See also:

Institutions for defectives, dependents, and

  delinquents 73

Science and the humanities 81

Education. 87

Trusts 429

Gift giving. 431

Investment. 454

Taxation 651

Church organizations 794

742 MEDICAL RESEARCH--extent of research in medicine, nutrition, and public health; integration with hospitals and medical schools; specialized personnel (e.g., researchers, technicians); laboratories and equipment; research institutes; administration of research; special objectives (e.g., control of cancer, of tuberculosis); finance (e.g., government aid, foundation grants, public drives); fund-raising organizations and techniques (e.g., Christmas seals, march of dimes); allocation of funds; etc. See also:

Veterinary science 232

Government support 654

Medical personnel 759

Development of biological science 815

Medical schools 874

743 HOSPITALS AND CLINICS--number and availability of special institutions for medical care; organization and operation of clinics and hospitals; personnel (e.g., administrative and medical staffs, nurses, orderlies, technicians); equipment; special services; charges and fees; sources of financial support (e.g., governmental, ecclesiastical, private); ambulatory clinics. See also:

Physicians, nurses, and medical care. 75

Hospital buildings 344

Care of war veterans 729

Institutions for the care of defectives 732

Care of alcoholics and drug addicts 733

Sanatoriums, convalescent homes,

  mental institutions, and leproseries 734

744 PUBLIC HEALTH AND SANITATION--organized measures for the prevention and control of infectious diseases and epidemics; degree of development and adequacy of public health services; specialized personnel (e.g., sanitary engineers, quarantine officers, inspectors); public health laboratories; public health activities (e.g., milk and meat inspection, imposition and enforcement of quarantines, control and extermination of disease vectors, sanitation); special control programs (e.g., yellow fever, venereal disease); public health legislation (e.g., pure food and drug acts); etc. See also:

Malnutrition 146

Incidence of disease 164

Municipal sanitation 364

Hygienic conditions in industry 466

Disposal of human excreta 514

Public welfare 657

Army sanitary corps. 708

Immunization and unspecialized preventive

  medicine 751

745 SOCIAL INSURANCE--prevalent types of social insurance (e.g., retirement pensions, old age pensions, sickness and maternity benefits, unemployment benefits); contributions (e.g., from employers, beneficiaries, government); administration of funds; premiums and payments; industrial and business

pension and benefit systems; social insurance legislation; systems sponsored and operated by the state (e.g., socialized medicine); etc. See also:

Annuities, individual insurance, and
   mutual benefit societies 456
Labor relations 466

Government expenditures for public welfare
   and pensions to government employees . . . 657
Pensions to war veterans 729
General data on medical care 758

746 PUBLIC ASSISTANCE--tax-supported agencies for the administration and dispensing of relief; categorical aid (e.g., grants to needy mothers, invalids, crippled children, dependent old people); unemployment relief (e.g., doles, public works programs); public welfare policies; justifications of public welfare as opposed to private relief; etc. See also:

Invalidism, poverty, and dependency 73
Incidence of unemployment 464

Public works 653
Expenditures for public welfare 657

747 PRIVATE WELFARE AGENCIES--private fund-raising organizations (e.g., community chests); private, semi-private, fraternal, and ecclesiastical operating relief agencies (e.g., Red Cross, Salvation Army, family welfare organizations); welfare institutions not elsewhere described (e.g., settlement houses, city missions, day nurseries, church community houses); organization, administration, financial support, and activities of each type; etc. See also:

Institutions caring for specific types of defectives, dependents, and delinquents 73

Church welfare work 794

748 SOCIAL WORK--specialization of training and techniques in the administration of relief and welfare activities; personnel (e.g., qualifications, education, organization); special types of social workers (e.g., visiting nurses, psychiatric social workers); employment of social workers by private, ecclesiastical, and governmental welfare organizations; social work policies, activities, and methods (e.g., family case work); etc. See also:

Social work schools 874

---

75 SICKNESS

75 SICKNESS--general statements covering several aspects of sickness. Ideas of the causation of sickness, with methods of cure, and with specialists in the treatment of disease, including bodily injuries and functional or neurotic ailments will be filed below in the appropriate three digit category.

751 PREVENTIVE MEDICINE--conception of health and hygiene; health regimen; protective measures (e.g., sun tan lotion, amulets, charms, spells, prophylaxis, immunization); etc. See also:

Incidence of disease 164
Diet 262

Health insurance 456
Personal hygiene 515

Exercise	526	Magic	789
Public health and sanitation	744	Infant care	854
Fetishes	778	Child care	855
Taboos	784	Prescriptions for longevity	886

752 BODILY INJURIES--theory of the causation of mishaps and accidental injuries; first aid; treatment of wounds, cuts, burns, frostbite, bruises, and sprains (e.g., ligatures, bandages, poultices, massage, cauterization); treatment of snake and insect bites; antidotes for poisoning; treatment of fractures (e.g., bonesetting, trepanation); surgical operations; use of sterile techniques; adjustments to pain (e.g., anesthetics); dental surgery; etc. See also:

Obstetrics	84	Accident insurance	456
Incidence of accidents	164	Bloodletting	757
Mutilation	304	Wound doctors, surgeons, and dentists	759
Surgical instruments	413	Ideas about human anatomy	826

753 THEORY OF DISEASE--extent of the attribution of disease to natural causes, to sorcery, and to supernatural aggression; prevalent theories of the supernatural causation of disease (e.g., soul loss, spirit possession, object intrusion, poison, evil eye, violation of taboos, pollution or contagion); special notions about loathsome diseases (e.g., leprosy); scientific theories of disease (e.g., transmission through germs); etc. See also:

Religious and magical beliefs	77	Development of biological science	815
Incidence of disease	164	Knowledge and beliefs concerning	
Medical research	742	human physiology	827
Conception of the causes of death	761	Interpretation of mental disorders	828

754 SORCERY--ideas of the causation of disease and death through witchcraft and sorcery; actual and reputed prevalence of sorcery; motives for practicing sorcery; methods (e.g., bone pointing, manipulation of effigies, exuvial magic, invocation of spirit aids); employment of sorcerers; witches, wizards, and sorcerers; physical, social and mental characteristics; sources of power, training; organization; special types of sorcerers (e.g., werewolves, vampires, individuals with the evil eye); evidence as to the efficacy of sorcery; reactions to sorcerers (e.g., witch hunts); etc. See also:

Ingroup antagonisms	578	Familiar spirits	776
Sorcery as a factor in social control	626	Uses of magic other than for the causation	
Punishment of sorcery	683	or cure of disease	789
Counter-measures to sorcery	755		

755 MAGICAL AND MENTAL THERAPY--individual therapeutic efforts (e.g., acts of faith, self-analysis); resorting to a specialized practitioner (e.g., circumstances, arrangements, payments); diagnosis (e.g., divination, interpretation of symptoms); therapeutic procedure (e.g., shamanistic seances, analytic couch); methods (e.g., interpretation of dreams, countermagic, exorcism, recapture of soul, sucking out of intrusive object, resort to spirit helpers); prescriptions (e.g., medication, purification, expiation, imposition of taboos);

prognosis; ritual banishment of disease (e.g., scapegoat); faith healing; scientific systems of psychotherapy (e.g., psychoanalysis, psychiatry, mental hygiene); evidence as to the effectiveness of magical and mental therapy; etc. See also:

Behavior processes and personality 15   Soul concepts 774
Shamanistic dances 535   Spirit possession and dream interpretation . . 787

756 PSYCHOTHERAPISTS--prevalent types of psychotherapists (e.g., shamans, faith healers, psychoanalysts, clinical psychologists); physical, mental, and social characteristics; source of power (e.g., inheritance, spirit helpers, specialized knowledge); training and initiation; prerogatives and disabilities; special paraphernalia and behavior; source of support (e.g., gifts, fees); penalties for failure; relations between practitioners (e.g., rivalry, organization); shamanism as a religious complex; special organizations (e.g., medicine societies, psychoanalytic societies); etc. See also:

Sorcery 754   Nontherapeutic functions of psychotherapists . .789
Familiar spirits. 776   Magicians and diviners 791
Revelation and divination 787   Transvestitism. 838

757 MEDICAL THERAPY--extent of differentiation of medical from magical and mental therapy; home remedies and self-medication; resorting to a specialized practitioner (e.g., circumstances, arrangements, payments); diagnosis (e.g., examination for symptoms, diagnostic aids); consultations; therapeutic principles (e.g., counterirritation, homeopathy); therapeutic methods (e.g., bloodletting, administration of cathartics and emetics, medication); prescribed regimen (e.g., rest, diet, isolation); remedies for specific complaints (e.g., fevers, colds, toothache, indigestion, rheumatism, infectious diseases); etc. See also:

Ideas about anatomy and physiology   82   Medical research   742
Obstetrics   84   Public health and sanitation   744
Materia medica and pharmacology   278   Surgery   752

758 MEDICAL CARE--regimen and care of sick persons (e.g., diet, rest, isolation); apparatus and paraphernalia of medical care (e.g., clinical thermometers, bed pans); general availability of medical advice, treatment, and care (e.g., organization, finance, services); etc. This category is intended for general information on medical care. For specialized data see relevant categories in 73, 74 and 75. See also:

Gift giving 431   Visiting 574

759 MEDICAL PERSONNEL--prevalent types of medical specialists (e.g., herbalists, diagnosticians, physicians, surgeons, dentists, nurses, technicians, midwives); qualifications, training, status, and activities of each type; prerogatives and disabilities of medical personnel; special garb, paraphernalia, and behavior;

remuneration (e.g., fees, salaries); penalties for failure; medical organizations; professional ethics; medical cults (e.g., acupuncture, osteopathy); examination and licensing of medical practitioners; etc. See also:

Medical personnel in institutions for defec-
    tives, dependents, and delinquents 73
Public health, hospital, and research personnel . 74

Psychiatrists, shamans, and medicine societies . 756
Role of midwives at childbirth 844
Medical and nursing schools 874

------

76 DEATH

76 DEATH--general statements dealing with several distinct aspects of death including ideas about death and with practices which accompany and follow the occurrence of death. For beliefs concerning a life after death see 775.

761 LIFE AND DEATH--theories about life and death; notion of a life force; conception of death (e.g., as natural, as unnatural); beliefs about the causes of death; attitude toward death (e.g., confidence, fear, fatalism); etc. See also:

Theories of health and disease. 75
Conception of fate, animistic beliefs,
    eschatology, and myths about origin of death . 77

Mortality statistics 165
Prescriptions for longevity. 886

762 SUICIDE--incidence of suicide; motives (e.g., humiliation, thwarted love); common methods (e.g., jumping, drowning, shooting, poison); stereotyped methods (e.g., suttee, hara-kiri); justifications; attitude toward suicides; etc. See also:

Personality disorders. 158
Punishment of attempted suicide. 682

763 DYING--omens and predictions of death; notions about dying; recognizing the approach of death; settlement of affairs; assembling of relatives; attempts to postpone death; preparing the patient for death (e.g., removal from dwelling, dressing in mortuary garments, last rites); preparing the funeral equipment (e.g., shroud, coffin); last words and last favors; criteria of death (e.g., coma, cessation of breath or heart action); attempts at revival; reaction to the impact of death (e.g., wailing, flight, self-mutilation); announcement of death; post-mortem examinations; etc. See also:

Deathbed testaments 428
Capital punishment 681

Omens 787

764 FUNERAL--attitude toward the corpse; mortuary toilet (e.g., dressing and decorating the body); laying out in state; preservative techniques (e.g., embalming, desiccation, mummification); determination of time, place, and mode of burial; interval between death and burial (e.g., duration, measures to prevent further deaths, manifestations of grief); vigils and wakes; place of disposal of corpse (e.g., cemetery, ossuary); receptacles (e.g., coffin, canoe, urn, tomb); method of disposal (e.g., abandonment, inhumation, cremation, sea burial, cave burial, tree or scaffold·burial); preparation of grave, pyre, or scaffold; transport of corpse to place of disposal; procession to grave; disposition of corpse (e.g., posture, orientation); funerary mounds, monuments, and memorials; burial rites; mortuary sacrifices; disposition of grave goods; roles of relatives at funerals; economic obligations of participants (e.g., fees, contributions); precautions against return of the soul (e.g., silence, disguise, doors of the dead); return from the funeral; purification of participants; etc. See also:

Commemorative statues and monuments 211   Blood vengeance 628
Dirges and laments 533   Eschatology 775
Posthumous marriages 588   Purification rites 783

765 MOURNING--duration of the mourning period; behavior of spouse and other relatives after the funeral (e.g., seclusion, mourning garb, observance of taboos, sacrifices); treatment of relics (e.g., preservation of skull or head, wearing of bones, use of hair for artifacts); visits to the grave; mortuary feasts; exhumation, second funeral, and reburial; ceremonies terminating mourning; etc. See also:

Mortuary cannibalism 266   Headhunting 721
Status of widows 589

766 DEVIANT MORTUARY PRACTICES--abbreviated and extended funerals; distinctive mortuary rites in special cases of death (e.g., for an enemy, stranger, executed criminal, pauper, slave, child, woman dying in childbirth, chief, shaman, warrior, person dying abroad, victim of accidental death, suicide, homicide, victim of epidemic or loathsome disease); ceremonies at the death of animals; etc. See also:

Disposition of war casualties 727   Disposition of miscarriages and stillbirths . . 845
Notions about loathsome diseases 753   Disposition of victims of infanticide 847
Human sacrifice 782

767 MORTUARY SPECIALISTS--burial associations; gravediggers; cemetery guards and caretakers; hired mourners; embalmers and undertakers; funeral parlors; status and remuneration of mortuary specialists; etc. See also:

Coroners 693

768 SOCIAL READJUSTMENTS TO DEATH--disposition of the possessions of the deceased (e.g., abandonment or relocation of dwelling, destruction or mutilation of movable possessions, redistribution of property); provision for support of spouse and children; residence changes of survivors; etc. See also:

Inheritance. 428   Rule of residence 591
Guardianship and administration. 429   Adoption 597
Insurance 456   Rules of succession 59, 61, 63, 622, 643
Heirlooms 523   Relief of widows and orphans 736
Remarriage 587   Social insurance 745
Status of widows 589

769 CULT OF THE DEAD--avoidance of graves and cemeteries; propitiation of
ghosts and ancestors; recurrent feasts of the dead; maintaining relations with
the long dead; ancestor worship; household cults; hero worship; etc. See also:

Family organization. 59   Idea of filial piety 577
Religious practices 78   Eschatology 775

77 RELIGIOUS BELIEFS

77 RELIGIOUS BELIEFS--general statements about several types of religious beliefs and ideologies. The behavioral and organizational aspects of religion
are treated, respectively, under 78 and 79.

771 GENERAL CHARACTER OF RELIGION--conception of what constitutes religion;
differentiation of the sacred and the profane; distinctions drawn between religion and superstition; relation of religion to the unknown and the unpredicta-
ble; relative prominence of magical and anthropomorphic elements; evidence
of the expression of projective mechanisms in religious beliefs; primary
orientation of the religious system (e.g., ancestor worship, nature worship,
totemism, ritualism, mysticism, redemptive religion); social and individual role of religion (e.g., services and disservices); incidence of faith, in-
difference, and skepticism; existence of nonsupernatural ideologies supported
with a faith akin to that in religion (e.g., ethical systems, political philoso-
phies); etc. See also:

Personality. 15   Magic. 789
Integration of religion with other aspects of   Religious sects 795
   culture 182   Philosophy 812
Ethical ideals. 577   Ideas about the social role of religion 829
Ancestor worship 769   Inculcation of religious beliefs 869
Extended discussions of theological systems . . 779

772 COSMOLOGY--conception of the universe; cosmological systems (e.g.,
heavens and hells); universal categories (e.g., dualism of nature); etc. See also:

Realm of the dead. 775   Ideas about cosmic phenomena 821
Conception of a moral order of the universe . . 812

773 MYTHOLOGY--cosmogony (e.g., theories and accounts of the creation of the
world and of man); mythical epochs (e.g., golden age, age of the gods, age
of animals); cataclysms (e.g., mythical floods and conflagrations); culture
myths (e.g., accounts of a culture hero, mythical explanations of culture
traits); myths about the origin of evil and death; nature myths; totemic myths;
theogonic myths; ancestor myths; etc. For texts of myths see 539. See also:

Historical traditions 173

774 ANIMISM--conception of the soul; number of souls; location in the body; characteristics (e.g., shape, visibility, separability); relation of the soul to the body, to the name, to the breath, to dreams, to shadows and reflections, and to life and death; notions of the temporary departure of the soul from the body; attribution of souls to animals and inanimate objects; etc. See also:

Personality 15
Names 551
Conception of conscience 577
Theories of disease and death 753, 761
Concepts of soul-stuff and animated fetishes . . 778
Spirit possession and dream interpretation. . . 787
Interpretation of shadows and reflections . . . 822
Ethnozoology 825
Ideas about breathing 827
Ideas about abnormal mental states 828

775 ESCHATOLOGY--conception of the survival of the soul; career of the soul after death (e.g., mode of departure from the body, temporary sojourn near place of death, indefinite sojourn as a disembodied soul or ghost, journey to a realm of the dead); notions about ghosts, specters, apparitions, and phantoms (e.g., shape, substance, propensities); behavior of departed souls or ghosts (e.g., haunting of houses and cemeteries, visitations); spiritualistic beliefs; conception of a realm of the dead (e.g., place, mode of life, rewards and punishment); duration of afterlife; belief in immortality; ideas of transmigration and reincarnation; conception of the survival of the body (e.g., resurrection); etc. See also:

Belief in witches, vampires, and werewolves. . 754
Cult of the dead 769
Communication with spirits. 787
Notion of death and rebirth in initiation
    ceremonies 881

776 SPIRITS AND GODS--conception of supernatural beings of a higher order than disembodied souls; indications of their genetic relationship to ghosts; prevalent types of supernatural beings (e.g., guardian and familiar spirits, tutelary divinities, tribal gods, nature spirits and gods, angels, animal and totemic divinities, fairies and sprites, demons, mythical monsters, deified heroes and saints, divine tricksters, occupational or functional deities, creator gods, rulers of the spirit world, high god or supreme being); attributes of individual deities and of categories of divine beings (e.g., name, sex, form, character, powers, functions, symbols); hierarchical arrangement (e.g., polytheistic pantheon, dualism, henotheism, monotheism); etc. See also:

Totemic beliefs associated with kin groups . . . 61
Religious practices 78
Hero worship 769

777 LUCK AND CHANCE--concept of good and bad luck; ideas about chance and probability; things associated with good or bad luck (e.g., lucky objects, luck-bringing formulas, lucky and unlucky numbers, propitious and unlucky days); techniques for controlling luck (e.g., wearing of luck amulets, reciting of lucky formulas); conception of fate; etc. See also:

Insurance 456
Gambling. 525
Protective amulets 751
Theory of accidental injuries 752
Divination. 787
Pattern numbers 801
Calendar 805
Scientific theory of chance 813

778 SACRED OBJECTS AND PLACES--conception of sanctity (e.g., possession by an indwelling or frequenting spirit, infusion with impersonal supernatural power); idols and fetishes; extraordinary objects (e.g., bezoar stones, albino animals, mandrake roots); sacred places (e.g., shrines, altars); places of asylum and sanctuary; notions of impersonal supernatural power (e.g., mana, soul-stuff); animatism; beliefs and practices of consecration and desecration; etc.

See also:

Churches and temples	346	Luck amulets	777
Heirlooms	523	Notions of uncleanness	783
Asylum	696	Taboos	784
Protective amulets	751	Phallic rites	786
Relics	765	Conception of magic force	789
Conception of the sacred and the profane	771	Holy men	792

779 THEOLOGICAL SYSTEMS--elaborated systems of religious beliefs (e.g., totemism, pantheism); state religions; revealed religions (e.g., Buddhism, Christianity, Mohammedanism); sacred books; content of complex, systems of dogma and theology; association of theological systems with ethics and philosophy; etc.

See also:

Totemic kin groups	61	Statements on the general character of religion	771
Ethical ideals	577	Sects	795
Ancestor worship	769	Theologians	812

78 RELIGIOUS PRACTICES

78 RELIGIOUS PRACTICES--general statements dealing with several aspects of the description and analysis of specific religious rites and practices or types thereof. Extended ceremonies, in which various rites are combined in sequential order, are presented as units under 796. For cult of the dead see 769; for transmission of religious beliefs see 869.

781 RELIGIOUS EXPERIENCE--emotional reactions experienced in religious behavior (e.g., oppressive fear of malevolent higher powers, overwhelming awe of divine might, luxurious sense of dependence upon a benevolent and all-knowing superior, reassuring feeling of security through conformity, prideful conviction of right, grateful release from the burdens of a guilty conscience, groveling humility of self-abnegation, ecstatic release of mysterious inner powers, mystic sense of identification with or absorption in the divine essence, esthetic thrill in religious art, music, or ceremonial); evidence as to the predominant type or types of religious experience in the particular society; emotional needs satisfied through religious behavior; etc. See also:

Personality	15	Ethical ideals	577
Fine arts	53	Conceptions of emotions	828
Esthetic ideals	517		

782 PROPITIATION--practices reflecting a sense of dependence and a desire to ingratiate or influence the supernatural; repudiation and intimidation; obeisances (e.g., bowing, genuflection); laudation; prayer; sacrifice (e.g., libations, food sacrifices, animal and human sacrifice, symbolic and vicarious sacrifices); vows; burning of incense; decoration of religious edifices; endowing of shrines and temples; etc. See also:

Philanthropy	73, 74	Desecration and consecration of sacred	
Hymns	533	objects and places	778
Etiquette	576	Stereotyped prayers	788
Mortuary sacrifices	764		

783 PURIFICATION AND EXPIATION--practices reflecting a sense of contamination or guilt; concept of ritual uncleanness; things and persons considered unclean or impure; purification rites (e.g., ritual ablutions and bathing); concepts of sin, salvation, and redemption; riddance of sin (e.g., confession, remission, atonement, penance, scapegoat); etc. See also:

Elimination	514	Ideas about corpses	764
Personal hygiene	515	Ideas about sexual intercourse	833
Ideas about unclean castes	564	Ideas about menstrual blood	841
Definitions of acts regarded as sinful	673	Ideas about the exuviae of childbirth	844
Punishment of ritual offenses	688		
Conception of pollution, contagion, and			
loathsome diseases	753		

784 AVOIDANCE AND TABOO--practices reflecting impulses to escape from fear or anxiety; techniques for avoiding malevolent spirits (e.g., flight, disguise, deception, disparagement); concept of taboo; imposition and removal of taboos; prevalent types of taboos (e.g., food taboos, property taboos, status taboos, word and name taboos, totemic taboos, sex taboos, reproductive taboos, therapeutic taboos, mortuary taboos); systematization of taboos; general discussion of taboos; list of taboos; specific taboos not classifiable elsewhere; supernatural punishments for violations of taboos and other offenses; etc. Since taboos commonly represent the negative aspects of cultural norms, information on taboos may be found under many categories, only a few of which are indicated in the cross-references below.

Totemic taboos	61, 82	Rest days	527
Mortuary taboos	76	Name taboos	551
Sex taboos	83	Avoidance relationships	602
Reproductive taboos	84	Taboos surrounding a chief or king	63, 622, 643
Cultural norms	183	Legal norms	671
Euphemisms	195	Definition of acts regarded as sins	673
Food taboos	262	Social Sanctions for violations of taboos	688

785 ASCETICISM--practices reflecting tendencies of self-abasement or self-torture; mortification of the flesh (e.g., flagellation, hookswinging, bed of spikes); fasting; sexual renunciation (e.g., continence); renunciation of comforts (e.g., vows of poverty, wearing sackcloth); abandonment of worldly affairs (e.g., becoming a beggar or hermit); etc. See also:

Personality 15   Suicide 762
Control of hunger 261   Ascetics 792
Mutilation 304   Idealization of continence and chastity . . . 831

786 ORGIES--practices reflecting hysterical tendencies or release from normal inhibitions; frenzied singing and dancing; ceremonial license (e.g., phallic rites, temporary lifting of sex restraints, ceremonial intoxication); bacchanalian revels; religious prostitution; induced hysteria, hallucination, and swoon; religious revivalism; etc. See also:

Sex taboos 83   Temple prostitutes 793
Drunkenness 273   Conception of abnormal mental states . . . 828

787 REVELATION AND DIVINATION--practices reflecting anxiety about the future and often also a sense of inspiration; quest for visions and guardian spirits; hallucinatory revelations; communication with spirits (e.g., through spirit possession, through inspired oracles, through mediums); prophesy; clairvoyance; acquiring mystic insight through concentration and contemplation; interpretation of dreams; omens and their interpretation; divinatory practices and techniques (e.g., haruspicy, hepatoscopy, necromancy, scapulimancy, scrying, sortilege, astrology); etc. See also:

Personality disorders 158   Cult of the dead 769
Judicial oaths and ordeals 695   Guardian spirits 776
Revelation and divination in the   Diviners, seers, and messiahs 791
    treatment of diseases 755   Ideas about dreams 828
Omens of death 763

788 RITUAL--practices reflecting relief of anxiety through performance of repetitive or obsessionally precise symbolic acts; compulsive gestures (e.g., sign of the cross); repetitive behavior (e.g., tolling of bells, burning of candles, sprinkling with holy water); recital of stereotyped formulas (e.g., blessings); mechanical praying (e.g., with rosary, with prayer wheel); recitation of litanies and liturgies (e.g., credos, masses); processions; making of pilgrimages; etc. See also:

Propitiation 782   Ritual numbers 801
Elaboration of rituals into extended
    ceremonies 796

789 MAGIC--practices reflecting confidence in the ability to manipulate supernatural forces; magical techniques of weather control (e.g., rain making); magical rites for increasing the food supply; exorcistic practices (e.g., driving off evil spirits with noise); potent formulas, incantations, and spells; curses; miracles; prevalent types of magic (e.g., imitative, contagious); concept of magical force; functions and social significance of magic; nonsupernatural magic (e.g., wonderworking, jugglery, legerdemain, fire-walking); etc. See also:

Magical rites in the food quest 22   Magic rites at funerals 764
Magic rites in agriculture 24   Luck magic 777
Magic rites in the reproductive cycle 84   Concept of mana 778
Magic as entertainment 545   Prevalence of nonlogical reasoning 811
Magic rites in warfare 726   Relation of magic to science 813
Sorcery, witchcraft, and evil eye 754   Love magic 832
Therapeutic magic 751, 755

123

79 ECCLESIASTICAL ORGANIZATION--general statements dealing with several aspects of the organization of religion, i.e., specialists, cult groups, and systematized ceremonial.

791 MAGICIANS AND DIVINERS--specialists in magic (e.g., wonder workers, exorcists, magicians, fakirs); specialists in divination (e.g., astrologers, oracles, diviners, fortune tellers, seers, mediums); characteristics of each (e.g., personality, sex, training, garb); sources of power; prerogatives and disabilities; organization; fees; etc. See also:

Magicians as entertainers 545   Divination 787
Witches, wizards, and sorcerers 754   Magic 789
Shamans and faith healers 756

792 HOLY MEN--prophets and messiahs; ascetics and anchorites; monks, friars, and nuns; monastic orders (e.g., mendicant, hermit, cenobite); monasteries and convents (e.g., organization, activities); monastic rules (e.g., poverty, celibacy); characteristics, status, and means of support of holy men; etc. See also:

Celibacy 589   Concept of sanctity 778
Divine rulers 643   Asceticism 785
Messianic movements 668   Oracles 787
Poverty and almsgiving 735

793 PRIESTHOOD--specialists in organized religious activities (e.g., priests, priestesses, clergymen, rabbis, mullahs); status and means of support; selection, training, and consecration; hierarchical organization (e.g., chief priests, bishops, cardinals, popes); prerogatives and disabilities of priests; characteristics (e.g., sex, garb, paraphernalia); distinctive behavior (e.g., celibacy); activities (e.g., conducting ceremonies, preaching, teaching, comforting); special priestly personnel (e.g., acolytes, temple prostitutes); etc. See also:

Celibacy 589   Shamans 756
Theocratic forms of government 642   Theologians 812
Military chaplains 708   Divinity schools 874

794 CONGREGATIONS--groups organized for common worship (e.g., kin and local groups, special cult groups, church congregations, parishes); lay organization (e.g., elders, deacons, committees); qualification for membership; admission and disciplining of members; fund raising; maintenance of place of worship; religious activities (e.g., sunday school); secular church activities (e.g., education, welfare work, church gambling, temple money lending); recreational facilities (e.g., parish houses); etc. See also:

Recreation 52   Relief and welfare 73, 74
Religious activities of kin and local groups . 61, 62   Education 87

Churches and temples. 346   Gambling 525
Banking. 453   Temple prostitution. 786

795 SECTS--organized groups of congregations with differing and unreconciled systems of beliefs; crucial divergences in dogma; organization of sects or denominations (e.g., episcopal, congregational); admission of members (e.g., baptism, confirmation); distinguishing characteristics of members (e.g., special garb or behavior); established churches; splinter sects; interdenominational conferences and federations; etc. See also:

Sectarian philanthropic institutions . . . . . 73, 74   Government support of established churches . 659
Sectarian educational institutions 87   Medicine societies 756
Castes 564   Associated theological systems 779
Secret societies 575   Baptism of infants 851

796 ORGANIZED CEREMONIAL--systematization of religious ritual; ceremonial calendar (e.g., fixed and movable religious holidays, rest days, and festivals); detailed description of the ceremonies regularly associated with each (e.g., participants, ceremonial attire and paraphernalia, prescribed succession of rites, accompanying music and dancing, symbolism); church and temple services; religious dramas and spectacles; notions of propitious and unlucky days for ceremonies; etc. See also:

Agricultural ceremonies 24   Spectacles 541
Music, dancing, and drama 53   Weddings 585
War ceremonies" 72   Installation of chiefs and kings 643
Specific cult practices. 78   Shamanistic performances 755
Annual cycle of economic activities. 221   Mortuary ceremonies 764
Housebuilding ceremonies 342   Calendar 805
Leisure-time activities 517   Rites of passage 88, 561, 852
Secular holidays, rest days, and festivals. . . 527

797 MISSIONS--religious proselyting and evangelism; religious conversions; organized missionary activities (e.g., by sects within the society, by missions from other societies, by foreign missions abroad); mission organizations; mission stations; missionaries or evangelists (e.g., qualifications, selection, prerogatives and disabilities, religious activities); secular activities of missions and missionaries (e.g., education, medicine, technological assistance); etc. See also:

Welfare missions 747   Religious revivalism. 786

798 RELIGIOUS INTOLERANCE--rivalry between sects; religious persecution and intolerance; concept of heretics; suppression of dissenters by established religions (e.g., massacres, inquisitions, discriminatory legislation); martyrdom and martyrs; antireligious proselyting; etc. See also:

Ethnocentrism 186   Civil liberties 641
Stratification 563   Religious skepticism 771
Ingroup antagonisms 578

80 NUMBERS AND MEASURES--general statements dealing with several aspects of mathematics, counting, and mensuration.

801 NUMEROLOGY--symbolic and mystical significance of numbers; ritual and pattern numbers (e.g., standard numerical repetitions of elements in folklore and ceremonial); lucky and unlucky numbers; etc. See also:

Ideas about luck . . . . 777 Ritual 788
Divination by numbers . . . . 787 Magic 789

802 NUMERATION--words for numerals (e.g., cardinal, ordinal); numerical signs and gestures; written numerals (e.g., Roman, Arabic); numerical system (e.g., quinary, decimal, vigesimal); methods of counting (e.g., on digits); aids to numeration (e.g., tallies, counters, abacus); upper limit of numerical reckoning; fractions and decimals; tabulations; etc. See also:

Demographic conformation . . . . 16 Writing 212
Vocabulary . . . . 192 Accounting 451
Gestures and signs . . . . 201 Census taking 659

803 MATHEMATICS--arithmetical calculation (e.g., addition, subtraction, multiplication; division); use of calculating machines; higher mathematical knowledge (e.g., algebra, geometry, calculus); mathematical theory, statistics (e.g., theory, methods, uses); etc. See also:

Use of sampling methods in field research . . . 12 Navigation 502
Sampling methods in public opinion polling . . 208 Games of calculation 524
Description of calculating machines . . . . . 405 Calendrical reckoning 805
Mathematical knowledge exhibited in   Logic 811
  accounting . . . . 451 Statistical methods in scientific research . . . 813
Mathematical knowledge exhibited in
  actuarial practice 456

804 WEIGHTS AND MEASURES--methods of measurement (e.g., comparison with parts of the body, use of mensurating tools, use of weighing and measuring machines); customary and standardized units (e.g., of length, area, volume, weight, heat, angles, electrical energy); complex techniques of measurement (e.g., surveying); governmental supervision of weights and measures; etc. See also:

Architectural draftsmanship . . . . 341 Money 436
Weighing and measuring machines . . . . . 405 Coast, geodetic, and geological surveys . . 654
Mensurating tools . . . . 413 Conception of space 822

805 ORDERING OF TIME--sense of time; conception of a minimal unit of time (e.g., a moment); divisions of the day and night (e.g., hours); divisions of the year (e.g., weeks, months, seasons); longer time spans; solar, lunar, and stellar reckoning of time; methods of dating; calendar and calendrical knowledge; use of aids to measure the passage of time (e.g., sundials, clocks); etc. See also:

Annual cycle of economic activities . . . . . 221 Holidays, birthdays, and anniversaries 527
Clocks and watches . . . . 405 Age levels and age terms 561
Routine activities of a typical day . . . . . . 512 Ceremonial calendar 796
                                                 Conception of time 822

81 EXACT KNOWLEDGE--general statements dealing with several aspects of the use of logic, scientific experiment, and other exact methods as means to the attainment of knowledge, and with the intellectual products of such methods. To the extent that exact knowledge is international or cross-cultural, only its degree of development in the particular society, not its detailed content, will be included in the categories below. For unsystematized ideas and theories about nature and man see 82.

811 LOGIC--prevailing canons and criteria of validity in thought and demonstration; prevalence of nonlogical methods of reasoning (e.g., by analogy, free or mystical association, post hoc ergo propter hoc, rationalization); degree of acceptance of precise principles of definition, classification, and use of terms; notions of correct predication; formal principles of logic; development and use of symbolic or mathematical logic; etc. See also:

Methods of problem solution 153   Mathematics 803
Magic. 789   Ideas about mental processes 828

812 PHILOSOPHY--degree of development and acceptance of elaborated metaphysical and epistemological systems (e.g., theories of being, of supersensible reality, of experience, of understanding, of knowledge); theoretical foundations of ethics (e.g., divine will, moral order of the universe, free will and moral accountability of the individual); ethical systems (e.g., hedonism, utilitarianism, perfectionism); teleological evaluations (e.g., theories of the highest good, idea of progress, pragmatism); theologians and philosophers (e.g., number, characteristics, status, sources of support, activities); etc. See also:

Ethos. 181   Cosmology. 772
Ethical ideals 577   Theological systems 779
Legal liability. 672   Social philosophy 829

813 SCIENTIFIC METHOD--relative prevalence of fact-thinking as opposed to wishful thinking; degree of reliance on common sense and experience; areas in which experimental evidence is normally accepted; degree of acceptance and use of exact methods (e.g., precise canons of historical and linguistic research, experimentation, comparative and statistical methods); philosophy of science; evidence bearing upon the relationship of science to magic, technology, and philosophy; etc. See also:

Practical or folk science 82   Magic. 789

814 HUMANISTIC STUDIES--historiography; archeology; biography; linguistic studies; research in literature and the fine arts; degree of interest, activity, and specialization in humanistic studies; etc. See also:

Data on history and archeology 17   Education. 87
The society's language 19   Architecture. 341
Records 21   Esthetic ideals, appreciation, and taste . . . 517
Cultivation of the fine arts 53   Public lectures. 544

815 PURE SCIENCE--degree of acceptance of theories of natural causation; extent and dissemination of scientific knowledge, degree of development of knowledge and research in the natural sciences (e.g., astronomy, physics, chemistry, geology, biology) and in the social sciences (e.g., psychology, geography, anthropology, sociology, economics); extent of laboratory and research facilities, scientists (e.g., number, characteristics, status, sources of support, activities); scientific associations (e.g., organization, membership, meetings); etc. See also:

Popular beliefs about nature and man	82	Foundation support	741
Education	87	Divination	787
Museums	217	Mathematics	803
Lectures	544		

816 APPLIED SCIENCE--extent to which exact science is applied to practical problems; areas of such application; proliferation of laboratory and research facilities; sources of support; applied scientists (e.g., number, activities, organizations); etc. See also:

Medical practice	75	Civil engineering	331
Conservation	185	Chemical engineering	381
Fisheries research	228	Mechanical engineering	401
Veterinary science	232	Navigation	502
Agricultural science	242	Aeronautic science	507
Pharmacology	278	Government-supported research	654
Forestry science	313	Military science	711
Mining engineering	316	Medical research	742
Metallurgy	325	Scientific education	874

---

82 IDEAS ABOUT NATURE AND MAN

82 IDEAS ABOUT NATURE AND MAN--general statements covering several types of speculative and popular notions concerning phenomena of the external world and of the human organism.

821 ETHNOMETEOROLOGY--ideas about night and day, dawn and twilight, rising and setting of the sun, phases of the moon, eclipses, solstices and equinoxes, and the succession of seasons; notions about heavenly bodies (e.g., sun, moon, stars, constellations, planets, comets, meteorites); ideas about meteorological phenomena (e.g., clouds and fog, frosts and drought, rain and snow, ice, hail and sleet, winds and whirlwinds, storms, thunder and lightning, rainbow, parhelion and aurora); associated behavior patterns (e.g., greeting the dawn, dispelling an eclipse); etc. See also:

Climate	132	Cosmology	772
Navigation	502	Nature spirits and gods	776
Reaction to disasters	731	Omens and astrology	787

Magical weather control 789   Development of scientific astronomy
Ordering of time 805   and meteorology 815
                                                      Association of lunation with menstruation . . 841

822 ETHNOPHYSICS--popular conceptions of matter, energy, and their properties; notions about space, time, and gravitation; ideas about form, color, and sound (e.g., color symbolism, patterned use of color); beliefs about shadows, reflections, and echoes; notions about electricity, magnetism, chemical properties (e.g., alchemy); etc. See also:

Telephone, telegraph, radio, and television . . 20   Chemical engineering 381
Ideas about heat, light, and fire 37   Mechanics 401
Art and music 53   Optical instruments 416
Data on sensation and perception 151   Ideas about the soul 774
Photography 215   Mensuration 804
Metallurgy 325   Development of scientific physics and
Civil engineering 331   chemistry 815

823 ETHNOGEOGRAPHY--notions about water; ideas about hydrographic phenomena (e.g., oceans and seas, waves and tides, currents and whirlpools, rivers and streams, lakes and springs, floods); ideas about topographic phenomena (e.g., hills and mountains, canyons and valleys, caves and grottoes, striking natural formations, volcanoes and earthquakes); notions about minerals, metals, and precious stones; geographical and geological lore; directions (e.g., upstream and downstream, cardinal points); ideas about the beauty of nature; associated behavior patterns (e.g., attempts to quell earthquakes); etc. See also:

Geographical environment 13   Disaster relief 731
Settlements 36   Flood myths and mythical cataclysms . . . 773
Place names 103   Nature spirits and monsters 776
Land use 311   Surveying 804
Water supply 312   Development of scientific geology and
Routes and maps 487   geography 815

824 ETHNOBOTANY--notions about plants in general; ideas about particular plants (e.g., mistletoe); cultural uses of plants; native terms for plants; knowledge of poisonous plants; associated behavior patterns; etc. See also:

Agriculture 24   Materia medica and pharmacology 278
Textile uses of plant fibers 28   Lumbering and forestry science 313
Native flora 137   Forest products 314
Collecting 222   Arrow poisons 411
Fish poisons 226   Development of scientific botany 815
Food taboos 262

825 ETHNOZOOLOGY--notions about animals (e.g., mammals, birds, reptiles, fish, crustaceans, insects); ideas about particular animals (e.g., snakes, fireflies); technological and other cultural uses of wild animals and their products; native terms for animals; associated behavior patterns (e.g., avoidance of snakes); etc. See also:

Collecting, hunting, and fishing 22   Native fauna 136
Animal husbandry 23   Proper names of animals 552

Public health and sanitation	744	Animal divinities	776
Remedies for snakebite	752	Totemism	61, 779
Germ theory of disease	753	Animal sacrifices	782
Vampires and werewolves	754	Development of scientific zoology	815
Animism	774		

826 ETHNOANATOMY--conception of ideal bodily proportions; ideas about the torso and its parts (e.g., belly, breasts, buttocks, navel, neck, spine), skin and pigmentation, hair (e.g., axial, body, facial, head, pubic), head and its parts (e.g., brain, ears, eyes, lips, mouth, nose, teeth, tongue), limbs (e.g., arms, legs, hands, feet, fingers, toes, nails), blood, veins and arteries, bones, fat and muscles, nerves and sinews, internal organs (e.g., heart, intestines, kidneys, liver, lungs, stomach); interpretations of physical abnormalities (e.g., albinism, clubfoot, cretinism, dwarfism, harelip, hermaphroditism, hunchback); associated behavior patterns; etc. See also:

Adornment	30	Defectives	732
Anthropometric measurements	141	Surgery	752
Bathing and laving	515	Use of hair and nails in sorcery	754
Athletic sports	526	Relation of body and soul	774
Race prejudice	563	Development of scientific anatomy	815
Blood brotherhood	608	Notions about the genitalia	831
Blood vengeance	628	Ideals of erotic beauty	832
Taking of trophies	727	Ideas concerning menstrual blood	841

827 ETHNOPHYSIOLOGY--ideas about anal reactions (e.g., urination, defecation, farting); circulatory reactions (e.g., heartbeat, pulse); dermal reactions (e.g., flushing, fever and temperature, perspiring, shivering, itching and twitching, sloughing of skin and hair); facial reactions (e.g., laughing, smiling, grinning, sneering, frowning); nasal and respiratory reactions (e.g., breathing, panting, sneezing, running of nose); ocular and auricular reactions (e.g., weeping, blinking, dilation of pupils, ringing of ears, secretion of wax); oral reactions (e.g., salivation, spitting, swallowing, vomiting, coughing, hiccoughing, yawning); ideas about digestion and respiration; notions about heredity; associated behavior patterns (e.g., scratching, congratulations upon sneezing); etc. See also:

Genetic and ontogenetic data	14	Eating	264
Drinking, smoking, and narcosis	27	Humor	522
Sleeping, elimination, and bathing	51	Sorcery with exuviae	754
Sickness and therapy	75	Relation of breath to soul concepts	774
Death and mortuary customs	76	Taboos on looking, listening, and speaking	784
Sex	83	Development of scientific physiology	815
Reproduction	84	Ideas about suckling	853
Ideas about language	191	Ideas about development and maturation	856
Gestures	201	Cleanliness training	863

828 ETHNOPSYCHOLOGY--ideas about impulses or drives; conceptualization of sensation, perception, and emotions; standards of sensory pleasantness and unpleasantness; ideas about conscious and unconscious mental processes;

130

notions about abnormal mental states (e.g., aphasia, catalepsy, coma, delirium, hallucination, hypnosis, hysteria, swoon); interpretations and explanations of neuroses and psychoses; ideas about habits, attitudes, and the learning process; concepts of the self, of human nature, of motivation, of personality, of character; associated cultural behavior; etc. See also:

Data on behavior processes and personality . . . 15
Use of alcohol, narcotics, and stimulants . . . 27
Ideas about sleep and elimination 51
Sex 83
Education 87
Patterned expressions of emotions 201
Gratification and control of hunger 261
Food preferences 262
Manifestations and control of thirst 271
Palliation of labor 461
Esthetic ideals and canons of taste 517
Appreciation of form and perspective 532
Ethics 577
Punishments for abnormal behavior 689
Ideas about blindness, deafmutism, and
    feeblemindedness 732
Use of anesthetics 752
Psychotherapy 755
Soul concepts 774
Types of religious experience 781
Divination and interpretation of dreams
    and hallucinations 787
Logic 811
Conception of free will 812
Development of scientific psychology 815
Ideas about form, color, and sound 822

829 ETHNOSOCIOLOGY--social philosophy; interpretations of the society's charter; native ideas about social relationships and social structure; concepts of society (e.g., social contract); notions about culture and cultural change; economics and political behavior (e.g., mercantilism), racial inequality; etc. See also:

Population policy 168
Sociocultural trends 178
National character 181
Social planning 185
Development of nationalism 619
Constitution 642
Principles of taxation 651
Policies of government regulation 656
Political movements 668
Jurisprudence 671
Criminology 674
Penology 681
Welfare policies 746
Theological systems 779
Missionary programs 797
Philosophical systems 812
Development of scientific anthropology,
    sociology, and economics 815
Educational policies 871

-----

83 SEX

83 SEX--general statements about several aspects of sexual ideas and behavior. For marriage see 58.

831 SEXUALITY--ideas about the male and female sex organs; conceptions of sexual physiology (e.g., erection, nocturnal emission); notions about seminal and vaginal secretions; favorable attitudes toward sex (e.g., as natural, necessary, amusing, sacred); idealization of sex (e.g., romantic love); unfavorable attitudes toward sex (e.g., as dangerous, debilitating, unclean, disgusting, sinful); idealization of continence and chastity; preoccupation with sex (e.g., sexual symbolism in religion and the arts, obscenity, pornography); etc. See also:

Description of secondary sexual characteristics . 142   Affection between husband and wife. 593
Sexual humor 522   Chastity as an ascetic ideal 785
Differences in sex status 562   Ideas about the sex impulse 828
Celibacy 589   Notions about puberty in each sex. 881

832 SEXUAL STIMULATION--ideals of erotic beauty and sexual attraction; enhancement of sexual appeal (e.g., through wearing of alluring garb, use of perfumes and cosmetics, artificial development of the breasts and genitalia); acts interpreted as erotic overtures; suggestive gestures (e.g., winking, staring); innuendoes; serenades; love magic; techniques of sexual approach; terms of endearment; caresses and embraces; kissing; coyness and bashfulness; etc. See also:

Use of cosmetics and perfumes 302   Courtship 584
Genital mutilations. 304   Magic 789
Love songs 533   Blushing 827
Erotic dancing 535

833 SEXUAL INTERCOURSE--sexual initiation (e.g., age and circumstances of first intercourse for each sex, preferred partner); defloration; times and places considered appropriate for coitus; degree of interest and enjoyment ascribed to and manifested by each sex; initiative in copulation; degree of elaboration of preliminary sex play; preferred, variant, and tabooed postures; accompanying behavior (e.g., biting, urination); frequency and duration of coitus; occurrence of female orgasm; artificial means of augmenting sensation; behavior after coitus (e.g., sexual hygiene); psychic difficulties in coitus; impotence and frigidity (e.g., prevalence, explanation, prevention, treatment); etc. See also:

Defloration rites at marriage. 585   Contraception 842
Regulation of intercourse under polygamy . . . 595   Sex training of children 864

834 GENERAL SEX RESTRICTIONS--sexual modesty and decorum; ideas of proper behavior between the sexes; sex taboos observed on particular occasions (e.g., before or during ceremonies, war, hunting, or special industrial activities); miscellaneous sex restrictions; etc. See also:

Effect of sexual repression on personality 15   Etiquette 576
Regulation of sex relations between classes,   Deferred consummation 585
 castes, and ethnic groups. 56   Sex regulation under polygamy 595
Sex behavior and taboos at menstruation and   Avoidance and joking relationships. 602
 during pregnancy 84   Punishable sex offenses 684
Euphemisms 195   Word taboos. 784
Modesty in dress 291   Asceticism 785
Modesty about elimination 514   Sex taboos during lactation 853
Modesty in bathing 515   Training of children in modesty 864

835 KINSHIP REGULATION OF SEX--incest taboos (e.g., between primary relatives, bilateral and unilinear extensions); patterned exceptions to primary incest taboos (e.g., ceremonial and dynastic incest); violations of incest taboos

(e.g., incidence, circumstances, notions of physical and social results, treatment of offspring); privileged and tolerated sex relations between kinsmen (e.g., between cross-cousins, between siblings-in-law); etc. See also:

Exogamous rules. 61   Patterned behavior between kinsmen 602
Regulation of marriage 582   Punishments for incest 684
Levirate and sororate marriages 587

836 PREMARITAL SEX RELATIONS--presence or absence of a standard of chastity for the unmarried; variations in the standard (e.g., by sex, by class status); basis of the standard (e.g., material or ethical considerations); prevalence of premarital liaisons; degree of social approval or disapproval; seduction; assignations; permanency and exclusiveness of premarital unions; reciprocal behavior of lovers; incidence of rivalry and jealousy; termination of liaisons; evidence as to infertility of premarital unions; etc. See also:

Fertility, contraception, abortion,   Idealization of chastity. 831
  infanticide, and illegitimacy. 84   Sex training. 864
Trial marriage 583   Adolescent activities. 883
Courtship and behavior during betrothal . . . 584

837 EXTRAMARITAL SEX RELATIONS--presence or absence of an ideal of marital fidelity; cultural definition of adultery (e.g., applying to both spouses, to wife only); allegations of promiscuity; incidence of adultery for both sexes; prevention (e.g., cloistering of women, chastity belts); initiation and conduct of adulterous liaisons; cicisbeism; keeping of mistresses; culturally sanctioned extramarital relations (e.g., wife lending, sexual hospitality); etc. See also:

Prostitution. 548   Ceremonial license 786
Concubinage 595   Privileged sex relationships 835
Punishment of adultery 684   Illegitimacy 848

838 HOMOSEXUALITY--conceptualization (e.g., as normal, as abnormal); prevalence for each sex; specific behavior patterns; regulation (e.g., by incest taboos and exogamous rules); institutionalization (e.g., in bachelor organizations); reactions of the community (e.g., toleration, disgust); variant attitudes correlated with sex, age, and marital condition; transvestitism; etc. See also:

Unconscious homosexual traits. 15   Celibacy. 589
Friendships 572   Legal definitions and sanctions 684
Marriages between persons of the same sex . . 588

839 MISCELLANEOUS SEX BEHAVIOR--incidence of nocturnal emission, masturbation, petting to orgasm, bestiality, necrophilia, sexual sadism and masochism, exhibitionism, voyeurism, sexual fetishism, and rape; personal and social characteristics, circumstances, methods, and social reaction for each type of behavior; eunuchs (e.g., number, status, activities); etc. See also:

Psychoses and neuroses 158   Asceticism. 785
Castration 304   Orgies 786
Irregular unions 588   Coitus interruptus 842
Punishable sex offenses. 684   Sexual behavior of infants and children. . . 864

84 REPRODUCTION--general statements dealing with several aspects of the cultural adjustments, behavioral and ideological, to the reproductive cycle in women.

841 MENSTRUATION--theory of menstruation and the menstrual cycle (e.g., association with lunation); beliefs about menstrual blood; associated practices (e.g., medicinal and magical uses of menstrual blood, avoidance of contact, methods of stanching and disposal); behavior and treatment of women during menses (e.g., isolation, imposition of food and sex taboos, purificatory rites); adjustments in behavior of spouse and parents; recognized symptoms of menstruation; explanation and treatment of irregular, excessive, or prolonged menses; etc. See also:

Physiological characteristics of menstruation . . 147   Purification 783
Menstrual lodges 343   Ideas about blood 826
Notions of the uncleanness of women 562   First menstruation 881
Medical therapy 757   Menopause 886

842 CONCEPTION--theory of impregnation and paternity; fertility and sterility (e.g., incidence, conceptualization); desire for children and preferences as to sex; methods of inducing conception and of counteracting barrenness and sterility; treatment of barren women and sterile men; methods of influencing conception (e.g., determining sex, preventing twins, inducing healthy offspring); prevention of conception (e.g., continence, coitus interruptus, contraceptive devices); attitudes toward birth control; etc. See also:

Sex behavior 83   Notions of reincarnation 775
Population policy 168   Ideas about heredity 827
Sterilization of defectives 732

843 PREGNANCY--theory of pregnancy; determination of pregnancy (e.g., from cessation of menses, darkening of areola, abdominal protuberance, fetal movements); forecasting time of delivery; predicting sex, etc.; treatment and behavior of the pregnant woman (e.g., relief from work, dealing with nausea and giddiness, gratification of food cravings, observation of food and sex taboos, regimen, isolation); associated rites and ceremonies; sympathetic behavior of husband; ideas about embryonic development; practices intended to facilitate delivery and insure healthy offspring; differences in treatment of first and subsequent pregnancies; miscarriages (e.g., disposal of fetus, associated beliefs and practices); etc. See also:

Maternity benefits 745   Abortion 847

844 CHILDBIRTH--ideas about childbirth; attitude of the community; importance of first and subsequent births; preparations for delivery; place of birth; witnesses, assistants, and excluded persons; role of midwives and obstetricians; onset and duration of labor; facilitation of delivery (e.g., pressure, massage); posture in childbirth; receiving the baby; severing and tying the umbilical cord; expulsion of placenta; disposal of exuviae; immediate care of mother

and child; cleansing, bandaging, and medication of mother; adjustments to postnatal hemorrhage; treatment of baby (e.g., initiation of respiration, cleansing, swaddling); etc. See also:

Birth statistics. 163   Hospitals. 743
Infant and maternal mortality 165   Medical personnel. 759
Birth registration. 217   Special mortuary rites 766
Birthdays 527   Omens, divination, and astrology 787

845 DIFFICULT AND UNUSUAL BIRTHS--explanations of prolonged, difficult, and fatal deliveries; methods of dealing with abnormal presentations; obstetrical surgery (e.g., use of forceps, Caesarian section); beliefs and practices connected with unusual births (e.g., premature births, caul births); stillbirths (e.g., conceptualization, disposal of stillborn infant); delivery and treatment of deformed infants; notions about birthmarks; multiple births (e.g., conception of causation, reaction of the community, treatment of twins); special observances and ceremonial associated with unusual births and persons distinguished by unusual births; etc. See also:

Incidence of stillbirths and   Treatment of defectives 732
   multiple births 163   Surgery 752

846 POSTNATAL CARE--care of postparturient mother during period of recuperation (e.g., rest, isolation, medication, sex and food taboos); duration of lochia and its disposal; visits and presents; resumption of normal life (e.g., gradual, after lapse of a specified time); purificatory rites; special care of child between birth and sloughing of umbilical cord; conceptualization and disposition of umbilical cord; treatment and disposition of motherless infants; special behavior of father (e.g., couvade); etc. See also:

Gift giving. 431   Purification. 783
Adoption 597   Infant feeding. 853

847 ABORTION AND INFANTICIDE--prevalence of abortion; reasons and circumstances (e.g., illegitimate pregnancy); methods; disposal of fetus; reaction of community (e.g., toleration, disapproval); prevalence of infanticide; reasons and circumstances (e.g., illegitimate pregnancy, deformity, death of father or mother); methods used; disposal of corpse; reaction of community; etc. See also:

Mortality. 165   Miscarriages. 843
Legal sanctions 682

848 ILLEGITIMACY--cultural definition of legitimacy and illegitimacy; frequency of illegitimate pregnancies; tests of legitimacy; behavior and treatment of mother (e.g., ordeals, confession); treatment of father (e.g., forced marriage); treatment of offspring; status of illegitimate children; etc. See also:

Legal sanctions. 684   Premarital sex relations. 836

85 INFANCY AND CHILDHOOD--general statements dealing with several aspects of the care, physical development, activities, and status progression of children from birth to puberty. For their socialization see 86.

851 SOCIAL PLACEMENT--assignment of infant to a male parent (e.g., under polyandry, in case of a posthumous child); public announcement of birth; formal acceptance of infant into a social group (e.g., by family head or chief); alignment with the supernatural (e.g., baptism); changes in marital status and social relationships wrought by birth of a child; etc. See also:

Affiliation of offspring of mixed marriages	56	Orphans	736
Naming ceremonies	553	Concept of reincarnation	775
Adoption	597	Adult baptism	795
Descent	611	Theory of paternity	842

852 CEREMONIAL DURING INFANCY AND CHILDHOOD--rites of passage prior to puberty; maturation ceremonies (e.g., at first step, at first tooth); rites associated with cutting of hair, ear piercing, and circumcision; ceremonies correlated with achievements (e.g., first animal killed, first cloth woven); adult guidance and sponsorship; participation of children in adult ceremonies (e.g., Christmas); etc. See also:

Mutilation	304	Artificial kin relationships	608
Birthdays	527	Baptism and confirmation	795, 851
Naming ceremonies	553	Religious ceremonial	796

853 INFANT FEEDING--conception of lactation, milk, and colostrum; beliefs about sucking; initiation of suckling in newborn infants; stimulation of the flow of milk; routine of nursing (e.g., posture, intervals); feeding problems; treatment and behavior of the nursing mother (e.g., diet, sexual abstention); communal nursing; fosterage; adjustments to death of mother; supplementary feeding (e.g., age at beginning, appropriate foods and their preparation); method of feeding (e.g., bottle, cup, spoon); etc. See also:

Malnutrition	146	Ideas about breasts	826
Dairy products	234	Weaning	862
Diet	262		

854 INFANT CARE--care of routine bodily needs; cleaning; dealing with excreta; clothing and swaddling; provisions for sleep (e.g., cradles, cribs); playing with infants (e.g., fondling, dandling, rocking, crooning); emotional care (e.g., distracting techniques, methods of soothing, guarding against emotional upsets); watching and tending; special dangers ascribed to period of infancy; protection from real and supernatural dangers; hygienic and therapeutic measures; methods of holding and carrying infants (e.g., on back, astride hip); distribution of care among members of the family; institutionalized care (e.g., nurseries); etc. See also:

Cradle songs and lullabies 533
Preventive medicine 751
Medical care 758

Disparagement 784
Cleanliness training. 863

855 CHILD CARE--supervision, care, and support of children from earliest independence (e.g., walking, talking) to puberty; distribution of responsibility
among parents and other relatives; institutionalized care (e.g., day nurseries);
beliefs and standards concerning proper clothing, feeding, and housing of children; provisions for physical and mental health; protection from physical and
social dangers (e.g., confinement, removal of dangerous objects); attitude of
adults toward children (e.g., indulgent, indifferent, censorious); spoiling and
coddling; mistreatment and neglect of children; etc. See also:

Discipline and training 86
Family relationships 593
Care of orphans 736

Preventive medicine. 751
Medical care 758

856 DEVELOPMENT AND MATURATION--concepts and standards of physical,
mental, and emotional development during infancy and childhood; methods of pro-
moting and influencing growth (e.g., molding of head, magical rituals); adjustments to growth; data on maturation (e.g., age at creeping, standing, walking,
talking, cooperation); attitudes toward and special treatment of developmental
events (e.g., teething, growth of hair and nails, increases in weight and stature);
reactions and adjustments to retardation and precocity; etc. See also:

Socialization 86
Education 87
Data on physical growth and mental
development 145

Cranial deformation 304
Ceremonies during infancy and childhood . . . 852

857 CHILDHOOD ACTIVITIES--extent to which a special culture of childhood exists;
children's play; imitative activities (e.g., make-believe); habits of rest and
sleep; children's playgroups, cliques, and gangs; quarreling and fighting; children's explorations and haunts; tasks performed by children and age at which
each is undertaken (e.g., errands, chores, care of younger children); etc. See also:

Socialization. 86
Education 87
Baby talk 195
Mutual aid 476
Daily routine 512
Children's games, toys, and playthings . . . 524

Age-grades 561
Primary groups 571
Ingroup antagonisms 578
Child betrothal 584
Residence changes by children. 591
Quest for guardian spirits 787

858 STATUS OF CHILDREN--cultural definition of status periods and progression of
statuses during infancy and childhood; rights, privileges, and powers of children
(e.g., special exemptions); restrictions and disabilities of infants and children
(e.g., special taboos); conception of legal minority; extent to which children are
treated as inherently inferior or merely as inexperienced adults; stereotyped ideas
about children (e.g., concepts of the good and the naughty child); differential expectations and treatment of children (e.g., according to age, sex), etc; See also:

Kin relationships 60
Guardianship 429
Age stratification 561
Marriageability of children 582

Family relationships 593
Legal liability 672
Juvenile courts 698
Special mortuary rites 766
Concept of legal majority 884

86 SOCIALIZATION--general statements dealing with several aspects of the basic
mechanisms of cultural transmission, especially the socialization of impulses
and the more informal educational processes. For formal education see 87;
for personality and its development see 15.

861 TECHNIQUES OF INCULCATION--ideas about childhood training; general
methods of inculcation and discipline; specific techniques of providing motivation (e.g., inciting, warning, scolding, threatening, punishing); specific techniques of guidance (e.g., leading, demonstrating, explaining, commanding);
specific techniques of providing rewards (e.g., helping, recompensing, praising);
special emphasis on particular techniques (e.g., in general, at different ages,
for particular types of training); consistency or inconsistency in the use of
techniques; ages at which conscious parental inculcation begins and ends; etc.
See also:

Data on habit formation	153	Military discipline	703
Family relationships	593	Native ideas about learning	828
Social control	626	Education through play	857
Legal sanctions	681	Educational theory	876

862 WEANING AND FOOD TRAINING--adult beliefs, standards, and aims concerning weaning and appropriate eating habits for children; special reasons for
weaning (e.g., insufficient lactation, illness or pregnancy of mother); normal
age at weaning (e.g., from breast, from bottle); abruptness or gradualness
of transition; method of weaning (e.g., separation from mother, ridicule,
application of bitter substances to nipple); reactions of children to weaning;
imposition of rules about eating; teaching of table manners; resistance of
children to food training; etc. See also:

Diet	262	Etiquette	576
Eating and table manners	264	Infant feeding	853

863 CLEANLINESS TRAINING--adult beliefs, standards, and aims concerning
sphincter control and cleanliness for children; normal age at beginning and
completion of bladder and bowel control; techniques employed; bladder and
bowel incontinence (e.g., incidence, parental reaction, treatment); methods
of teaching children to wash, bathe, and groom themselves; inculcation of
standards of cleanliness, neatness, and orderliness, reactions of children to
cleanliness training; etc. See also:

Elimination	514	Ideas about anal reactions	827
Personal hygiene	515	Infant care	854

864 SEX TRAINING--adult beliefs, standards, and aims concerning sex behavior in children and methods of sex training; incidence of specifically sexual
behavior in infants and children (e.g., masturbation, fingering of genitals,
exhibitionism, sex play); rules for the control of such behavior (e.g., imposition, inculcation, enforcement); training in sexual modesty; imparting of

knowledge and beliefs about sex and reproduction; reactions to curiosity of children about sex; normal age for each aspect of sex training; reactions of children to sex training; etc. See also:

Personality 15   Ethical ideals 577
Sex 83   Initiation 881

865 AGGRESSION TRAINING--adult beliefs, standards, and aims concerning aggression in children and means of controlling it; incidence and treatment of physical aggression (e.g., striking, biting, kicking, hair-pulling); incidence and treatment of verbal aggression (e.g., insults, profanity, teasing); incidence and treatment of annoying behavior (e.g., crying, whining, noisiness); incidence and treatment of disobedience, defiance, and temper tantrums; incidence and treatment of rivalry and jealousy in children; rules governing the control of aggressive behavior (e.g., imposition, inculcation, enforcement); approved forms of and occasions for aggression (e.g., rules, inculcation); etc. See also:

Profanity 195   Warlikeness 721
Insults and quarrels 578   Obscenity 831
Crime 674   Quarreling and fighting among children 857
Litigation 691

866 INDEPENDENCE TRAINING--adult beliefs, standards, and aims concerning dependence in children and the development of independence; culturally prescribed age levels for the achievement of independence; incidence and treatment of dependent behavior (e.g., clinging to parents, tattling); induration to heat, cold, pain, and fatigue (e.g., exposure, ordeals, flogging); inculcation of courage; teaching of self-reliance and readiness to assume responsibility; inculcation of cooperation and competitiveness; instilling of levels of aspiration (e.g., for knowledge, for skills, for social advancement); reactions of children to demands for independence; etc. See also:

Economic cooperation and competition. . . . 47   Military training 702
Social mobility 55   Vision quest 787
Cooperativeness and competitiveness 157   Activities of children 857
Age stratification 561

867 TRANSMISSION OF CULTURAL NORMS--inculcation of norms concerning appropriate behavior for children (e.g., rest and sleep routines); initiation of children into social relationships (e.g., teaching to share and take turns, instruction in etiquette and kinship behavior); training in sex-typed attitudes and values (e.g., ladylikeness, manliness); instilling of respect for property; instruction in social, ethical, legal and political norms; techniques for inculcating morals and character; etc. See also:

Personality 15   Labor and leisure. 461
Mutual aid and competition. 47   Occupational specialization 463
Kinship behavior 60   Standard of living 511
Social norms 183   Sleeping 513
Public opinion 208   Esthetic ideals 517

Status and role	554	Citizenship	641
Interpersonal relations	571	Legal norms	671
Etiquette	576	Juvenile delinquency	674, 738
Ethical ideals	577	Taboos	784
Social control	626		

868 TRANSMISSION OF SKILLS--acquisition of language; teaching children to walk and swim; techniques for inculcating manual dexterity and technological skills; teaching and learning of economic skills appropriate to each sex; informal instruction in occupational skills; acquisition of artistic skills (e.g., playing of musical instruments); relative importance of imitation, practice, and instruction in the transmission of skills; etc. See also:

Language	19	Motor habits	516
Fine arts	53	Athletic sports	526
Division of labor by sex	462	Military training	702
Occupational specialization	463	Age at walking and talking	856
Locomotion	481	Formal vocational education	874

869 TRANSMISSION OF BELIEFS--special techniques for the inculcation of beliefs, attitudes and values not covered elsewhere in this section (e.g., supernatural beliefs, beliefs concerning phenomena of the external world); manipulation of anxiety in support of beliefs (e.g., arousing it for motivation, relieving it for reinforcement); role of accident and coincidence in confirming supernatural beliefs (e.g., rain following a rain-making rite, winning a race while wearing a luck charm); extent to which reality testing is inhibited or encouraged in children; etc. See also:

Religious beliefs	77	Types of religious experience	781
Beliefs about nature and man	82	Formal religious instruction	794, 872
Theories of disease	753		

---

87 EDUCATION

87 EDUCATION--general statements dealing with several aspects of the more formal and institutionalized aspects to the educational process, especially instruction conducted in schools, by specialized tutors, or through formal apprenticeship. For informal education see 86.

871 EDUCATIONAL SYSTEM--degree of development and elaboration of formal education; prevalent types of educational specialization (e.g., schools, tutors, apprenticeship); source of support of teachers and educational institutions (e.g., fees from students, ecclesiastical aid, private gifts and endowments); systematization of education (e.g., local school boards, state educational agencies, voluntary organizations of educational administrators); degree of standardization as to levels, policies, and curricula; primary objectives of

formal education (e.g., piety, morality, citizenship, vocational skills, intellectual leadership); diffusion of education (e.g., educational statistics); etc. See also:

Literacy	212	Reformatories	738
School buildings	346	Philanthropic foundations	741
Public support of education	658	Sunday schools	794

872 ELEMENTARY EDUCATION--tutorial education; primary schools (e.g., private, parochial, public); periods of instruction (e.g., terms, vacations, hours per day, days per week, weeks per year, years required for graduation); compulsory or voluntary attendance; objectives (e.g., universal literacy); curriculum (e.g., subjects and their progression); grading and advancement; educational aids (e.g., textbooks, stationery, blackboards); ceremonial (e.g., graduation); special institutions for very young children (e.g., nursery schools, kindergartens); etc. See also:

Books and writing materials	21	Ethical ideals	577
Religious beliefs	77	Civics	641
Traditional history	173	Arithmetic	803
Reading, writing, and spelling	212	Ethnogeography	823
School buildings	346	Informal transmission of social norms	867
Music	533	Teachers	875

873 LIBERAL ARTS EDUCATION--existence, number, and variety of institutions on the secondary and college levels devoted to instruction in the liberal arts; special objectives (e.g., inculcation of aristocratic ideals, preparation for democratic leadership, refinement of personal tastes, preparation for rational choice of careers); sources of financial support; administration; scholarships; curricula; courses and terms; educational aids (e.g., libraries); grading and advancement; degrees; ceremonial (e.g., commencement); student organizations; extracurricular activities (e.g., sports, politics, debating); special institutions (e.g., finishing schools, adult education); etc. See also:

Fine arts	53	Esthetic ideals	517
Humanistic studies, philosophy, and science	81	Public lectures	544
Ideas about nature and man	82	Student uprisings	664
Cultural participation	184	Mathematics	803
Libraries	217		

874 VOCATIONAL EDUCATION--institutionalized vocational apprenticeship (e.g., skills thus taught, terms and conditions of apprenticeship); number and variety of educational institutions specialized for vocational training; general types (e.g., trade schools, correspondence schools, professional schools); special types (e.g., barber schools, secretarial schools, radio schools, police schools, social work schools, business schools, journalism schools, agricultural schools, military schools, art schools, normal schools, engineering schools, divinity schools, law schools, medical schools, graduate schools); sources of support; administration; courses and curricula; degrees; facilities; etc. See also:

Occupational specialization 463   Physicians 759
On-the-job training 466   Priesthood 793
Craft guilds 467   Applied science 816
Lawyers 693   Informal transmission of skills 868

875 TEACHERS--number of general and specialized teachers; degree of training and proficiency; social status of teachers (e.g., prerogatives, disabilities); mode of selection; fees and salaries; tenure and advancement; degree of academic freedom; organization (e.g., associations, unions); extracurricular activities (e.g., research, community activities); etc. See also:

Government pensions 657   Normal schools 874

876 EDUCATIONAL THEORY AND METHODS--dominant and alternative theories of education; favored methods of instruction (e.g., collective recitation, rote memorizing, systematic classification, case analysis); system of rewards (e.g., praise, prizes); prevalent and eschewed methods of punishment (e.g., ridicule, corporal punishment, deprivation of privileges); special techniques for handicapped and backward pupils; educational psychology; examining and testing methods; use of visual and auditory aids, degree of individuation in instruction (e.g., cultivation of uniformity, encouragement of independence and initiative); educational experiments and innovations (e.g., progressive education); etc. See also:

Informal techniques of instruction 86   Social control 626
Evidence on habit formation 153   Ethnopsychology 828
Educational motion pictures 546

---

88 ADOLESCENCE, ADULTHOOD, AND OLD AGE

88 ADOLESCENCE, ADULTHOOD, AND OLD AGE--general statements dealing with several aspects of the age-graded statuses and associated activities in the individual life cycle from puberty to old age.

881 PUBERTY AND INITIATION--ideas, beliefs, and practices associated with first emissio seminis and first menstruation; rites of passage at or near puberty; prevalence of special initiation rites for each sex; ceremonial sponsors; function and purpose of ceremonial; mystery and seclusion; taboos; ordeals and tests; inculcation of secret lore; special instruction in sex life; ideas of death and rebirth; etc. See also:

Age at puberty 145   Artificial kin relationships 608
Mutilation 304   Concept of reincarnation 775
Masks 532   Taboos 784
Bullroarers 534   Religious confirmation 795
Age-grades 561   Religious ceremonial 796
Initiation into clubs and secret societies 575   Menstruation 841
Tests of marriageability 582   Sex training 864

882 STATUS OF ADOLESCENTS--cultural definition of adolescence (e.g., age limits); beliefs and attitudes about adolescents; prerogatives and disabilities of adolescents; relaxing or tightening of social control for each sex; residence shifts at puberty (e.g., removal of boys to men's house or to home of a grandparent or maternal uncle); readjustment of social relationships; etc. See also:

Age stratification	561	Social control	626
Men's clubs	575	Legal liability	672
Residence rules	591		

883 ADOLESCENT ACTIVITIES--behavior patterns characteristic of adolescents (e.g., dating, loitering); economic activities expected of adolescents; adolescent organizations (e.g., work groups, cliques, bachelors' clubs); adolescent recreations (e.g., expeditions, picnics); adolescent problems (e.g., reactions to social pressures for adult behavior); etc. See also:

Cliques, gangs, clubs, and visiting	57	Mutual aid	476
Welfare organizations	74	Athletic sports	526
Socialization	86	Dancing	535
Education	87	Courtship	584
Slang	192	Juvenile delinquency	674, 738
Loafing and loitering	461	Premarital sex relations	836
Child labor legislation	466		

884 MAJORITY--concept of legal majority if differentiated from puberty; criteria for its attainment by each sex (e.g., age); ceremonies of admission to full manhood or womanhood; readjustments of behavior and social relationships; etc. See also:

Sex	83	Full citizenship status	641
Age at marriage	582	Conception of legal minority	858
Celibacy	589		

885 ADULTHOOD--conception of the prime of life; cultural definition of adult status; differential status and activities of adult males and females prior to and subsequent to marriage; concepts of the ideal man and the ideal woman; etc. See also:

Social mobility	55	Ethical ideals	577
Leisure-time activities	517	Activities of newly married persons	585
Age stratification	561	Celibacy	589
Sex status	562	Civil rights	641

886 SENESCENCE--cultural criteria of senescence and the onset of old age; menopause (e.g., cultural interpretation, adaptive changes in behavior); attitude toward growing old (e.g., resignation, simulation of youth); prescriptions for longevity and rejuvenation; preparations for old age (e.g., insurance); retirement from active life (e.g., gradual, at a prescribed retirement age); etc. See also:

Physical senescence	145	Attitude toward death	761
Insurance	456	Menstruation	841

887 ACTIVITIES OF THE AGED--regimen of the aged (e.g., diet, exercise, rest); economic tasks performed by the aged; leisure time activities of the aged; sexuality in old age; professional activities of the aged; other functions and activities of the aged (e.g., ceremonial, political); etc. See also:

Domestic authority of the aged 59   Educational and disciplinary functions
Authentic cases of extreme longevity 165   of grandparents 603

888 STATUS AND TREATMENT OF THE AGED--cultural definition and explanations of old age; idealized and derogatory evaluations of old age; conception of the ideal old man and old woman; symbols and synonyms for age and longevity; prerogatives and disabilities of the aged; special exemptions (e.g., from legal sanctions, from taboos); etiquette toward the aged; treatment of the aged (e.g., exploitation, neglect, obedience, respect); support of the aged (e.g., investments, fees for services, annuities, pensions, assistance from relatives); care of the aged; customs of abandoning and killing the aged; etc. See also:

Investment. 454   Polygamy 595
Insurance and annuities 456   Legal liability 672
Age stratification 561   Incidence and relief of old age dependency. . 737
Etiquette 576   Social insurance 745
Status of widows 589   Last favors before death 763
Family relationships 593

INDEX

Abacus, use, 803; description, 405

Abandonment, of aged, 888; of dying, 763; of infants, 847; of sick, 758; criminal, 684

Abduction, of bride, 583; criminal, 674, 683

Ablutions, 515; ritual, 783

Abnormal behavior, 158; conception of, 828; penalties for, 689

Abnormality, physical, 143, 732; ideas about, 826

Abortion, 847; penalties for, 682

Absentee ownership, 423, 427

Abstention, from food, drink, and drugs, 261, 273, 276, 785; sexual, 834

Accidents, conception, cause and treatment of, 752; incidence of, 164, 165; liability for, 672

Accommodations, aircraft, 506; boat, 501; railway, 497; travellers', 485

Accountants and accounting, 451

Accounts, government, 652

Accounts and deposits, bank, 453

Acculturation and culture contact, 177

Accumulation, of food supply, 251; of wealth, 454, 556

Acids, 385

Acquired drives, 152

Acquisition and relinquishment of property, 425

Activities of the aged, 887

Actors, 536; in motion pictures, 546; in radio and television, 207

Actuarial theory and practice, 456

Adaptation, physical, 147

Adat, 671

Addiction, to drugs or alcohol, 158, 733

Address, terms of, 551, 601

Adjustment processes, 154

Adjustments, to disaster, 731; wartime, 722

Administration, colonial, 636; of property, 429; public, 647

Administrative, agencies, 647; law, 671

Adolescence, 882, 883; adulthood and old age, 88

Adolescent activities, 883

Adoption, 597; of slaves, 567

Adornment, 30

Adult education, 873

Adulteration, legal offense, 685

Adultery, 837; penalties for, 684

Adulthood, 885

Advertising, 447

Aeronautic science, 507

Affection, expressions of, 201, 832

Affiliations, cultural, 101

Afterbirth, 844

Afterlife, conceptions of, 775

Aftermath of combat, 727

Age, at creeping, standing, talking, walking, 856; clothing differentials by, 291; differentiation by linguistic styles, 195; at marriage, 582

Age-grading, 561

Age stratification, 561

Aged, activities, 887; dependency, 737; status and treatment, 888

Agency, legal, 676

Ages, mythical, 173, 773

Aggression, control and repression of, 578; definitions of and sanctions for, 683; expressions of, 201; incidence and quality of, 152; control of in children, 865; training, 865

Agrarian movements, 668

Agricultural by-products, 24

Agricultural machinery, 407; manufacture of, 392

Agricultural science, 242

Agricultural tools, 412; manufacture of, 391

Agriculture, 24; government subsidies to, 654

Air conditioning, 354; manufacture of apparatus for, 394

Air force, 707

Air lanes, 487

Air transport, 489, 509; military, 705

Aircraft, 506; industry, 399; operation of, 507

Airfields, 508; military, 712

Airport facilities, 508; availability and location of, 368

Albinism, human, 143, 826; animal, 137, 825; as sacred animal, 778

Alchemy, 822

Alcohol, potable, manufacture of, 274; use of, 273; non-potable, 38

Alcoholic beverages, 273

Alcoholism, 733

Aliases, 551

Aliens, 167; attitudes toward, 186; treatment of, 609; civil status, 641

Allegory, 538

Alliances, international, 648

Almanac, 787, 805

Almsgiving, 735

Alphabets, 212

Altars, 778

Altruism, 577

Ambassadors, 648

Amber, 314

Ambil-anak, 611

Ambition, incidence and quality of, 152

Ambivalence, 152

Amitate, 604

Amnesty, 696

Amok, 158, 579

Amortization, 426, 451

Amulets, 778; wearing of for luck, 777; as preventive medicine, 751; magical, 789

Amusement, 52, 53, 54

Anal humor, 522

Anal reactions, ideas about, 827

Analogy, use of in reasoning, 811

Anarchism, 668

Ancestors, worship of, 769, 771

Anchorites, 792

Anchors, 501

Anesthetics, 752

Angels, 776

Anger, 152

Animal breeding, 23; as a hobby, 523

Animal by-products, 237

Animal energy, as a source of power, 379

Animal husbandry, 23

Animal pens and corrals, 417

Animal racing and fighting, 541

Animal transport, 492; as urban traffic, 363

Animals, legal liability of, 672; as literary characters, 538; as message carriers, 202; ideas about, and native terms for, 825; principal species of, 136; proper names of, 552; taming and domestication of, 231; sacred, 778

Animated cartoons, 546

Animatism, 778

Animism, 771, 774

Anniversaries, 527

Annual cycle, 221

Annuities, 456

Annulment, of marriage, 586

Antagonisms, ingroup, 578

Anthropology, 815; applied, 816

Anthropometry, 141

Anthropomorphism, 771, 776

Anti-aircraft installations, 712

Antidotes, for poison, 752, 278

Antique collecting, 523

Anxiety, incidence and quality of, 152; manipulation of, 869; modes of resolving, 154; as a personality disorder, 158

Apartheid, 563, 656

Aphasia, incidence of, 158; notions about, 828

Aphrodisiacs, 832

Apothecaries, 278

Apparatus, 417

Apparitions, 775

Appetites, drink, 271; food, 261; sexual, 831

Appliances, 416; electrical, 403; heating and lighting, 354

Applied animal science, 232

Applied science, 816

Apprentices, 467, 874

Appropriations, governmental, 652

Aptitude and intelligence tests, 125, 816; results of, 153

Aqueducts, 312

Arbitration, international, 648; judicial, 628, 695; labor, 468

Arboriculture, 245

Archeology, 172; as a study, 814; use of in supplementing field work, 127

Architecture, 341; landscape, 351

Archives, 217

Archivists, 814

Argot, 198

Argument, 578

Arising, time of, 512

Aristocracy, 565

Arithmetical calculations, 803

Armed forces, 70

Armistice, 726

Armor, 713, 714

Arranging a marriage, 584

Arrests, 694; statistics of, 674

Arsenic, deposits, 317

Arson, 685

Art, 53; appreciation of, 517; exhibitions, 543; galleries, 346, 368; lapidary, 306

Art supplies industry, 549

Artificial insemination, in animals, 232; in humans, 842

Artificial kin relationships, 608

Artisans, skilled, 463

Artists, 532

Artists' tools, 413

Asceticism, 785

Ascetics, 792

Assassination, 682

Assault, physical, 683

Assemblies, political, 646

Assignation, 836, 837

Assimilation of ethnic groups, 563

Associations, trade, 441; voluntary, 575; mutual aid, 452

Astrologers, 791

Astrology, 787

Astronomy, 815

Asylum, for mentally ill, 734; places of, 778; for slaves, 567

Atheism, 771

Athletic fields, 345, 367, 542

Athletic sports, 526

Athletics, amateur, 526; professional, 542

Atomic energy, 378

Atonement, 783

Attitudes, 181, 208; ideas about, 828, 829

Attorneys, 693

Auctioning, 437

Auguries, 787

Auricular reactions, notions about, 827

Authority, locus of in household, 592; in extended family, 596; in nuclear family, 594; of military leaders, 701

Authors, 538

Autocracy, 642

Automobile, 493; clubs, 485; industry, 398; shows, 543; as urban traffic, 363

Auxiliary corps, 708

Auxiliary highway services, 495

Avatar, 775

Aviation, 507

Avocation, 523

Avoidance and taboo, definition of, 784; of graves and cemeteries, 769; of mother-in-law, 606; as stereotyped pattern of kinship behavior, 602

Avoidances, food, 262

Avuncular and nepotic relatives, 604

Avunculate, 604

Avunculocal residence, 591

B

Baby talk, 195

Bachelors' clubs, 883

Bachelors, prevalence of, 589

Bad luck, concept of, 777

Bailment, 426

Bakeries, 256; equipment of, 252

Baldness, 142

Ball fields, 542

Ball games, amateur, 526; commercial, 542

Ballets, 535, 545

Balloons, 506, 524

Balloting, 666

Banditry, 579

Bands, migratory, 621; musical, 533

Banking, commercial, 453; temple, 794

Bankruptcy, 426; administration of, 429

Banks, government, 652, 655

Banquets, 574

Baptism, 795; infant, 851

Barbers, 305

Bargaining, collective, 468

Bark cloth, 287

Barns, 343

Barrenness and sterility, incidence and treatment of, 842

Barrio, 621

Bars, 275

Barter, 437

Baseball, 526

Bashfulness, 157, 832

Basis of marriage, 581

Basketry and matting, 285

Bathing, 515

Battles, 726; sham, 541

Bazaars, 443

Beauty, sexual, ideals of, 832

Beauty specialists, 305

Bedding, 513

Beds, 352

Beekeeping, 231

Beggars and begging, 735

Behavior, abnormal, 158; penalties for, 689

Behavior processes and personality, 15

Behavior toward nonrelatives, 609

Bequests, 428

Berserker, 158, 579

Bestiality, 839; penalties for, 684

Betel, 276

Betrothal, 584

Betting, 525

Beverage industries, 274

Beverages, nonalcoholic, 272; alcoholic, 273

Bibliography, 11

Bilinear kin groups, 617

Bilingualism, 191

Billeting, military, 726

Bills of exchange, 452

Biographical materials, 159

Biology, scientific, 815

Bird lime, 223

Birth, 844; control, 842; rates, statistics, 163.

Birthmarks, ideas about, 826

Black markets, 437

Blacksmiths, 326

Blasphemy, 688

Blindness, 732

Blood brotherhood, 608

Blood, conceptions of, 826; groupings, 143; menstrual, 841

Blood-typing, as a field technique, 125

Blowgun, 411

Boasting, 521

Boathouses, 343

Boats, 501; construction of, 396; names of, 552; races, 526, 542

Bodily injuries, 752

Body, ideal proportions of, 826; injuries to, 752; lice, 515; painting of, 302; postures, 516

Body odor, 147

Bonds, corporation, 473; government, 652

Bone, work in, 321; industrial use of, 237

Bookkeeping, 451

Books, publication of, 214

Bootlegging, 548

Boroughs, 632

Borrowing and lending, 426; cultural, 177; government, 652

Botanical gardens, 367

Boundary marks, 423

Bounties, 654

Bourgeoisie, 565

Boycotts, 468

Braiding, 283

Brawls, riots and banditry, 579

Breach of contract, penalties for, 686

Breaches of etiquette, 576; of ethics, 577; of legal norms, 672

Breakwaters, 503

Breathing, ideas about, 827

Breeding, selective, in animals, 232; in plants, 242

Brewing, 273, 274

Bribery, 661, 662, 687

Brick manufacture, 323, 339

Bricks, use of, 333

Bride-price, bride-service, 583

Bridges, 49

Brokers, marriage, 584; stock, 454

Buddhism, 779

Budgets, family, 511; government, 652

Building and construction, building trades, 33

Building equipment and maintenance, 35

Building supplies industry, 339

Buildings, domestic, 342, 343; nondomestic, maintenance of, 358; as property, 423; public, construction of, 653

Bullroarers, 534

Buoys, 502

Burden carrying, 482

Bureaucracy, 647

Burial, time, place, and mode of, 764, 766

Buses, 493; manufacture of, 398; operation of, 494; services of, 365; terminals for, 368, 498

Business, cycles, 458; entrepreneurs, 463; facilities, 366; industrial organization, 47; state operated, 475, 655; structures, 347

Business machines, 405

Businessmen, businessmen's organizations, 441

Buying and selling, 432

C

Cabinet, governmental, 645

Cabinet making, 322

Calculating machines, 405, 803

Calculation, 803; games of, 524; of odds, 525

Calendars, 805; ceremonial, 796

Calisthenics, 526

Calligraphy, 212

Cameras, 416; manufacture of, 395

Camp, military, 712; nomadic, 361

Campaigns, military, 723; political, 665, 666

Camphor, 314

Camping, 484; military, 726

Canals, 487; description of and building, 503; boats, 501; navigation, 502

Candles, 354; religious use of, 788

Candy, consumption, 262; manufacture, 257

Canes, 481

Cannibalism, 266

Canning, 251; industry, 255; machinery, 402

Canoes, 501

Capital, 471

Capital goods industries, 39

Capital punishment, 681

Capitalism, theory of, 471

Captives, as slaves, 567; war, 727

Caravans, 484; routes of, 487

Cardinal points, 823

Caretakers, 357, 358

Carnivals, 541

Carpentry, 335

Carrier birds and animals, 202

Cartels, 477

Cartoons, 532; animated, 546

Carts, 493; as urban traffic, 363

Carving, 531; in the round, 532; of tombstones and monuments, 324

Case records, personal, 159

Caste, 564; loss of, 558

Castration, 304

Casualties, military treatment of, 727

Cataclysms, 731; mythical, 773

Catalepsy, 158; notions about, 828

Catapult, nonmilitary, 406

Cathartics, 757

Cattle, breeding, 23; as source of wealth, 556

Caucus, 665

Celebrations, 527

Celibacy, 589; religious, 793; rules of, 792

Cement, use of, 333; manufacture of, 339

Cemeteries, 764; avoidance of, 769

Cenotaph, 211

Censorship, 656

Census, data, 162; taking of, 659

Ceramic industries, 323

Cereal agriculture, 243

Cereal industry, 256

Ceremonial calendar, 796

Ceremonial, court, 644; license, 786; religious, 796; secular, 527

Ceremonial during infancy and childhood, 852

Chains, 401

Chambers of commerce, 441

Chance, concepts of, 777

Change, cultural, 17

Changeling, 776

Channels, radio and television, 207; regulation, 656

Channels, ship, 487, 503

Chanting, 533

Character, concepts of, 577, 828; national, 181

Charcoal, production of, 314

Charity, 73, 74

Charms, 751, 777, 789, 832

Charts, 102, 487

Chastity, notions about, 831; premarital, 836

Chemical engineering, 381

Chemical industries, 38

Chemical processing machinery, 402

Chewing gum, 261

Chief executives, 643

Chief priests, 793; as local officials, 624

Chiefs, 622; war, 624; exemptions from legal responsibility, 672

Child care, 855

Child labor, 464, 857

Child marriage, 584, 582

Childbirth, 844; difficult and unusual, 845

Childhood, 85; activities, 857; training, 861

Children, 85; adoption of, 597; changes of residence by, 591; desire for, 842; neglect of, penalties for, 684; sex behavior, 864

Children and parents, behavior between, 593

Children-in-law, 606

Chivalry, 562

Choirs, 533

Choreography, 535

Chores, daily, 512

Christening, 553, 852

Christianity, 779

Church, buildings, 346; government support of, 659; organizations, 79

Churches, location of, 368; secular activities of, 794, 797

Cicatrization, 304

Cicisbeism, 548, 837

Circulatory reactions, notions about, 827

Circumcision, 304; rites associated with, 852, 881

Circuses, 541

Cities, 36, 633

Citizenship, 641

City planning, 185, 361

Civic virtue, notions of, 641

Civil and civic registers, 217

Civil defense, 722

Civil engineers, 331

Civil law, 671

Civil rights, 641; deprivations of, 681

Civil service, 647

Civil wars, 669

Clairvoyance, 787

Clan, 618, 621

Class consciousness, 186, 565

Class, social, 56

Classes, 565

Clay, deposits of, 317

Cleanliness training, 863

Clearing houses, 453

Client-patron relationship, 466, 565, 566

Climate, 132

Climbing, 481; as sport, 526, 542

Clips, 414

Cliques, 573; children's, 857; adolescent, 883

Clitoridectomy, 304

Clocks, 405, 805

Clothing, 29

Clothing manufacture, 294

Clowns, 522, 536

Clubhouses, 345; location of, 368

Clubs, 529, 575

Coal, deposits of, 135; mining of, 316; products, 382; uses of, 37

Coast guard, 706

Coastal surveys, 654

Cock fighting, 541

Codes, criminal, 681; legal, 671; signal, 202

Coffee, consumption of, 272; growing of, 245

Cognition, 153

Coiling, in mats and basketry, 285

Coinage, 436

Coitus, 833

"Cold" vs. "hot" classification - see "hot" vs. "cold"

Collaborators, punishment of, 687

Collecting, food, 222

Collective bargaining, 468

Collective farming, 241, 474

Collective ownership of the instruments of production, 471

Colleges, 873

Colonial administration, 636, 645, 648

Colonies, 631, 636

Color, ideas about, 822
Color-blindness, 143
Colostrum, conception of, 853
Coma, notions about, 828
Combat, 72
Combs, description of, 412; manufacture, 303; use, 302
Comedians, 522
Comedy, dramatic, 536
Comic strips, 522
Comments, 114
Commerce, 44, 47
Commercial facilities, availability and location of, 366
Commercialized sports, 542
Commissariat, military, 705
Communalism, 476
Communication, 20
Community, 62; structure, 621
Compass, mensurating, 413; as navigational instrument, 416; use in navigation, 502
Competition, 477
Competitiveness, inculcation of, 866; occurrence of, 157, 476
Compliments, 576
Composition of population, 162
Conception, 842
Concerts, 545
Concubinage, 595
Condiments, 263
Confectionery industries, 257
Confederation, 631, 642
Confession, 783
Confirmation, religious, 794
Confiscation, 425, 651, 681
Conflict, ingroup, 578; personal, 154; prevention of, 626
Conformity, incentives to, 626
Congregations, 794
Conjugal relationships, 58, 59, 833
Conjuring, 789
Consanguinity, 60
Conscience, conception of, 577
Conscientious objectors, 577, 721
Conscription, labor, 651; military, 702
Consecration, 778; of priesthood, 793
Conservation policies, 185
Constitutional types, 142
Constitutions, 642

Construction, 33, 331; public works, 499, 653
Consular service, 648
Consultant, 445
Contact, cultural, 174, 177
Containers, 415
Contests, 524, 525, 526
Continence, 589, 785, 831, 842
Contraception, 842
Contractors, 331
Contracts, 675; penalties for breach of, 686; violations of, 673
Convents, 792
Conversations, 521
Conversion, religious, 781, 797
Cooking, 252
Cooperation, 476
Cooperativeness, inculcation of, 866; occurrence of, 157, 476
Cooperative organization, 474
Copra making, 245
Copyrights, 424
Cordage, 283, 288
Cork, manufacture of, 322
Corporal punishment, 681, 861
Corporate organizations, 473
Corpse, attitude toward, 764
Corruption, political, 662, 667
Corvée, 466, 651
Cosmetics, 302; preparation of, 303
Cosmogony, 773
Cosmology, 772
Cost of living, 511
Costume, 29, 30; for performances, 535, 536
Cottage industries, 438, 463, 472
Cotton, 248; cotton oil, 258, 388
Coughing, ideas about, 827
Councils, 63, 623
Counterfeiting, 436; penalties for, 687
Counting, 802
Coups d'etat, 669
Courage, as an ideal, 577; as a military virtue, 703; inculcation of, 866
Couriers, 202
Court etiquette and personnel, 644

Courthouses, 344
Courts of law and justice, 69
Courtship, 584
Courtyard, 351
Cousins, 605
Couvade, 846
Covenants, 675
Cradles and cradleboards, 352, 854
Craft guilds, 467
Crafts, 28, 32, 33
Cranial deformation, 304; molding, 856
Creation myths, 773
Creator gods, 776
Credit, 45
Credos, 779, 788
Creeping, age at, 145, 856
Cremation, 764
Criers and heralds, 203
Crime, 68, 674
Criminal law, 671
Cripples, 732
Crocheting, 286
Crops, 24
Crutches, 481
Cryptography, 202
Cultivating machines, 407
Cultivation, 241; of fish, 228
Cults, 794; of the dead, 769; medical, 759
Cultural change, 177; ideas about, 829
Cultural goals, 185
Cultural participation, 184
Cultural summary, 105
Culture, characterizations of, 181
Culture hero, 554, 773
Curators, 217
Curfew, 656
Curiosity, incidence of, 152
Currency, 436, 652; controlled, 457
Curses, 578, 754
Custom, 183
Customary law, 671
Customs duties, 651; inspections, 489
Cutting tools, 412
Cybernetics, 815
Cycle, annual, 221
Cyclical trends in culture, 178

D

Daily routine, 512

Dairying, 234

Damages, legal, 681

Dams, 312; government construction of, 653

Dancing, 535; in religious ceremonies, 796; relation of drama to, 536

Day and night, divisions of, 805; ideas about, 821

Dead, communication with, 787; cult of, 769; disposal of, 764, 766; marriage of, 588; realm of, 775

Deaf-mutism, 732

Death, 76; myths about origin of, 773

Death rates, 165

Debates, public, 544

Debits and credits, accounting of, 451

Debt, public, 652; slavery, 567

Debts, 426; enforcement of, 686

Decision-making within social groups, general statements, 571

Decoration, interior, 353

Decorative art, 531

Decorum, 576, 834

Deeds, property, 423

Defecation, ideas about, 827; postures in, 514

Defectives, 732; as wards, 429

Deflation, 458

Defloration, 833; rites, 585

Deformed infants, 845, 847

Deformities and defects, bodily, 732

Deification, 769, 776

Delinquency, 674, 738

Deme, 621

Democracy, 642

Demography, 16

Demons, 776

Dental ailments, 164

Dentistry, 757

Dentists, 759

Dependencies, territorial, 636

Dependency, 736

Depilation, 302

Depression, economic, 458; mental, 152

Derision, expressions of, 201

Descent, rule of, 611

Descriptive somatology, 142

Desertion, marital, 586; military, penalties for, 687

Detergents, manufacture of, 388

Development and maturation, 856

Deviant mortuary practices, 766

Devils, 776

Diagnosis, medical, 755, 757

Dialects, 197

Diary, keeping of, 538

Diet, 262; adequacy of, 146; of infants and nursing mothers, 846, 853

Difficult and unusual births, 845

Diffusion, 171, 177

Digestion, theories of, 827

Digging tools, 412

Dikes, 312, 731

Diplomacy, 648

Dirges, 533

Disasters, 731

Discipline, of children, 861; in armed forces, 703; religious, 794

Disease, statistics of, 164; treatment of, 75; animal, 231

Disposal, of garbage, waste and sewage, 364

Dissemination of news and information, 203

Distance, ideas about, 822

Distilling, 273, 274

Distributional evidence, 171

Divination, 787

Divine kingship, 643

Diviners, 791

Diving equipment, 293, 481, 526

Divorce, 586

Doctors, 759

Dogma, 779

Doles, 735

Dolls, 524

Domestic animals, 231; servants, 463; service, 357

Domestic trade, 438

Downward mobility, 558

Dowry, 583

Draftsmanship, 341, 532

Drainage, systems, 312; of highways, 491

Drama, 536; religious, 796

Drawing, 532

Dreams, 159; interpretation of, 787; ideas about dreaming, 828

Dress, 29; accessories to, 293

Drink, drugs and indulgence, 27; offering, to visitors, 574

Drinking, establishments, 275; etiquette in, 576; social, 574; songs, 533

Drives and emotions, 152; ideas about, 828

Droughts, 132, 731

Drug addiction and alcoholism, 733

Drugs, 276; manufacture of, 278

Drums, 534

Drunkenness, 276, 733; penalties for, 689

Dualism, in supernatural beings, 776, 812; in nature, 772

Duels, as entertainment, 541; in ingroup antagonisms, 578; in warfare, 726

Dwellings, 342

Dyes, manufacture and use, 386

Dying, 763

Dynastic lists, 173

E

Ear piercing, 304, 852

Earth moving, 332, 483; machinery, 406

Earthquakes, 133, 731; ideas about, 823

Eating, 26; etiquette in, 264

Eating utensils, description, 412; use, 264; manufacture, 391

Ecclesiastical organization, 79

Echoes, beliefs about, 822

Eclipses, ideas about, 821

Ecology, 13; urban, 361

Economic activities, 47

Economic theory, 815

Economy, productive capacity, 433

Education, 87; church, 794; public, 658; elementary, 872

Educational facilities, 346; availability and location of, 368

Educational system, 871

Educational theory and methods, 876

Election, 666

Electric, lights, 354; power, 377; stoves and furnaces, 354

Electrical engineering, 377, 403; installation, 337; machines and appliances, 403; supplies industry, 393

Electricity, 377; notions about, 822

Elevators, 406

Elimination, 514

Elites, 571

Elopement, 583

Embalmers, 767

Embalming, 764

Embargoes, 439

Embezzlement, 685

Embraces, 832

Embroidery, 294, 531

Emetics, 757

Emigration, 167

Emotions, 152; concept of, 828

Employment and labor supply, 46

Endogamy, caste, 564; local, 591; kin group, 61

Endowments, philanthropic, 741

Energy and power, 37; atomic, 378; conceptions of, 822

Engagements, marital, 584

Engineering, chemical, 381; civil and structural, 331; electrical, 377, 403; mechanical, 401; military, 711

Engines, description of, 40; manufacture of, 39

Engraving, 531

Entertainment, 54; of visitors, 574

Entrails, industrial use of, 237; divinatory use of, 787

Entrepreneurs, 463, 472

Epicures, 261

Epidemics, occurrence of, 164, 731; prevention of, 744

Epilepsy, 158; ideas about, 828

Equipment and maintenance of buildings, 35

Erosion, 134

Eschatology, 775

Espionage, peacetime, 648; wartime, 687, 708, 726

Esprit de corps, 703

Esthetic ideals and principles, 517

Ethics, 577; and religion, 771, 779; theoretical systems of, 812

Ethnic stratification, 563

Ethnoanatomy, 826

Ethnobotany, 824

Ethnocentrism, 186

Ethnogeography, 823

Ethnometeorology, 821

Ethnophysics, 822

Ethnophysiology, 827

Ethnopsychology, 828

Ethnoscience, 82

Ethnosociology, 829

Ethnozoology, 825

Ethos, 181

Etiquette, 576; court, 644; drinking, 273; eating, 264

Eugenics, 842, 847

Eunuchs, 839

Euphemisms, usage of, 195

Euthanasia, 732, 734, 888

Evangelism, religious, 797

Evil eye, 753, 754

Evolution, cultural, 178

Exact knowledge, 81

Exchange, 43; foreign, 457; of names, 553; marriage by, 583; medium of, 436; of services, 476; transactions, 437

Exchanges, stock and produce, 455

Excise taxes, 651

Excommunication, 794, 795

Excretion, 514

Execution of justice, 696

Executioner, 693

Executions, 541, 696

Executive household, 644

Executives, business, 47, 473; governmental, 63, 64

Exercise, forms of, 526

Exhibitionism, sexual, 839; in infants and children, 864

Exhibitions, 543

Exhumation, 765

Exogamy, local, 591; caste, 564; kin group, 61

Exorcism, 755, 789

Exploitation, political, 661

Exploitative activities, 31

Exploring expeditions, 484; government, 654

Explosives, manufacture of, 389

Exports, 439

Exposition, 543

Express, railway, 497

Extended family, 596

Extension services, 654; agricultural, 242

Extortion, 685

Extramarital sex relations, 837

F

Fable, 538

Fabrics, woven, 286; nonwoven, 287

Facial reactions, interpretations of, 827

Factories, 348

Fair trade agreement, 435, 477

Fairs, local, 543

Fakirs, 791

Falconry, 223, 224, 231

Family, 59

Family relationships, 593

Famines, prevalence of, 731

Farm implements, 412

Farming, 23, 24

Farting, 514

Fashions, change in, 178; in dress, 291

Fasting, 785

Fate, conception of, 777

Fatigue, ideas about, 828

Fauna, 136

Fear, expressions of, 201; incidence and quality of, 152

Feasts, mortuary, 765; bridal, 585; ceremonial, 796; secular, 527; as hospitality, 574

Featherwork, 287

Felonies, 68, 673

Felting, 287

Feminism, 562, 668

Fences, 351, 417

Fertility, 842

Fertilizer, industry, 387; use of, 241

Festivals, 527; religious, 796
Fetishes, 778
Feudalism, 421, 631, 642
Feuding, 578, 627, 628
Fiction, 538
Field data, 117
Field methods, 12
Fighting, 578, 726; among children, 857
Film industry, 546
Finance, 45; public, 652
Fine arts, 53; government support
    of, 658
Fines, 681; as public income, 651
Fire, 372
Fire protection services, 368, 659
Fire regulations, 656, 659
Fire-walking, 789
Fireplaces, 354
Firewood, gathering of, 313
Fireworks, 389; display of, 541
Fish, species, 136
Fisheries, 228
Fishing, 226; gear used in, 227
Flags, in communication, 202, 502;
    national, 186; of truce, 726
Floods, 133, 731; mythical, 773
Flora, 137
Floriculture, 247
Flower arrangement, 353
Folk medicine, 755, 757
Folktales, 538; texts, 539
Folkways, 183
Food, consumption of, 26; containers
    for, 415; division of products in
    food-getting activities, 22, 23, 24;
    offering of, to visitors, 574; quest,
    22; taboos, 26, 784; catering, 265;
    preparation, 252; processing, 25
Food service industries, 265
Forage crops, 246
Foreign advisors, 645, 648
Foreign aid programs, 648
Foreign exchange, 457; trade, 439
Foreign policy, 648
Foreigners, attitude toward, 186, 609
Foresight, 185
Forest fires, 731
Forest products, 314
Forestry, 313; government re-
    search in, 654
Forests, distribution of, 137, 311;
    national and state, 659

Fornication, 684
Forts, 712
Forums, public, 544
Fossils, 133
Fosterage, 608, 853
Fowling, 223
Fowls, 136; domesticated, 235
Fraternities, 575
Fraud, 685
Freight services, 497, 505;
    by air, 509
Friendship, 572
Frigidity, 833
Frogging, 224
Fruits, growing of, 245
Frustration, 154
Fuels, 372, 375
Function, 182
Funerals, 764, 766; secondary, 765
Fur, industrial use of, 237;
    preparation of, 281
Furnaces, 354, 394
Furniture, 352; arrangement of, 353;
    manufacture of, 322

G

Gaits, 481
Gambling, 525; church, 794;
    establishments, underworld,
    548; inveterate, 738
Game laws, 22
Games, 524
Gang wars, 579
Gangs, 573; children's 857, 883
Garb, 29
Garbage, disposal of, 364
Gardens, 351; flower, 247
Garments, 29; cleaning, repairing,
    and preservation, 296
Gas, 375, 382; wells, 315
Gates, 351, 417
Genealogical kinship charts, 601
Genealogies, 173
Genealogists, 814
General character of religion, 771
General sex restrictions, 834
General tools, 412
Genetics, 143
Genitals, ideas about, 826; mutila-
    tion of, 304
Geodetic surveys, 13, 654

Geographical, location, 131;
    lore, 823
Geography, 13
Geology, 133, 134, 135
Geophagy, 261
Gerontocracy, 561, 642
Gerrymandering, 665
Gestures and signs, 201; in art,
    53; in numeration, 802; sug-
    gestive, 832
Ghosts, notions about, 774, 775;
    ghost dance, 668, 769
Gift giving, 431; of property, 425;
    exchange of, in marriage, 583
Glass manufacture, 323
Glossary, 104
Gloves, wearing of, 291
Glue, manufacture, 381
Goals, cultural, 185
Godparents, 608
Gods, 776; as literary characters,
    538
Goggles, snow, 293
Gossip, 521, 626
Government, 65; lotteries, 525;
    insurance organizations, 456;
    military, 727; officials, 463, 647;
    enterprises, 655; regulation, 656
Graft, 661, 667
Grains, 243, 256
Grammar, 193
Grandparents and grandchildren, 603
Gratification and control of hunger,
    261
Graves, 764; avoidance of, 769
Greetings, 576
Grooming, 515; of domesticated
    animals, 231
Ground combat forces, 704
Grounds, 351
Group solidarity, 571
Groups, age, 561; cooperative work,
    476; kin, 61; social, 57; socially
    ranked, 56
Growth, 145, 856
Guano, use, 237; collecting, 317
Guardian, spirits, 776; quest for, 787
Guardianship, 429
Guest house, structure, 343; as travel
    service, 485
Guests, 574; accommodations for, 485

Guides, 485

Guilds, merchant, 441; craft and labor, 467

Guilt, sense of, 783

Gunpowder, 389, 713, 719

Guns, 411, 713, 719

Gunsmiths, 326

H

Habit, formation, 153

Habits, ideas about, 828; idiosyncratic, 157

Hacienda, ownership, 471

Hair, growth of, attitude toward, 856; ideas about, 826; styles and care of, 302; description, 142

Hallucination, 158; notions about, 828

Hammock, 352

Handedness, 145, 828

Handicrafts, 463

Hangings, public, 541; as sanction, 681

Harbors, 504

Hardware, 41, 391

Hardware manufacture, 391

Harem, 595

Harvest, 24; celebration, 527

Headhunting, 721, 727

Headmen, 622

Healing, 75

Health and welfare, 74; conception of, 751; public, 657

Hearse, description of, 493

Hearths, 354

Heat, 374

Heating and lighting equipment, 354

Heavens, 772, 775

Heirlooms, 523

Heirs, 428

Hells, 772, 775

Hemophilia, 143

Hepatoscopy, 787

Heralds, 203, 624

Herding, 233

Heresy, 798

Hermaphrodites, 143

Hermits, 792

Hero worship, 769

Heroes, deified, 776

Hides, industrial use of, 237; preparation of, 281

Highways, 491; construction of, 499; construction of, by government, 653; services, 495; transport, 494

Historical reconstruction, 174

Historical research, 127

Historiography, 814

History and culture change, 17

Hoarding, 454

Hobbies, 523; supplies, 549

Holidays, religious, 796; secular, 527

Holy men, 792

Holy war, 721, 798

Home economics, 816

Home industry, 438, 472

Homicide, 682

Homosexuality, 838; organized, 548

Hops, cultivation of, 245

Horoscopes, 787

Horse racing, 541, 542

Hospitality, 574; sexual, 837

Hospitals, 344; clinics, 743

"Hot" vs. "cold" classification, 82; of foods, 261; of diseases, 753

Hotels, 485

House, upkeep of, 356

Household, 592

Household machines and appliances, 404

Housekeeping, 356

Houses, names of, 552

Housewarming, 527

Housing, 362

Human biology, 14

Human energy, as power source, 379

Human nature, concept of, 828

Humanistic studies, 814

Humor, 522

Hunger, 261; ideas about, 827, 828

Hunting and trapping, 224, 225

Husbandry, animal, 23

Hydrographic phenomena, ideas about, 823

Hygiene, conception of, 751; personal, 515; sexual, 833

Hypergamy, 564, 582

Hypnosis, 755; notions about, 828

Hysteria, 158; notions about, 828; religious, 786

I

Idealism, 577, 812

Ideals, 577; cultural, 183

Ideas about nature and man, 82

Identification, 101

Idiots, 732

Idling, 461

Idols, 778

Illegitimacy, 848

Illness, 75

Illumination, 354, 373

Imitation, 861; in learning, 153, 861

Immigration and emigration, 167

Immortality, belief in, 775

Immunity, diplomatic, 648; to disease, 164, 147, 751

Immunization, 751

Impeachment, 687

Imports, 439

Impotence, 833

Impregnation, theory of, 842

Imprisonment, 681

Incantations, 754, 789

Incense, 356, 782

Incest, penalties for, 684; taboos, 835

Incestuous unions, 588

Inclined plane, 401

Income and demand, 434

Income, government, 651; national, 434

Incontinence, 831

Incorporeal property, 424

Indemnity, 681

Independence training, 866

Individual enterprise, 472

Individual ownership, 421

Individual, in relation to society and culture, 156

Individuation and mobility, 55

Industrial areas, 361; entrepreneurs, 463, 472; labor organization, 467; machinery, 402; organization, 47; uses of animal by-products, 237

Industrial structures, 348

Industrialist, 441, 471

Industrialization, 47, 178

Industry, home or cottage, 438, 472

Industry (specialized), aircraft, 399; automobile, 398; beverage, 274; capital goods, 39; chemical, 38; coal products, 382; electrical supplies, 393; fertilizer, 387; iron and steel industry, 327; machine, 392; motion picture, 546; petroleum, 382; railway equipment, 397; recreational and art supplies, 549; rubber, 383; synthetic, 384; tobacco, 277

Infancy and childhood, 85

Infant, betrothal, 584; mortality, 165; sexuality, 864

Infant care, 854; feeding, 853

Infanticide, 847

Infectious diseases, incidence of, 164; treatment of, 757

Inferiority, incidence of, 152

Infibulation, 304

Inflation, 458; of currency, 652

Informal in-group justice, 627; inter-group justice, 628

Informants, 115

Information, dissemination of, 203; gathering of, for press, 204

Ingestion, ideas about, 261, 827

In-group, antagonisms, 578; exaltation of, 186

Inheritance, 428; taxes, 651

Initiation of judicial proceedings, 694

Initiation, puberty, 881; into age grades, 561

Injuries, treatment of, 752

Innovation, 176

Inns, 265, 275, 347, 485

Insane persons, care of, 758; exemptions from legal responsibility, 672

Insanity, incidence of, 158; treatment of, 755

Insecticides, manufacture of, 38, 278, 314; use, animals, 231; human, 751

Insects, protective measures taken against, 751; incidence of, 136; measures to protect animals from, 231, etc.; paraphernalia worn as protection against, 293; mosquito netting, 513; body lice, 515

Insignia, 301; as prestige symbols, 554; military, 703, 714

Instigation of war, 721

Instincts, 152

Instruments, 41; aircraft, 506; musical, 534; navigation, 416, 502

Insults, 578

Insurance, 456; social, 745

Insurrections, 669

Integration, cultural, 178, 182; personal, 154, 155

Intellectuals, intelligentsia, 517; as a social group, 571

Intelligence tests, 125; results of, 153

Intent, legal definition of, 672

Interaction, social, 571

Inter-community relations, 628

Intercourse, sexual, 833

Interest, 426; on public debt, 652

Interior decoration and arrangement, 353

Internal migration, 166

International relations, 648

Interpersonal relations, 57

Interpreters, selection and use of, 124

Intertribal relationships, 648

Interviewing, 124

Intimidation of gods, 782

Intoxicants, 273

Invalidism, 734

Inventions, 176; as property, 424

Investment, 454

Iron and steel industry, 327

Ironworking, 326

Irredentism, 563, 648

Irregular unions, 588

Irrigation, 312

J

Jails, 697

Jealousy, 152

Jesters, 522

Jewelers, 306; tools, 413

Jewelry manufacture, 306

Jokes, 522

Joking relationships, 602

Judicial authority, 692

Juggling, 524

Juries, 693

Jurisprudence, 671

Jus primae noctis, 585

Justice, 69; as an ideal, 577

Justice, informal in-group, 627; informal inter-group, 628

K

Kaolin, 317

Kava, as a beverage, 272; as a stimulant, 276

Kidnapping, 673

Killing humans, 682

Kin groups, 61

Kin relationships, 602

Kindreds, 612

Kingship, divine, 643

Kinship, 60

Kinship regulation of sex, 835

Kinship terminology, 601

Knitting, 286

Knives, forks, spoons, 412

Knife sheaths, 412

Knots and lashings, 284

Kraal, 351, 361, 592

Kula, 431

L

Labor, 46; division of, between town, country, 438; drafts, 466, 653; levies, 651; by age, 561; by sex, 462

Labor and leisure, 461

Labor organization, 467

Labor relations, 466

Labor supply and employment, 464

Laboratories, chemical research, 381; medical, 742

Labret, 301

Lac, 231, 237

Lace making, 286; embroidery, 531

Lactation, 853

Ladders, 417

Lag, cultural, 182

Laments, 533

Lamps, 354

Land, as property, 423; as source of wealth, 427, 556; clearing of, 241

Land reform, specific, 423

Land transport, 49
Land use, 311; acquisition of, 425
Landlords, absentee, 427
Landscape architecture, 351
Landscaping, 247, 351
Language, 19; ideas about, 191; structure of, 193
Lapidary art, 306
Lashings and knots, 284
Lassos, 233
Latah, 158, 579
Latches, 414
Lathes, 402
Latrines, 343, 514
Laughter, 522
Laundering, 296; appliances, 404
Law, 67; constitutional, 642; international, 648; martial, 722; of property, 421; of sales, 432; of trusts, 429; tax, 651
Laziness, 461
Leadership, in cliques, 573; political, 665, 668; military, 701
Leasehold, 425
Leasing and leases, 427
Leather, 28, 237
Leather industry, 282
Leather, textiles, and fabrics, 28
Lectures, public, 544
Legacies, 428
Legal and judicial personnel, 693
Legal norms, 671; violation of, 672, 673
Legends, 538, 539
Legerdemain, 789
Legislation, child labor, 464; minimum wage, 465
Legislation, financial, 652; labor, 466; public health, 744
Legislative bodies, 646
Legislators, 63, 646
Legitimacy, cultural definitions of, 848
Leisure, 461
Leisure-time activities, 517
Lending, 426
Lens-grinding, 395
Lese majesty, 687
Lessee, and lessor, rights, etc. of, 427
Level (measuring), 413

Levers, 401
Levirate, 587
Lex talionis, 681
Liability, 672
Libations, religious use of, 782
Libel, 683
Liberal arts education, 873
Libraries, 217, 346, 368; government supported, 658
Lice, body, 515
License, orgiastic ceremonial, 786
Licensing, 656
Life and death, theories about, 761
Life expectancy, 165
Life force, notion of, 761, 812
Life history, materials, 159; techniques of interviewing, 124
Life, offenses against, 682
Light, 373
Light and power systems, 365, 377
Lighthouses, 349, 502
Lighting and heating equipment, use of, in home, 354
Lights, portable, 416
Lineages, 613
Linguistic identification, 197
Linguistic studies, 19, 814
Liquor, 273
Liquor business, 274; illicit, 548
Litanies, recitation of, 788
Literacy, 212
Literary, styles, 538; texts, 539
Literati, 517
Literature, 538; research in, 814
Litigation, 691
Litters, 493
Liturgies, recitation of, 788
Livery stables, 495
Living standards and routines, 51; ideal and actual, 511
Loading facilities, aircraft, shipping, 504, 508
Loafing, 461
Loans, 45, 426; by churches, 794
Loans and debts, 426
Lobbying, 664
Local officials, 624
Location, 131
Lochia, 846
Locks, 414
Locomotion, 481

Locomotive works, 397
Lodges, 575
Logic, 811
Logistics, 724
Loitering, 461
Longevity, 165, 888; prescriptions for, 886
Longshoremen, 505
Loquacity, 521
Lots, building, 351
Lotteries, 525
Love, as an emotion, 152; romantic, 831
Love songs, 533
Loyalty, as an ideal, 577
Luck and chance, 777
Lucky numbers, 801
Lullabies, 533
Lumbering, 313; machinery, 402
Luxury, standards of, 511
Lying, 577, 689
Lynching, 578, 627

M

Machine, designing, 401; industries, 392; tools, 402
Machinery, aircraft and boat, 501, 506
Machines, 40
Magazines, 204
Magic, 789; black, 754; love, 832; luck, 777; relations of science, technology and philosophy to, 813; specialists in, 791; therapeutic, 755
Magical, therapy, 751, 755
Magicians and diviners, 791
Mails, 205
Maintenance, of buildings, 35; of nondomestic buildings, 358; of public works, 653; of railway equipment, 496; of roadways, 363, 491
Majority, 884
Maladjustment, 158
Malingering, 461
Malnutrition, 146
Mammals, 136
Man and nature, ideas about, 82
Mana, 778
Managerial personnel, 463

Mandrake, 778

Manias, 158

Manipulative mobility, 557

Manners, 264, 576

Manslaughter, 682

Manufacture of explosives, 389

Manufacture of heating and lighting appliances, 394

Manufacture of optical and photographic equipment, 395

Manufacture of toilet accessories, 303

Manufacture of vehicles, 398

Manumission, 567

Map making, 126, 823

Maps, 102; route, 487

Marine gathering, fauna, 226; flora, 222

Marine, hunting, 225; industries, 228; insurance, 456

Marital fidelity, 837; offenses, 684

Maritime customs and regulation, 502

Marketing, 44

Markets, 366, 443

Marriage, 58; regulation, caste, 564; by slaves, 567; of convenience, 557; temporary, 583

Martial law, 722

Martyrs, 798

Masks, 532

Masochism, 158; sexual, 839

Masonry, 333

Mass movements, 668

Masturbation, 839; in infants and children, 864

Match manufacture, 381; use, 372

Materia medica, 278

Mathematics, 803

Mats and basketry, 285

Matter, conceptions of, 822

Maturation, 856; ceremonies, 852

Maturity, 145, 884

Meals, 264

Measures, 80

Measuring machines, 405

Meat packing industry, 253

Mechanics, 401

Medals, as prestige symbols, 554; religious, 788; as protection, 751

Medical, care, 75; personnel, 759; research, 742; therapy, 757

Medicine, 75, 278; men, 756; preventive, 751; research in, 654, 742; socialized, 758

Medium of exchange, 436

Menarche, 145, 841, 881

Mendicant monastic orders, 792

Menopause, 145, 886

Menstruation, 145, 841

Mental states, ideas about, 828

Mercantile business, 441

Mercenaries, 702

Merchandising, 44

Merchant marine, 505

Merchants, 44; guilds, 441

Messages and messengers, 202

Messiahs, 792

Messianic political movements, 668

Metabolism, 147

Metallurgy, 325; non-industrialized, 326

Metals, mining of, 316; nonferrous metal industry, 328; notions about, 823

Metaphysics, 812

Metate, 412

Meteorology, 132, 815, 821

Meteors and meteorites, notions about, 821

Methodology, 12

Metropolis, 361, 633

Midwives, 759; role in childbirth, 844

Migration, 166, 167; seasonal, 221

Military aircraft, 717

Military alliances, 648

Military engineering, 711

Military establishment, 70; government expenditures for, 659

Military government, 727

Military installations, 712

Military operations, 72

Military organization, 701

Military schools, 874

Military technology, 71

Military vehicles, 715

Militia, 701

Milk and milking, 234

Milling machinery, 402

Mills, grain, 256

Mimicry, 536

Mineral resources, 135

Minerals, exploitation of, 315, 316, 317; notions about, 823

Mining and quarrying, 316

Miscarriages, 843

Miscegenation, 144, 563

Miscellaneous building equipment, 355

Miscellaneous building trades, 338

Miscellaneous food processing and packing industries, 258

Miscellaneous government activities, 659

Miscellaneous hardware, 414

Miscellaneous power production, 379

Miscellaneous sex behavior, 839

Miscellaneous structures, 349

Miscellaneous urban facilities, 368

Misdemeanors, 673

Missions, religious, 797

Mnemonic devices, 211

Mobility, social, 55

Mode of marriage, 583

Modeling, 532

Modesty, 291, 834; in elimination, 514; training in, 864, 867

Modification of behavior, 153

Moieties, 616

Monarchy, 642

Monasteries, 792

Money, 436; lending, 45; as a source of wealth, 556; changing, 453

Money lenders, 426

Monogamy, 595

Monopolies, 477; government, 655; prices, 435

Monotheism, 776

Monuments, 211, 764; as structures, 349

Moon, ideas about, 821

Morale, armed forces, 703; civilian, 722

Morality, 577, 779

Morbidity, 164

Mores, 183

Morphology, grammatical, 193

Mortality, 165

Mortars, 412

Mortgages, 426

Mortuary specialists, 767

Motion picture industry, 546

Motivation, 152; concepts of, 828
Motivational research, 208, 816
Motor disturbances, 158
Motor habits, general information,516
Motor transport, 494
Motors, electric, 393, 403;
   gasoline, 398, 399
Mourning, 765
Mulberry, 245, 246, 248
Mummification, 764
Municipalities, 36, 632, 633
Munitions industry, 719
Murder, 682
Museums, 217, 346, 543
Music, 533; in religious cere-
   monies, 796
Musical instruments, 534; techniques of
   playing, 533; technics of playing, 534
Musical and theatrical productions,545
Musicology, 533
Mutilation, 304
Mutiny, 687
Mutual aid, 476
Mutual benefit societies, 456
Mysticism, 771
Mythical beings, 776
Mythology, 773
Myths, texts of, 539

N

Nakedness, attitudes toward, 291
Namedays, 527
Names, animals and things, 552;
   personal, 551; place, 103
Naming and namesakes, 553
Narcotic addiction, 674, 733
Narcotics and stimulants, 276, 278;
   illicit trade in, 548
Narration, oratory 537; literary,538
Nasal reactions, ideas about, 827
National character, 181, 829
National heroes, nationalism aspects,
   186; for status, role aspects, 554;
   if dead and/or deified, 769, 776
National income, 434
Nationalism, 186, 619, 668
Native policy, 657
Native texts, 539
Nativism, 177, 668
Naturalization, 641

Nature, ideas about, 82
Nature worship, 771
Nautical gear, 501
Naval vessels, 716
Navigation, aerial, 507;
   water, 502
Navy, 706
Necromancy, 787
Necrophilia, 839
Neighborliness, 572, 621
Nepotism, political, 661;
   friendship,572; kinship, 602
Netting, 286; use of in hunting
   and fishing, 223, 224, 226
Neuroses, 158; explanations of,828
News, dissemination of, 203
Newspapers, 204
Nicknames, 551
Night clubs and cabarets, 547
Night and day, divisions of,805;
   ideas about, 821, 822
Noblesse oblige, 576
Nomadism, 221, 233, 361
Nonalcoholic beverages, 272
Nonferrous metal industries, 328
Nonfulfillment of obligations,686
Nonwoven fabrics, 287
Normal garb, 291
Norms, 183; legal, 671; social
   transmission of, 867
Nuclear family, 594
Nudity, 291
Nuisances, commission of, 689
Numbers, lucky and unlucky, 777,
   801
Numbers and measures, 80
Numeration, 802
Numerology, 801
Nuns, 792
Nuptials, 585
Nurseries, 854, 855; as welfare
   institutions, 746, 747
Nurses, 743, 759
Nursing, of infants, 853
Nutrition, 146

O

Oaths, social control, 626; religious, 782; allegiance, 641; legal,
   627, 695; profane, 195, 578

Obesity, 142
Objets d'art, 353
Obscenity, 831
Observational role, 123
Observatory, 346
Obstetrics, 844, 845
Occultism, 789
Occupational specialization,463;
   deities, 776
Oceans, ideas about, 823
Ocular reactions, notions about, 827
Offenses against life, 682; against
   the person, 683; against the state,
   687
Offenses, common and rare,674;
   and sanctions, 68
Officials, government, 64, 463;
   local, 624; political hierarchy
   of, 631
Oil, edible, processing, 258
Oil and gas wells, 315; refining,
   382
Oil pipelines, 315
Ointments, use of, 302; prepara-
   tion, 303
Old age dependency, 737;
   preparation for, 886
Oligarchy, 642
Omens, 787; of death, 763
Ontogenetic data, 145
Opera, 545
Opera houses, availability and
   location of, 368
Operations, surgical, 752
Opium, as a crop, 249; use of,
   276, 278; addiction to, 733;
   dens, 548
Optical equipment, manufacture
   of, 395
Optical instruments, 416
Oracles, 791; use of, 787
Oral reactions, ideas about, 827
Oratory, 537
Orchestras, 533, 545
Ordeal, trial by, 627, 695
Ordeals, as independence train-
   ing, 866
Ordering of time, 805
Ordinances, 671
Ordnance, 713
Ores, refining and smelting of, 325
Organization of results, 128

Organized ceremonial, 796
Organized vice, 548
Orgasm, 83
Orgies, 786
Orientation, 10
Ornament, 301
Orphans, as dependent, 736
Orthographies, 104
Ostracism, 626
Outbuildings, 343
Outlawry, 681
Ovens, 252, 354
Ownership and control of capital, 471
Ownership, types of, 421

P

Pack animals, 492
Pageants, 527, 541
Pain, ideas about, 828
Paint and dye manufacture, 386, 549
Painters, house, 338
Painting, 531, 532; of buildings, 353, 358; body, 302; war, 714
Palaces, 344, 644
Paleontology, 133
Pantheism, 779
Pantheon, 776
Pantomime, 535, 536
Paper hangers, 338
Paper industry, 289
Parades, 541
Paraphernalia, 293; dancing, 535; religious, 793, 796
Pardons for crimes; reasons for, etc., 696
Parents-in-law and children-in-law, 606
Parishes, 632, 794
Parks, municipal, 367; national and state, 529
Parliaments, 646
Paroles, 696
Parricide, 682
Parties, political, 665; social, 574
Partnerships, 472
Parturition, 844
Passive resistance, 668
Passports, 486

Passwords, 192
Pastimes, 517, 523
Pastoral activities, 233
Patents, 424
Paternity, theory of, 842
Paths, 363, 487
Patriotic celebrations, 541; occasions, 527
Patriotism, 186, 619, 668
Patterns, cultural, 18
Pawn shops, 426
Peacemaking, 728
Peasantry, 369, 565
Peat, 314
Pedestrians, 363
Pemmican, 251, 262
Penalties, 68
Penance, 783
Penology, 681
Pensions, 745; civil service, 657; military, 729; private business, 466
Peonage, 566
Perception, acuity of, 151; ideas about, 828
Perfumes, 302, 303
Perjury, 687
Permits for travel, 486
Persecution, 186; religious, 798
Personal hygiene, 515
Personal names, 551
Personality, 15; ideas about, 828; development, 155; disorders, 158; traits, 157; basic type, 157
Personality types, statuses adapted to, 554
Petroleum and coal products industries, 382
Petroleum, 135, 315; industries, 382
Petting, 832, 839
Phallicism, 831; religious, 786
Pharmaceuticals and pharmacology, 278
Pharmacists, 278
Philanthropic foundations, 741
Philanthropy, 741
Philatelic equipment, and stamps, 549; philately, 523
Philosophy, 812; of science, 813; and theology, 779

Phobias, 158
Phonemics and phonetics, 194, 195
Phonograms, 212
Phonographs, 216, 405; phonograph records, 216; publishers, 214
Phonology, 194
Photography, 215; equipment and supplies, 395
Phratries, 615
Physical abnormalities, incidence of, 143, 164; ideas about, 826
Physical types, ideal, 826
Physical typology, 142
Physiological data, 147
Physiology, ideas about, 827
Picketing, 468, 664
Picture writing and pictographs, 212
Pier and breakwater construction, 503
Piers, 504; availability and location of, 368
Piety, 781
Pigmentation, skin, notions about, 826
Pigments, 386, 549
Pilgrimages, 484, 788
Pillory, 681
Pins, 291, 414
Pipe, 414; manufacture of, 391
Pipes, 276
Piracy, 579, 721; sanctions for, 685
Pisciculture, 228
Pisé de terre, 333
Place names, 103
Plaiting, mats, 285; for cordage, 283
Planets, ideas about, 821
Planning, social, 185; city, 361
Plantation, 24; ownership, 471
Planting, 241; machines, 407
Plants, breeding of, 242; ideas about, and native terms for, 824
Plasterers, 338
Plastics industries, 384
Play, 52; children's, 857
Playgrounds, 367
Plays, as fine art, 536; as commercialized entertainment, 545, 546
Playthings, 524
Playwrights, 536
Plows, 407
Plumbing, 336; plumbing fixtures, 414

Plutocracy, 642
Pocketbooks, 293, 415
Poetry, 538
Poison, 278; antidotes for, 752; use of in hunting and fishing, 224, 226
Poisonous plants, knowledge of, 824
Police, 625; government expenditure for, 659
Political authority, system of, 642
Political behavior, 66
Political divisions, 63
Political intrigue, 662
Political machines, 667
Political movements, 668
Political offenses, 687
Political parties, 665
Political riots, 579, 668
Political theory, 814
Polls, of public opinion, 208
Polygamy, 595
Polytheism, 779
Population, 16; policy, 168
Pornography, 522, 831
Port facilities, 504
Portaging, 502
Porters, 482
Portraiture, 532
Possessions, 42
Post offices, 205, 344, 368
Post stations, 495
Postal system, 205; government, operation of, 655
Post-mortem examinations, 763
Postnatal care, 846
Posture, 516; during sleep, 513; during elimination, 514; in the arts, 535, 536; during sexual intercourse, 833
Potlatch, 431, 556
Pottery, 415; manufacture of, 323
Poultry, raising of, 235
Poverty, 735
Power development, 371
Power and energy, 37
Power generating machines, 402
Power and light systems, municipal, 265
Power relationships, 66
Practical preparations, 122
Prayer, 782; mechanical, 788
Preaching, 793

Precocity, reaction to, 857
Pregnancy, 843
Prejudice, 56, 186
Premarital sex relations, 836
Prenatal care, 843
Preschool education, 872
Preservation and storage of food, 251
Press, 204
Pressure groups, 664
Pressure politics, 664
Prestige, 554
Preventive medicine, 751
Price cutting; price agreements, 477
Price and value, 44, 435
Priesthood, 793
Primaries, political, 665
Primary drives, 152
Primary groups, 571
Prime minister, under constitutional monarchy, 643; under absolute monarchy, 645
Primogeniture, 428
Printing, 213; machines, 402; supplies, 218
Prisoners, 697; war, 727
Prisons, 344
Prisons and jails, 697
Privacy, 362
Private welfare agencies, 747
Privateering, 721
Privileges, class status, 55, 56
Probability, ideas about, 777
Probate law, 428
Processing of basic materials, 32
Processions, religious, 788; secular, 541
Procreation, 842
Produce exchanges, 455
Production figures, national, 433; regional, 438
Production and supply, 433; local and regional specialization, 438
Profane and sacred, differentiation of, 771
Profanity, 195
Professions and professionals, 463
Progress, concept of, 185; socio-cultural trends, 178

Proletariat, 565
Promiscuity, 836, 837
Propaganda, 208
Property, 42; offenses, 685; respect for, instilling of, 867; taboos, 784; taxes, 651; in movables, 422
Property system, 421
Prophecies, 787
Prophets, 792
Prophylaxis, 751
Propitiation, 782
Propriety, 576
Prose, 538
Prosperity and depression, periods of, 458
Prosthetic devices, 732
Prostitution, 548; penalties for, 684; religious and temple, 786, 793
Proverbs, 538
Provinces, 635
Psycholinguistics, 196
Psychological tests, 15, 125
Psychological warfare, 723
Psychoses, 158
Psychotherapy, 755; psychotherapists, 756
Puberty and initiation, 881; rites of passage prior to, 852
Public administration, 647; safety, 659; utilities, 365; welfare, 657; works, 653; assistance, 746
Public baths, 368
Public education, 658
Public finance, 652
Public health and sanitation, 744
Public lectures, 544
Public opinion, 208
Public service, 663
Public structures, 344
Publishing, 214
Pulley, 401
Pulp, 289; pulp mills, 313
Punishment, 681
Pure science, 815
Purification and expiation, 783
Purification, religious rites, 783
Puzzles, 524

Q

Quarantine, 744
Quarreling, 578; among children, 857

R

Race, mixture, 144; prejudice, 186, 563; riots, 579; notions about, 829
Racial amalgamation and assimilation, 563; affinities, 144
Racing, 526, 541
Radar, 207, 507, 718
Radio and television, 207
Rail transport, 497
Railway equipment industry, 397
Railways, 496; construction, 499
Rain gear, 292
Rainfall, 132
Rainmaking, 789
Ramages, 612
Rape, 839; penalties for, 684
Rationalization, 811
Rationing, 434, 656; of food, 262
Reading, incidence of, 212; hobby, 523; tastes, 517
Real property, 423
Reason, conception of, 828
Rebirth, ideas about, 881
Reburial, 765
Recipes, 252, 424
Recitation, 538; of litanies, 788
Recording and collecting, 126
Records, financial, 451; historical, 175; mnemonic, 211; sound, 216
Recreation, 52, 517; supplies, 549; facilities, 368, 529; structures, 345
Recruitment and training, 702
Refining, of minerals, 325, 382
Reflections, beliefs about, 822
Reformatories, 738
Refrigeration, 251; industry, 254
Regency, 643
Regional differences, general, 184; for differences in clothing, 29; in food, 262; in housing, 342
Regulation of marriage, 582
Regulation of travel, 486

Reincarnation, belief in, 775
Relatives, 60
Relaxation, 461, 512
Relief agencies, fraternal and religious, 746; government, 73, 74, 657
Religion, 77, 78, 79
Religious and educational structures, 346
Religious experience, 781; foundations, 741; instruction, 869, 872, 794; intolerance, 798; offenses, 688; practices, 78
Remarriage, 587
Renting and leasing, 427, 434
Repairs, see service industries or general services, 445; building, 356, 358; clothing, 296; boat, 396; for repair of other items see the appropriate descriptive category
Representative art, 532
Reproduction, 84
Reproductive taboos, 784
Research and development, 654, 815, 816
Reservations, ethnic group, 657
Reservoirs, 312, 653
Residence rules, 591
Residential areas, 361
Resorts, 528, 529
Respiratory reactions, ideas of, 827
Rest, 461; children's habits of, 857
Rest days and holidays, 527
Restaurants, 265
Resthouses for pilgrims, 485
Resurrection, ideas about, 775
Retail businesses, 444; marketing, 443
Retainers, of executive household, 644
Retirement, from active life, 886; military, 701; pensions, 745
Revelation and divination, 787
Revenue, public, 651; statistics of, 652
Revivalism, religious, 786
Revolution, 669
Revolutionary movements, 668

Rice, as a crop, 243
Riddles, 524
Ridicule, as sanction, 681; as expression of ingroup antagonism, 578; social control, 626
Riding, 526; animals, 492
Rights, property, 421
Riots, 579
Rites, of passage, 561, 852, 881; purification, 783; scatological, 514
Ritual, 788; offenses, 688
Ritualism, 771
Rivalry, among children, 865; between moieties, 616; sports, 526
Rivers, navigable, 487, 133
Rochdale plan, 474
Roles, dramatic, 536; social, 554
Romantic love, 581, 831
Routes, 487
Routines of living, 51
Royalty, 565, 643
Rubber industry, 383
Rubber, plantation, 249; wild, 314
Rule of descent, 611
Rumor, 203
Rural life, 369

S

Sacrament, 788
Sacred, books, 779; music, 533; objects and places, 778
Sacred and profane, differentiation of, 771
Sacrifice, religious, 782
Saddles, description and use of, 492
Sadism, 158; sexual, 839
Safe conduct, 486
Safes, safe deposit boxes, 454
Safety, public, government expenditure for, 659
Sagas, 538
Sailing, 501, 505
Saints, 776
Salaries, 465
Sales and selling, 43, 44
Salt, extraction of, 317; deposits, 135
Salutations, 576
Salvage, 502
Salvation, concepts of, 783

Sanatorium, 734

Sanctions, social, 68; supernatural, 784

Sanctity, conception of, 778

Sanctuary, places of, 778

Sanitary facilities, 364, 514, 515

Sanitation and public health, 744

Saving and investment, banks, 454

Sawmills, 313

Scaffolds, 417

Scales, 405

Scapegoats, ethnic, 186; religious,
  783

Scapulimancy, 787

Scarecrows, 241

Scarification, 304

Scatological rites, 514

Schedules, railway, 497; sailing,
  505; flight, 509

Schools, 87, 346; availability and
  location of, 368

Schools, parochial, 872; Sunday, 794

Science, applied, 816; pure, 815;
  aeronautic, 507; applied, government research in, 654; pure, government support of, 658

Scientific method, 813

Screw, 401, 414

Scribes, 212

Sculpture, 532

Sea lanes, 487

Seances, as therapy, 755

Seasonal activities, 221

Seasons, 132; reckoning of, 805

Seaweed, collecting, 222, 228

Secondary marriages, 587

Secret societies, 575

Sects, 795

Secular festivals, 527; pageants, 541

Securities, corporate, 473

Seduction, 836; penalties for, 684

Seers, 791

Selling, 432

Semantics, 196

Senescence, 145, 886

Sensation and perception, 151;
  conception of, 828

Sensory reactions, notions about, 827

Serfdom and peonage, 566

Servants, domestic, 357; as members
  of household, 592

Service industries, 445

Services, transportation, 48, 49, 50

Settlement houses, 746

Settlement patterns, 361

Settlements, 36, 311, 621

Sex, 83; behavior of children,
  864; training, 864; delinquency, 738; division of labor
  by, 462; offenses, 684

Sexes, respective statuses of, 562

Sexual intercourse, 833

Sexual stimulation, 832

Sexuality, 831

Sewerage system, 364

Sewing, 294

Shadows, beliefs about, 822

Shamans and shamanism, 755, 756, 791

Sharecropping, 427, 465

Sheath, penis, 291

Sheep, 231, 233, 236

Shellfish, cultivation of, 228

Shellwork, 321

Shields, 714

Shipbuilding, 396

Shipping crews, 505

Ships, 501

Shoemaking, 294, 295

Shoes, 291

Shrines, 346, 778; in home, 353

Siblings, half, behavior between,
  593; in polygamous families, 595

Siblings-in-law, 607

Sibs, 614

Sickness, 75; benefits, 745

Siestas and naps, 513

Sign language, 201

Signaling, 202

Signposts, 487

Signs, numerical, 802

Silverwork, 306, 328

Silviculture, 245

Singing, 533

Sinks, 355

Sins, 673, 688, 783

Skates, 481

Skating, figure, 535

Skepticism, religious, 771

Skills, transmission of, 868

Skins, work in, 281

Skis, 481

Slander, 683

Slang, 192

Slaughtering of animals, 22,
  231, 253

Slavery, 567

Sleep, 513

Slums, 362

Smelting, 325

Smiths and their crafts, 326

Smoking, 276

Smuggling, 439, 687

Snake charming, 789

Snowshoes, 481

Soap and allied products, manufacture of, 388; use of, 515

Social, control, 626; groups, 57;
  insurance, 657, 745; offenses, 689;
  problems, 73; stratification, 56;
  personality, 156

Social placement, 851

Social readjustments to death, 768

Social relationships and groups, 571

Social sciences, 815

Social work, 657, 747, 748

Socialization, 86

Societies, secret, 575

Society, native concepts of, 829

Socio-cultural trends, 178

Sod, construction, 333

Sodalities, 575

Soil, 134

Solar energy, 379

Soldiers, 70

Sonar, 207, 718

Songs, 533; texts of, 539

Sorcery, 754; penalties for, 683

Sororate, 587

Soul, 77

Sound records, 216

Sources consulted, 112

Sources processed, 111

Spas, 529

Special clothing industries, 295

Special courts, 698

Special crops, 249

Special garments, 292

Special languages, 198

Special military equipment, 718

Special mineral deposits, 317

Special tools, 413

Specialization, occupational, 463

Spectacles and pageants, 541; religious, 796
Speculation, 455
Speech, 191
Spells, 751, 789
Spinsters, 589
Spirits, 776; communication with and possession by, 787
Spirits and gods, 776
Spitting, 514
Spoils system, 665, 667
Sports, 526; commercialized, 542
Squatters, 361, 423, 563
Stage productions, 545
Stamps, postal, 205; revenue, 651; collecting, 523
Standards of living, 511
State, activities of, 65; enterprise, 475; offenses against, 687; organization of, 63, 64
State socialism, 475
Statesmanship, 663
Stationery, 218
Statuary, 211, 532
Status of adolescents, 882; of children, 858
Status, role and prestige, 554
Status and treatment of the aged, 888
Steatopygia, 142
Steel industry, 327
Stem family, 596
Stenographers, 212
Stepchildren and stepparents, behavior between, 593; in polygamous families, 595
Sterility, 842
Stillbirths, 845
Stilts, 481
Stimulants, 273
Stock exchanges, 455
Stockholders and management, 473
Stoicism, 152, 812
Stone, deposits of, 135; quarrying of, 316; industry, 324
Storage, 488, 498
Stores, 443
Stories, 538; texts, 539
Strangers, attitudes toward, 186, 609
Straw, 243
Streets and traffic, 363
Strikes, 468

String figures, 524
Structural steel work, 334
Structures, 34
Stuttering, 191
Styles, art, 53; clothing, 291; hair, 302
Stylistics, linguistic, 195
Subcultures, 184
Suburbs, or satellite areas, 361, 369, 621
Succession, 643
Suffrage, 641
Sugar, 249, 257, 263
Suicide, 682, 762
Sulphur, 135, 317
Sumptuary laws, 434
Sun protection devices, 293, 751
Sunburn, as affecting skincolor, 142; as an ailment, 164
Supernatural, ideas about, 77
Superstitition, 77, 78, 79
Supply and commissariat, 705
Surgery, 752
Surveying, 804
Surveys, geographical, 654, 816
Suttee, 762
Sweathouses, 343
Swimming, 481; as sport, 526, 542
Symbiosis, 177, 437, 439
Symbolism, art, 53; religious, 796; status, 55; linguistic, 196
Synthetics industry, 384

T

Taboos, general, 183, 784
Tactics, military and resistance movements, 725; revolutionary and counter-revolutionary, 669
Tailors, 294
Talent mobility, 555
Tales, 538
Talisman, 751, 777
Talking, age at, 145, 856
Tanning, 281
Tapirage, 232
Tariffs, 651
Taste, acuity of, 151; canons of, 517

Tattooing, 304
Taverns, 265
Taxation, 651
Taxation and public income, 651
Tea, as a crop, 245; as a beverage, 272
Teachers, 875
Teaching, 86, 87
Techniques of inculcation, 861
Technology, relationship with science, 813
Teeth, beliefs about, 826; eruption of, 145, 856; filing of, 304; care of, 515; industrial use of, 237; use as ornament, 237, 301, 321
Teknonymy, 551
Telegraph, 206, 655; equipment, 403
Telemetering, 207, 804
Telephone equipment, 403
Telephone and telegraph, 206
Telescopes, 417
Television, 207; equipment, 403; manufacturing of, 393
Temple prostitution, 786, 793
Temples, 346, 778; availability and location of, 368
Tenancy, prevalence of, 427
Tents, 342
Terminal facilities, 498
Termination of marriage, 586
Territorial hierarchy, 631
Territorial organization, 63
Tests and schedules, 125
Textile agriculture, 248
Textiles, production of, 28; industries, 288
Texts, 116; native, 539
Theaters, 345, 545
Theft, 685
Theologians, 812
Theological systems, 779
Theology, 779
Theoretical orientation, 121
Theory of disease, 753
Therapy, medical, 757
Thermal power, 375
Thermostats, 405

Thirst, 271; ideas about, 828
Thrift, 454
Tidal power, 379
Tides, 133
Tillage, 241
Time and motion studies, 461
Time, notions about, 821, 822; ordering of, 805
Tithes, 794
Titles, assumption of, 553; as prestige symbols, 554; buying of, 556
Tobacco, consumption, 276; industries, 277; as special crop, 249
Toilet, 302; facilities, 514
Tolls, 494, 651
Tomb stones, 764; carving of, 324
Tools and appliances, 41; machine, 402; manufacture of, 391
Topography and geology, 133
Torches, 372, 416
Tornadoes, 132, 731, 821
Torts, 673
Torture, 681; in initiation, 575, 881; judicial, 695; of self, 158; of war prisoners, 727
Total culture, 18
Totemic, myths, 773; gods, 776; increase ceremonies, 789
Totemism, of kin groups, 61; religious, 771, 779
Tourists, tourism, 457, 484, 486
Towels, use of, 515; manufacture of, 288
Town meetings, 623
Towns, description of, 36; political organization, 632
Toys, 524
Trade agreement, international, 648
Trade associations, 441
Trade centers, 366
Trade, domestic, 438; foreign, 439
Trade routes, 487
Trade schools, 874
Trading expeditions, 437, 439, 484
Trading post, 443
Traditional history, 173
Traffic, air and water, 50; land, 49; regulation of, 363, 486
Trance, hysterical, 158; religious, 787

Transhumance, 221, 361
Transliteration systems, 104
Transmigration, belief in, 775
Transmission of beliefs, 869; of cultural norms, 867; of messages, 202; of skills, 868
Transportation, 48, 489; land, 49; military and naval, 724; water and air, 50
Transvestitism, 838
Traps, 22
Travel services, 485
Travel and transportation, 48, 484; vacations, 528
Treason, definition of and punishment for, 687
Treasury, governmental, 652
Treaties, peace, 728; capitulation, 641, 648; international, 648
Trespass, 685
Trial marriage, 583
Trial procedure, 695
Trials, adolescent, 881; judicial, 695
Tribe and nation, 619
Tribute, as public income, 651
Truces, 726, 728
Trusts, of property, 429
Tumpline, 482
Tunnels, highway, 491; railway, 496; construction of, 499
Tutors, 871, 875
Twins, reaction to, 845
Typhoons, reaction to, 731

U

Ultimogeniture, 428
Umbilical cord, severing and tying of, 844; disposition of, 846
Umbrellas, 293
Undertakers, 767
Underworld activities, organization of, 548; relation with politics, 667
Unemployment, incidence of, 464; insurance, 456; benefits, 745
Uniform and accouterment, 714
Unions, labor, 467
United Nations, 648
Universe, conception of, 772
Universities, 873, 874

Urban and rural life, 369
Urbanism, 36; urbanization, 369, 178
Urination, ideas about, 827; postures in, 514
Urine, industrial use of, 237
Usury, 426
Utensils, 415; manufacture of, 391
Utilities, public, 365
Utopias, 185

V

Vacations, 528, 529
Vaccination, 751
Vagina, ideas about, 831
Vagrancy, 484, 461, 689
Values, cultural, 185; ethical, 577
Vampires, 754
Vegetables, production of, 244
Vehicles, 493; manufacture of, 398
Vending machines, 405
Vengeance, blood, 628, 627
Ventriloquism, 198
Veterans, military, 729
Veterinary science, 232
Vice, organized, 548; sanctions against, 684
Village patterns, 361
Virginity, of bride, 585
Vision quest, 787
Visiting and hospitality, 574; etiquette in, 576
Vital statistics, 163, 164, 165
Vitamins, 146; manufacture of, 258
Vocabulary, 192
Vocational education, 874; guidance, 463
Vogues, 178
Voting, 666; machine, 405
Vows, religious, 782

W

Wagers, 525
Wages and salaries, 465
Walking, 481; age at, 856
War, 72; civil, 669
War veterans, 729

Ward, as an urban division, 621; as a dependent, 429
Warehousing, 488
Warfare, 726
Warriors, status of, 701
Wartime adjustments, 722
Washing, 515
Waste, collection of, 364
Water and air transport, 50
Water, ideas about, 823; ideas and practices about drinking of, 271; purification systems, 364; power, 376; transport, 501, 505
Waterways improvements, 503
Waterworks, 312
Wealth, accumulation of, 556
Weaning and food training, 862
Weapons, 411
Weather control, magical, 789
Weaving, 286; machinery, 402; tools, 413
Weddings, 585
Wedge, 401
Weighing, measuring, and recording machinery, 405

Weight moving, 483
Weight-moving machinery, 406
Weights and measures, 804
Welfare organizations, 747
Wells, gas and oil, 315; water, 312
Werewolves, 754
Wergild, 681
Wheat, as a crop, 243
Wheel, 401
Whistling, 198, 533
Widows, status of, 589
Wife lending, 837
Wigs, 301
Wills and testaments, 428
Windmills, 379, 402
Wire, telegraph or telephone, utilized by primitives, 325; acquired by primitives, 316
Witchcraft, 754
Witness, 675, 695
Woodworking, 322
Wool production, 236
Work in bone, horn and shell, 321
Work in skins, 281
Woven fabrics, 286

Writing, 212; instruments, 413.
Writing and printing supplies, 218
Writs, legal, 694
Wrongs, 673

X

X-ray, 416

Y

Yawning, ideas about, 827
Year, divisions of, 805; notions about, 821
Yodeling, 198

Z

Zero, concept of, 802, 803
Zodiac, 787, 805, 821
Zoning, 361
Zoological gardens, 367
Zoology, prescientific, 825; scientific, 815
Zoomorphism, 776